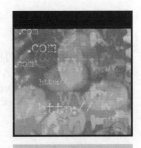

Common Warehouse Metamodel

John Poole
Dan Chang
Douglas Tolbert
David Mellor

John Wiley & Sons, Inc.

NEW YORK · CHICHESTER · WEINHEIM · BRISBANE · SINGAPORE · TORONTO

Publisher: Robert Ipsen
Editor: Robert Elliott
Assistant Editor: Emilie Herman
Managing Editor: John Atkins
Associate New Media Editor: Brian Snapp
Text Design & Composition: D&G Limited, LLC

Library of Congress Cataloging-in-Publication Data:

ISBN: 0-471-20052-2

Printed in the United States of America.

10 9 8 7 6 5 4 3 2 1

To my Mother, Josephine F. Poole, for her love and encouragement, and for teaching me the value of science at an early age, and to the memory of my father, John R. Poole, a true man among men.

—John

To my wife, Hedy, and my daughters, Lillian, Anne, and Vivian, who are the best in my life.

—Dan

To Margaret and Lindy.

—Doug

To my wife Michele, for her boundless love, support, and encouragement, and to the memory of my father, Richard G. Mellor.

—David

Advance Praise for *Common Warehouse Metamodel*

"Business intelligence applications have become the new data processing 'stove pipes' within the departments of an organization. In order for the analytics of these solutions to benefit the entire enterprise, standards such as CWM are essential. This book is an outstanding primer on CWM, not only giving the technical foundation behind this standard, but detailing the value of its application."

John Kopcke
Chief Technology Officer, Hyperion Solutions Corporation

"The CWM standard is one of the most important standards in the business intelligence and meta data repository market segments. Anyone in the business of building a meta data repository—whether for a software product or a corporate repository—needs to own a copy of this book."

David Marco
President, Enterprise Warehousing Solutions, Inc.

"For all but the smallest of organizations, high-quality business intelligence or decision support requires the integration of multiple information technologies—such as relational and multidimensional databases, data mining, and visualization—within a domain-specific solution-oriented framework. Unfortunately, the disparity of implicit modeling frameworks and meta data between different types of analytical technologies, not to mention between different vendors' products of the same type, has kept the benefits of integration beyond all but a few of the most price-insensitive applications. The OMG's Common Warehouse Metamodel represents an important step in the direction of multi-technology integration for enterprise decision support.

This book provides a timely, well-organized, clearly written, and comprehensive overview of CWM. I highly recommend it for practitioners who need to build CWM-based solutions, data-warehousing and decision support managers who need to understand the changing landscape of technology options, and for anyone interested in standards initiatives for data warehousing and decision support."

Erik Thomsen
Chief Scientist, DSS Lab

"It is easy to dismiss the Common Warehouse Metamodel (CWM) specification as 'just another three-letter acronym.' The sometimes-arcane world of data modeling and information architecture can seem impenetrable at times. But the emergence of this single worldwide standard for data warehousing is critical to solving the problem every CIO has: leveraging existing information assets to deliver new goods and services. Poole, Chang, Tolbert, and Mellor provide the first comprehensive introduction and guidebook to this all-important specification in a clear, concise, and complete book. It belongs on the bookshelf of every information architect, data-modeling professional, and database administrator."

Dr. Richard Mark Soley
Chairman and CEO, Object Management Group, Inc.

"Now that information is regarded by leading organizations as the fourth pillar of enterprise assets (in addition to financial, material, and human capital), formal meta data management has emerged as a key enabler of improved information asset valuation. Managing and leveraging information simply cannot be accomplished effectively without meta data. Until this book, only abundant, redundant, and incoherent meta data theory has been available. This book's treatment incorporates the gritty specifics craved by practitioners and product developers. Based on the leading meta data standard, this text diametrically details the approach to implementing practicable meta data solutions as part of custom information management applications or commercial offerings."

Doug Laney
Vice President, Application Delivery Strategies (ADS), META Group

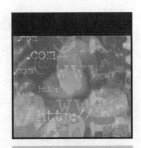

2001 OMG Press Advisory Board

OMG Press Books in Print

For complete information about current and upcoming titles, go to http://www.Wiley.com/compbooks/.

- *Building Business Objects* by Peter Eeles and Oliver Sims, ISBN: 0471-191760.
- *Business Component Factory: A Comprehensive Overview of Component-Based Development for the Enterprise* by Peter Herzum and Oliver Sims, ISBN: 0471-327603.
- *Business Modeling with UML: Business Patterns at Work* by Hans-Erik Eriksson and Magnus Penker, ISBN: 0471-295515.
- *CORBA 3 Fundamentals and Programming, 2nd Edition* by Jon Siegel, ISBN: 0471-295183.
- *CORBA Design Patterns* by Thomas J. Mowbray and Raphael C. Malveau, ISBN: 0471-158828.
- *Enterprise Application Integration with CORBA: Component and Web-Based Solutions* by Ron Zahavi, ISBN: 0471-32704.
- *Enterprise Java with UML* by CT Arrington, ISBN: 0471-386804
- *Enterprise Security with EJB and CORBA* by Bret Hartman, Donald J. Flinn and Konstantin Beznosov, ISBN: 0471-150762.
- *The Essential CORBA: Systems Integration Using Distributed Objects* by Thomas J. Mowbray and Ron Zahavi, ISBN: 0471-106119.
- *Instant CORBA* by Robert Orfali, Dan Harkey, and Jeri Edwards, ISBN: 0471-183334.
- *Integrating CORBA and COM Applications* by Michael Rosen and David Curtis, ISBN: 0471-198277.
- *Java Programming with CORBA, Third Edition* by Gerald Brose, Andreas Vogel, and Keith Duddy, ISBN: 0471-247650.
- *The Object Technology Casebook: Lessons from Award-Winning Business Applications* by Paul Harmon and William Morrisey, ISBN: 0471-147176.
- *The Object Technology Revolution* by Michael Guttman and Jason Matthews, ISBN: 0471-606790.
- *Programming with Enterprise JavaBeans, JTS and OTS: Building Distributed Transactions with Java and C++* by Andreas Vogel and Madhavan Rangarao, ISBN: 0471-319724.
- *Programming with Java IDL* by Geoffrey Lewis, Steven Barber, and Ellen Siegel, ISBN: 0471-247979.
- *Quick CORBA 3* by Jon Siegel, ISBN: 0471-389358.
- *UML Toolkit* by Hans-Erik Eriksson and Magnus Penker, ISBN: 0471-191612.

About the OMG

The Object Management Group (OMG) was chartered to create and foster a component-based software marketplace through the standardization and promotion of object-oriented software. To achieve this goal, the OMG specifies open standards for every aspect of distributed object computing from analysis and design, through infrastructure, to application objects and components.

The well-established CORBA (Common Object Request Broker Architecture) standardizes a platform- and programming-language-independent distributed object computing environment. It is based on OMG/ISO Interface Definition Language (OMG IDL) and the Internet Inter-ORB Protocol (IIOP). Now recognized as a mature technology, CORBA is represented on the marketplace by well over 70 ORBs (Object Request Brokers) plus hundreds of other products. Although most of these ORBs are tuned for general use, others are specialized for real-time or embedded applications, or built into transaction processing systems where they provide scalability, high throughput, and reliability. Of the thousands of live, mission-critical CORBA applications in use today around the world, over 300 are documented on the OMG's success-story Web pages at www.corba.org.

CORBA 3, the OMG's latest release, adds a Component Model, quality-of-service control, a messaging invocation model, and tightened integration with the Internet, Enterprise Java Beans, and the Java programming language.

Widely anticipated by the industry, CORBA 3 keeps this established architecture in the forefront of distributed computing, as will a new OMG specification integrating CORBA with XML. Well-known for its ability to integrate legacy systems into your network, along with the wide variety of heterogeneous hardware and software on the market today, CORBA enters the new millennium prepared to integrate the technologies on the horizon.

Augmenting this core infrastructure are the CORBAservices, which standardize naming and directory services, event handling, transaction processing, security, and other functions. Building on this firm foundation, OMG Domain Facilities standardize common objects throughout the supply and service chains in industries such as Telecommunications, Healthcare, Manufacturing, Transportation, Finance/Insurance, Electronic Commerce, Life Science, and Utilities.

The OMG standards extend beyond programming. OMG Specifications for analysis and design include the Unified Modeling Language (UML), the repository standard Meta-Object Facility (MOF), and XML-based Metadata Interchange (XMI). The UML is a result of fusing the concepts of the world's most prominent methodologists. Adopted as an OMG specification in 1997, it represents a collection of best engineering practices that have proven successful in the modeling of large and complex systems and is a well-defined, widely accepted response to these business needs. The MOF is OMG's standard for metamodeling and meta data repositories. Fully integrated with UML, it uses the UML notation to describe repository metamodels. Extending this work, the XMI standard enables the exchange of objects defined using UML and the MOF. XMI can generate XML Data Type Definitions for any service specification that includes a normative, MOF-based metamodel.

In summary, the OMG provides the computing industry with an open, vendor-neutral, proven process for establishing and promoting standards. OMG makes all of its specifications available without charge from its Web site, www.omg.org. With over a decade of standard-making and consensus-building experience, OMG now counts about 800 companies as members. Delegates from these companies convene at week-long meetings held five times each year at varying sites around the world, to advance OMG technologies. The OMG welcomes guests to their meetings; for an invitation, send your email request to info@omg.org.

Membership in the OMG is open to end users, government organizations, academia, and technology vendors. For more information on the OMG, contact OMG headquarters by phone at 1-508-820-4300, by fax at 1-508-820-4303, by email at info@omg.org, or on the Web at www.omg.org.

CHAPTER

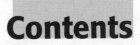

Contents

Foreword

The world of meta data began with simple listings that came from early compilers. From that humble origin came directories, then data dictionaries, then repositories and sophisticated end-user tools. The Internet came along and opened up the doors of computing into venues never before imagined, and meta data grew once again.

The corporate information factory (CIF) gave these different forms of computing a cohesive framework. From the data warehouse–centric CIF came the ODS, data marts, DSS, applications, exploration warehouses, data mining warehouses, and alternate storage. They required coordination across the framework. It naturally fell to meta data to provide the means for communication across the different components of the CIF.

The need for meta data began with simple documentation. System designers and developers, and later data modelers, found they needed meta data. Next systems integration consultants discovered that meta data was the glue that held things together. Finally the architect of the CIF came to the conclusion that without meta data, the CIF was just a bunch of architectural components operating independently and in chaos. Without meta data, one architectural component was singing rock and roll, another architectural component was singing rhythm and blues, and yet another component was singing country and western. The resulting cacophony was hardly pleasing to the ear. To get the components singing together, meta data across the CIF was essential.

Today the world of meta data has extended well beyond the simple technical origins of data dictionaries into the world of distributed processing, business meta data, and the Internet. Yet there is still surprising resistance to the standardization of meta data: From vendors who are determined not to let their meta data fall into the hands of other vendors, resulting in an industry full of proprietary meta data without standardization; From venture capitalists who prefer dot-com opportunities to financing new meta data projects; and from academics who are so far removed from the real issues of the day that any practical approach to meta data seems to elude them.

The time has come for consumers to step forward and specify a standard for meta data semantics and exchange. This book is an important step toward that goal. It will be a lodestone for future products and collaborative efforts across the corporate information factory.

W.H. Inmon
www.billinmon.com

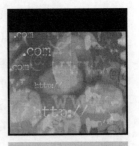

Acknowledgments

The Common Warehouse Metamodel specification would never have been possible without the efforts and contributions of many individuals. The authors wish to acknowledge and thank their many colleagues who participated in, contributed materially to, reviewed, and strongly supported, the CWM specification. This includes (in alphabetical order):

Steve Allman—Dimension EDI

Don Baisley—Unisys Corporation

Christian Bremeau—Meta Integration Technology, Inc.

Gorden Callen—Oracle Corporation

Cory B. Casanave—Data Access Technologies

J. J. Daudenarde—IBM Corporation

David S. Frankel—Genesis Development Corporation

Jack J. Greenfield—InLine Software

Tina Groves—Cognos, Inc.

Hans-Peter Hoidn—UBS AG

Mark Hornick—Oracle Corporation

Sridhar Iyengar—Unisys Corporation

David Last—Oracle Corporation

Debra LaVergne—IBM Corporation

Christoph Lingenfelder—IBM Corporation

Phil Longden—Genesis Development Corporation

Chuck Mosher—Sun Microsystems, Inc.

Jishnu Mukerji—Hewlett-Package Company

Chris Nelson—Dimension EDI

Robin Noble-Thomas—IBM Corporation

Jeffrey Peckham—UBS AG

Pete Rivett—Adaptive Ltd.

Karsten Reimer—Sun Microsystems, Inc.

Vilhelm Rosenqvist—NCR Corporation

Charles E. Simon—Aonix

David C. Smith—Deere & Company

Anders Tornqvist—Dimension EDI

Barbara Walters—SAS Institute, Inc.

Yuichi Yagawa—Hitachi, Ltd.

David Zhang—Hyperion Solutions Corporation

The authors would also like to express their gratitude to the following individuals who provided considerable support and backing to the CWM specification effort:

Ravi Dirckze, Susan Donahue, Giuseppe Facchetti, Robert Kemper, Suresh Kumar, James Jonas, Joanne Lamb, Don Lind, Tony Maresco, Bruce McLean, Karel Pagrach, William Perlman, Jeff Pinard, Curtis Sojka, Chris de Vaney, Robert Vavra, Adriaan Veldhuisen.

And, of course, tremendous thanks go to the fine editorial staff at John Wiley & Sons, who recognized the importance of this book and made its publication possible:

John Atkins, Julie Frigo, Robert M. Elliott, Emilie Herman, Theresa Hudson, and Kelly D. Dobbs.

CHAPTER

1

Introduction to the Common Warehouse Metamodel

Meta data: data describing data, or information about data; generally comprised of descriptions of information structures. Meta data is critical to achieving integration between dissimilar software systems and products from multiple vendors. If heterogeneous software products, applications, reporting tools, and databases are to interoperate effectively, they must have a common understanding of each other's information structures, which requires a common language in which to describe and communicate meta data. They must also have standard interfaces and protocols that support meta data interchange.

This fact is perhaps most relevant in the data warehousing and business analysis domains, in which the various components comprising the *information supply chain* (for example, operational data stores, relational databases, OLAP servers, analysis, visualization, and reporting tools) possess rich meta data structures. These components rely heavily on this meta data as the foundation of their operations and services. However, it is nearly impossible for most commercial software products and systems to readily share meta data. Most products coming from different vendors have dissimilar meta data models (or *metamodels*) and proprietary interfaces exposing their meta data. These differences result in considerable cost and diminished return-on-investment to both vendors and customer organizations attempting to integrate products, tools, and applications.

Nearly all integration efforts require the construction of custom *bridges* between dissimilar metamodels. This construction is time consuming, costly, and results in the creation of many software modules that perform essentially the same function but cannot readily be reused in other integration efforts.

As data warehousing becomes increasingly Web-centric (for example, using data warehouses to store and analyze clickstreams for online retailing and other e-commerce applications), an even greater requirement exists for robust meta data-level integration, especially as data warehouse components are deployed in totally heterogeneous, collaborative, and distributed application environments. The current climate of merger and acquisition, as well as the general desire to avoid single vendor lock-in and to combine best-of-breed products in the building of an information system, also places considerable pressure on vendors to provide readily interoperable tools, products, and applications.

The CWM Solution

The Common Warehouse Metamodel (CWM) is a recently adopted standard of the Object Management Group (OMG) for meta data interchange in the data warehousing and business analysis environments. CWM provides the long sought-after common language for describing meta data (based on a generic, but semantically replete, common data warehousing and business analysis domain metamodel) and an XML-based meta data interchange facility. CWM is rapidly gaining momentum within the data warehousing and business analysis communities and is being incorporated into various vendors' next generation of data warehousing products and tools.

Now that a single, industry-wide standard for meta data interchange exists, vendors finally have the common metamodel and interchange mechanism they need to build truly interoperable databases, tools, and applications. Customers will benefit by being able to select from best-of-breed product offerings while remaining confident that their investments will not be diluted by the inability of tools to interoperate.

From a technical standpoint, CWM extends the OMG's established meta-modeling architecture to include data warehousing and business analysis domain concepts. CWM supports a model-driven approach to meta data interchange, in which formal models representing shared meta data are constructed according to the specifications of the CWM metamodel (essentially an object technology approach to achieving data warehouse integration). These models are stored and interchanged in the form of XML documents. Meta data can be defined independently of any product-specific considerations or formats. It can be stored externally to products as an information commodity within its own right and is readily used by products as generic definitions of information structures.

Data warehousing and business analysis tools that agree on the fundamental domain concepts and relationships defined by CWM can understand a wide range of models representing particular meta data instances. Tools, products, and applications can integrate at the meta data level, because they have a common language in which to externalize their meta data and do not require knowledge of each other's proprietary information structures and interfaces.

Mission of This Book

The mission of this book is to provide a single, coherent, and comprehensive overview of the OMG's Common Warehouse Metamodel, which is easy to read. Prior to this book's publication, no such single source of information on CWM was readily available. Nearly all of the available information on CWM was scattered over the Internet, largely comprised of the CWM specifications themselves, numerous presentation slides, position papers, press kits, analyst reports, various summaries, and overviews. Readers needed to sift through a prohibitively large and rather fragmentary collection of information to gain even a rudimentary understanding of CWM and the value it provides to both vendors and their customers.

The intent of the book is basically threefold:

■ Fill the aforementioned information gap with a concise and highly readable primer on CWM, written by several of the core developers of the CWM standard.

■ Build interest, awareness, and understanding of CWM and its value in the data warehousing and business analysis marketplaces. The authors want to ensure that broad adoption of CWM is not inhibited by a dearth of reader-friendly and sensibly organized information on CWM.

■ Serve as an introduction and overview for the forthcoming *Common Warehouse Metamodel Developer Guide*, published by John Wiley & Sons, which will serve practitioners who are attempting to implement CWM within their own products or deploy CWM-enabled tools within their own organizations and data warehouses.

Perhaps the most ambitious goal of this book is to impart on the reader a CWM conceptual understanding or worldview comparable to that possessed by those individuals who participated in the actual development and implementation of CWM. This level of understanding is critical for those who want to deploy or use CWM in achieving meta data-based interoperability and integration in data warehousing and business analysis projects.

How This Book Is Organized

The organization of this book introduces the reader to the Common Warehouse Metamodel in a reasonably straightforward and logical manner. Each chapter builds upon preceding chapters and chapters should generally be read in order, although readers generally familiar with the problems of meta data integration and wanting to get immediately into the details of CWM may safely skip the first two chapters and start with Chapter 3, "Foundation Technologies."

Chapter 2, "The Value Proposition for CWM," introduces the overall problems associated with attempts at integrating the products and tools comprising the information supply chain in data warehousing environments. This chapter details the value proposition for CWM—that is, why a CWM-based solution to data warehouse integration enhances the overall return-on-investment (ROI) of the data warehouse—and provides a detailed overview of the model-driven approach to integration espoused by CWM.

Chapter 3, "Foundation Technologies," provides an overview of the various foundational technologies of the OMG's metamodeling architecture that are leveraged by CWM. These technologies include the OMG's Meta Object Facility (MOF), Unified Modeling Language (UML), XML Meta Data Interchange (XMI), and Interface Definition Language (IDL). The Java programming language also is discussed as the implementation language of choice for most CWM implementation efforts.

Chapter 4, "An Architectural Overview of CWM," continues the discussion by examining how CWM extends the OMG metamodeling architecture into the data warehousing and business analysis domains. CWM is notably the first OMG standard to extend this architecture into a specific problem domain. A detailed survey of CWM's own layered architecture is presented, including CWM core components and extension packages.

Concrete examples of how CWM is used to model various real-world data warehousing situations are presented in Chapter 5, "Using CWM." Descriptions of how CWM relates to several of the more traditional data warehousing models are provided, along with general guidelines for constructing CWM models.

The planning, design, implementation, and deployment of CWM within the context of data warehousing architectures and cohesive meta data management strategies are described throughout Chapter 6, "Developing Meta Data Solutions Using CWM," and Chapter 7, "Implementing CWM." Collectively, these chapters unite much of the higher level, business value proposition discussions presented in Chapter 2 with the more detailed, technical information presented in Chapters 3 through 5.

Finally, Chapter 8, "Conclusions," discusses how CWM relates to established and forthcoming standards for system integration and interoperability, such as CORBA, XML, and Web-oriented data-interchange protocols. It provides speculation on the technical evolution of the CWM standard and recommendations for further reading and research.

Who Should Read This Book

This book is intended for a moderately technical audience. The majority of our readers will be software developers, system integrators, software and data warehouse architects, database administrators, technical managers, product managers, marketing managers, planners, and strategists working primarily in the data warehousing and business analysis domains. The book will be of benefit to anyone who needs to rapidly build a coherent CWM knowledge base.

Technology-aware, high-level administrators, executives, and other decision-makers responsible for the overall management and integration of their organization's data warehouses, data warehousing, business analysis product offerings, and corporate-wide meta data strategies will find this book highly useful. Academicians and engineers from other disciplines who are interested in learning more about standards-based data warehousing and integration should also find this book very useful.

What's on the Web Site

This book is accompanied by the Web site www.wiley.com/compbooks/poole. This free site provides updated information on the ongoing evolution of the CWM standard as it affects the content and goals of the book. Also provided are links to vendors offering CWM-enabled data warehousing and business analysis tools, as well as links to other active or developing sources of information on CWM.

A Brief History of CWM

A considerable amount of history in the field of meta data standardization and integration preceded the development and adoption of CWM, and the following discussion attempts to summarize much of that history.

The OMG's adoption of the UML as a standard in 1997 is the first significant event leading to the genesis of the CWM. UML is a formal language for modeling discrete systems. Although most people familiar with UML tend to view it as a visual modeling language for designing object-oriented software systems, UML is not necessarily tied to this particular usage. Because UML is a formally defined language, artifacts modeled in UML (for example, descriptions of data warehousing concepts, in the case of CWM) are easily translated to other notations (such as XML), which are not necessarily visual in nature. These other notations may provide other benefits, however, including the easy communication of model contents between software processes.

The second major antecedent event to the creation of CWM was the adoption of the MOF as an OMG standard, also in 1997. MOF defines an abstract syntax for describing models of meta data (that is, metamodels). MOF is based on a subset of the UML and can describe metamodels such as the UML and CWM metamodels and even the MOF itself. In practical terms, MOF defines how meta data repositories might be structured and what capabilities and interfaces repositories need to provide to ensure that all supported metamodels have a common linguistic framework.

XMI was the third major cornerstone technology paving the way for CWM. The XMI specification defines how MOF-based meta data is represented in XML. Meta data is stored in an XML document, and XML tags provide definitions of the meta data elements. XMI is a significant foundational technology for CWM, because it provides a low-cost and Web-enabled interchange mechanism for meta data. XMI was adopted by the OMG as a standard early in 1999.

While the foundations for CWM were being developed within the OMG, several other significant meta data standardization efforts and trends were taking place in the industry. As early as 1993, the Electronics Information Group published the CASE Data Interchange Format (CDIF), a standard for interchanging meta data generated from Computer Aided Software Engineering (CASE) tools. CDIF gained some degree of industry acceptance but had perhaps arrived on the scene at the wrong time (after CASE tools had begun to fall out of the industry's favor but prior to the meta data efforts that started in the mid-to-late 1990s).

In October 1995, the Meta Data Coalition (MDC) was formed by a number of IT industry leaders. In April 1996, the MDC released the Meta Data Interchange Specification (MDIS) Version 1.0. MDIS was a product-neutral mechanism for the interchange of meta data between MDIS-enabled tools and consisted of a metamodel, an access framework specification, and a tag-oriented language for specifying meta data instances. In retrospect, MDIS was considerably narrower in scope than CWM, focusing primarily on the interchange of meta data-defining database schemas. Its specification and interchange languages were also proprietary to MDIS, in contrast to the use of UML and XML in the CWM (UML and XML had not been widely received by the industry when MDIS was drafted). MDIS was a note-worthy attempt, however, and represents one of the first *linguistic* (that is, metamodel and tag language-oriented) approaches to the meta data interchange problem.

At about the same time MDIS was being developed by the MDC, Microsoft Corporation was developing the Open Information Model (OIM), along with several other contributors, and in October 1996, an early draft of OIM was made available. What was significant about OIM was that it leveraged UML as its specification language and was based heavily on repository technologies developed largely by Microsoft and other contributors.

About two years later, several significant events occurred that brought about the recent competition between emerging meta data standards in the IT industry. In September 1998, the OMG published its RFP for a *Common Warehouse Meta Data Interchange* specification that was to build upon existing OMG technology standards for meta data and repository architectures (that is, UML, MOF, and XMI). In early 1999, several OMG member organizations (primarily IBM, Unisys, and Oracle) decided to collaborate on the joint submission of a proposal in response to this RFP. An intercompany team comprised of software architects from IBM, Unisys, NCR, Hyperion, Oracle, UBS AG, Genesis, and Dimension EDI set about developing this metamodel-based solution, under the leadership of Dr. Daniel T. Chang of IBM's Silicon Valley Laboratories. This effort produced what subsequently became known as the OMG's *Common Warehouse Metamodel* (CWM).

Meanwhile, in December 1998, Microsoft joined the MDC and submitted OIM to the MDC, ensuring that OIM would be developed further as an open standard. Representatives from the various MDC member companies subsequently released OIM Version 1.0 in July 1999. The subsequent submission of the initial CWM specification to the OMG occurred in September 1999, and this was immediately followed by an interoperability demonstration of CWM technology by several of the cosubmitting organizations that following November. It became readily apparent that the industry was now faced with the prospect of two competing and closely related specifications for meta data integration. This situation was met with considerable concern. How could true meta data integration be achieved if different products embraced different standards? Were the two standards reasonably similar to one another or highly divergent and fundamentally incompatible? Could the two standards somehow be merged, or otherwise bridged?

The OIM, like CWM, was based heavily on UML and relied on an XML-encoding of its meta data to provide a meta data interchange format. The OIM metamodel represented enterprise-wide IT architectures, including elements representing the system analysis and design process, component-based deployment, database, data warehousing, and knowledge management. In many ways, the scope of OIM was broader than that of CWM, focusing on the overall IT environment; whereas CWM focused specifically on data warehousing and business intelligence. Where the two standards converged (that is, data warehouse architecture and business analysis), CWM provided complete coverage of OIM semantics. This was due, in part, to the fact that OIM had served as one of the major design references in the development of CWM. The other reference standards included CDIF, MDIS Version 1.1, which was subsequently absorbed by OIM Version 1.0, and the OLAP Council's Multidimensional MD-API Version 2.0.

Therefore, where CWM and OIM intersected, CWM supported all of the capabilities of OIM and possessed an open standards-based repository infrastructure and meta data interchange mechanism. Those areas where OIM and CWM diverge generally reside outside the scope of data warehousing and business analysis. However, the most promising area for meta data-based ROI currently resides more in the area of data warehousing and business analysis tool integration and less in the broader areas of enterprise-wide environments. Therefore, although the CWM solution was narrower in overall scope than OIM, it had greater focus on a solution space that promised a much more immediate ROI and a greater probability of near-term success. It offered more bang for the buck (more on this in Chapter 2).

As a first step toward ensuring some level of convergence between the two standards, the OMG and MDC established reciprocal membership and representation between both organizations. An ongoing dialog took place, along with sharing of information and work products. It was even proposed that the two standards could possibly be bridged at the interchange level using standard XML transformations, and a proof-of-concept demonstration of this approach was performed.

However, in June 2000, the OMG Board of Directors approved the second edition of the CWM as an OMG *Adopted Technology Specification*. That September, given the support for CWM building within the industry, the MDC membership voted to discontinue its efforts on OIM in favor of joining ranks with the OMG and focusing on the continued development of the CWM standard. From this point on, the industry finally had a single, open standard for meta data integration with broad vendor support.

Much of the subsequent effort on CWM consisted of initial product-level implementations of the CWM standard. This culminated in the presentation of a multivendor *CWM Enablement Demonstration* at the OMG Technical Conference in December 2000. The experiences gained from initial product-level implementations were used to further tune the specification, leading to the submission of CWM Version 1.0 to the OMG. CWM Version 1.0 was approved by the OMG membership in March 2000, and this was immediately followed by another multivendor interoperability demo at the Meta Data Conference/DAMA Symposium, also in March. The OMG Board of Directors formally adopted CWM Version 1.0 as an OMG *Available Technology Specification* the following month, during the April OMG Technical Conference in Paris.

As part of the CWM adoption process, a CWM Revision Task Force has been formed to take ownership of CWM and further the evolution of the CWM standard through the formal OMG revision process. The membership of the current CWM RTF includes a number of previous supporters and developers of OIM.

The Value Proposition for CWM

The Common Warehouse Metamodel is an open industry standard defining a common metamodel and XML-based interchange format for meta data in the data warehousing and business analysis domains. We need to establish, however, why CWM is important to the data warehousing and business analysis communities. Why should software vendors invest time and effort in enabling their products to use CWM? Even more importantly, why should customers invest in CWM-enabled products or demand that their vendors include CWM support in their product offerings? Like everything else in the computer industry, an economic underpinning exists to technology efforts like CWM. And, the underlying economic justification is ultimately based on the value that a given technology provides to customers of computing systems and software products.

This chapter describes the economic benefits ultimately realized by CWM-enabled data warehousing and analysis products and tools. In this chapter, we analyze the economic impact facing the data warehousing community when meta data integration is not readily available, why the CWM approach is the best bet to achieving integration, and how CWM is used to integrate diverse, multivendor software products and applications. Because all useful technologies also have their limitations, this chapter delineates the boundaries of CWM and describes aspects of data warehouse integration that CWM is not intended to solve.

Analysis of the Problem Domain: The Information Supply Chain

The typical data warehousing and business analysis environment is often described in terms of an *information supply chain* (ISC) (Kimball, 1996) or *information economy* (Thomsen, 1997) These metaphors reflect the fact that information in this environment flows from its sources (that is, providers of *raw data*) through a sequence of refinements that ultimately yield *information products* that are of great strategic value to corporate decision-makers. Figure 2.1 provides an illustration of a typical ISC.

In many ways, the ISC resembles the manufacturing and distribution of durable goods. In a durable goods supply chain, raw materials (wood, iron or steel ore, petroleum, and so on) are refined through a number of distinct manufacturing steps and are finally assembled into useful consumer products. These products are stored in a warehouse until customer orders for the products are secured, at which point products are shipped out of the warehouse, either directly to the customer or perhaps to some intermediate distribution center. In the ISC analog to the manufacturing-distribution process, raw data is first acquired at the start of the chain and then is subjected to a number of refining transformations before being passed to the end consumer (the corporate decision-maker, in this context).

For example, consider how a typical point-of-sale system works. A sales transaction is completed at a cash register terminal, and the terminal transmits an electronic message to a transaction processing system. Each message is converted into a sales transaction record and entered into an online database (for example, a relational database or key-sequenced file system). At this point, data in its most elemental form has been transformed into something more refined (a database row or record) and something certainly more useful. We can now perform simple inquiries against this online database and view the

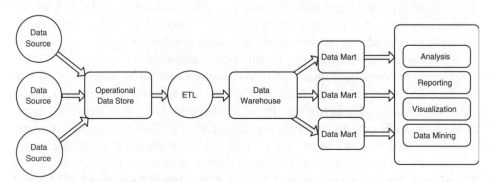

Figure 2.1   The information supply chain.

actual sales transactions, and we readily can examine specific properties of each transaction (date and time of sale, dollar amount, tax applied, and so on).

Data at this stage of refinement is more useful than it was in its initial form, which consisted of not much more than a sequence of electrical signals. However, its overall value as *information* is still limited. Much of the truly valuable business information, such as certain inter-relationships between different data elements (for example, how much was sold during a certain calendar period for stores in a specific geographic region) is not readily discerned from transaction records. Furthermore, transaction systems often differ considerably in the kinds of transactions they support, the format and storage of transaction records, how data elements are represented, peak times of online operation versus off-peak times when data inquiries can be performed in a relatively nonintrusive manner, and so on. These differences result from the fact that most transaction applications were developed to address very specific tactical problems (for example, sales transactions versus inventory transactions versus customer service transactions).

Therefore, the next refinement step in the ISC usually consists of reconciling diverse transactional data into something with a more uniform representation. This step comes under various names, including *data extraction, transformation, and loading* (ETL); *data normalization; data warehouse building; data cleansing and reconciliation*, and so on. Regardless of the terminology used, this step consists of scheduled acquisitions of data from the various transaction systems, the translation of that data into some common format, and the subsequent storage of that transformed data in a special-purpose database. This special-purpose database greatly enhances the transformed data's capability to serve as strategic information to decision makers, as opposed to detailed records of individual business events. Interestingly enough, this specialized database of strategic information (refined and assembled information products) is often called a *data warehouse*, in a manner consistent with our manufacturing-distribution analogy.

Therefore, one may compare the initial step of converting messages into transactions to converting raw materials into basic components or parts. Similarly, the transformation and cleansing step, which assembles the basic information elements and stores them in the data warehouse is equivalent to the storage of finished products in a manufacturer's warehouse prior to their distribution to customers. However, in this case, the manufactured product is an information product rather than a durable good, but that information is just as valuable to its customers as any manufactured product.

Perhaps the most significant feature about the data warehouse is that it organizes refined data in a manner that greatly facilitates advanced analyses, which are critical to the ongoing success of a business. Data warehouses are usually *dimensional* in nature; that is, they organize data in a uniform manner according to the various *dimensions* of the business: accounts, products, geographic regions, sales units, stores, and so on. These business dimensions serve as search keys that identify the data. Data warehouses are invariably organized by time, as well. For example, a business analyst might use a data warehouse to compare sales of a particular product line for different geographic regions over different fiscal periods. The data residing in a data warehouse may have been acquired from highly diverse transaction systems, but the variations in the transaction data are abstracted away by the dimensional organization of the data warehouse. Data warehouses ultimately facilitate business analysis by transforming raw business data into *strategic business information*.

In the manufacturing world, products are often sold by their primary producers to secondary manufacturers who further combine or transform those products into new products that satisfy very specific customer needs. These secondary manufacturers are *value-added resellers* (VARs), or *original equipment manufacturers* (OEMs). The relationship between the initial producer or supplier and VAR or OEM is a highly symbiotic one. The initial producer is provided with an entrèe into new markets that he otherwise might not possess the resources or expertise to pursue, which results in an increased volume of sales. The VAR or OEM focuses on serving their particular markets, using their expertise while reducing costs by not having to engage in the earlier stages of the manufacturing process.

An analog to VARs and OEMs exists in the information economy—the use of departmental data marts and advanced analysis and reporting tools as clients of the central data warehouse. A data mart is basically a scaled-down version of the data warehouse, which serves the analytical needs of a specific department or division within the organization. The data mart usually extracts some portion of the information available from the data warehouse, possibly reorganizing or embellishing that information in some manner. Data marts are often used as the basis for exploratory *what-if analyses*, because the local information can be modified without affecting the content of the central data warehouse.

Advanced analysis and reporting tools may work directly off the data warehouse or may attach to data marts. These tools add considerable value to the information available from the data warehouse. Although the data warehouse establishes the dimensional view of information, analysis and reporting tools provide unique capabilities, such as manipulation of dimensionally organized data and specialized operations or visualization. For example, an advanced financial analysis and modeling package might perform complex statistical analyses of the basic dimensional information. The analysis package also might leverage the capabilities of an OLAP server or data-mining tool. Advanced reporting and visualization tools add value by enabling the end-user to view the analysis results in highly useful and diverse ways. This includes the use of various types of charts, graphs, color codes, alerts, or multidimensional visual constructs and images that the end-user can manipulate directly (rotate, pivot, reshape, resize, and so on).

Data marts, advanced analysis tools (including software-based analysis packages, OLAP servers, and data mining packages), and reporting and visualization tools collectively represent the final refinement step in the ISC, in which strategic, dimensional business information is effectively transformed into *business knowledge*, *insight*, or *vision*. The business insight pyramid, shown in Figure 2.2, is another useful metaphor for describing the ISC from a knowledge-centric viewpoint.

Integrating the Information Supply Chain

We have seen that the information supply chain is a useful metaphor for describing the manner in which most business analysis is performed, and we have seen that data warehousing and business analysis tools are critical components of the ISC. Obviously, these tools must work together effectively if the ISC is to flow smoothly. More often than not, constructing an ISC and integrating its various component tools is a difficult and costly undertaking.

One of the key points brought out in the preceding discussion is the fact that different types of manufacturers of durable goods have expertise and capital

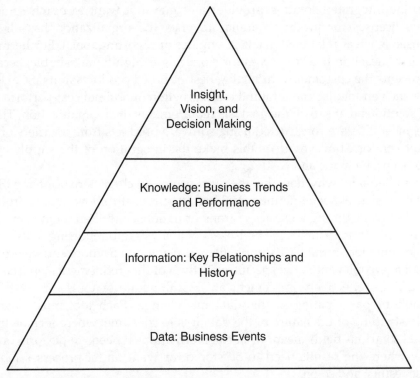

Insight,
Vision, and
Decision Making

Knowledge: Business Trends
and Performance

Information: Key Relationships and
History

Data: Business Events

Figure 2.2   The business insight pyramid.

investments in specific areas, and they find it economically unfeasible (and generally unnecessary) to pursue all aspects of the manufacturing-distribution supply chain. Manufacturers buy finished or partially finished products from other manufacturers or suppliers and combine them to produce new items that satisfy their customers' needs.

A similar situation exists in the information economy. More often than not, different software vendors supply the tools used to implement each step in an ISC. For example, a relational database vendor has expertise in relational database management systems and has invested considerable capital in the creation, sale, and support of her relational database products. But this does not necessarily mean that the vendor is in a good position to develop ETL or data quality tools for front-ending their relational databases in a data warehouse implementation. The same may be true of transaction system vendors and transaction-oriented applications. Similarly, ETL and data quality tools, as well as advanced analysis and reporting and visualization tools, tend to be manufactured by niche players with expertise in highly specialized areas.

Rarely does one vendor have the economic wherewithal or breadth of domain expertise to provide a completely integrated, end-to-end, ISC solution. Even when a complete solution is available from one vendor, investing in the single-vendor solution is not always the best approach. An organization may already have significant investments in products from vendors other than the integrated solution provider and may not want to purchase additional licenses for products similar to ones the organization has already licensed (such as relational database engines or reporting tools). Furthermore, locking oneself in to a single vendor's offering is highly undesirable, because it prevents the customer from mixing best-of-breed products in its ISC. Using only one vendor also can inhibit the construction of optimal cost-performance ISC solutions that satisfy the analysis requirements of an organization. Therefore, most ISCs are constructed using software products from a variety of different vendors. But why does this make the integration of the supply chain steps so problematic and costly?

To understand why, note that the most profound characteristic of any ISC is that it consists of a well-defined (and highly purposeful) flow of data, from its initial sources, through a series of transformations, and then on to some ultimate destination (usually, the end-users of analysis and reporting tools). Each refinement step in the ISC is implemented using one or more software products that are relevant to the specific objectives of that refinement step (see Figure 2.1). To effectively implement an ISC, the suite of tools must be fully capable of participating in this data interchange. Each tool must have an understanding of the nature of the data it is to consume: where it came from; what its various fields mean; what transformations it needs to perform on the data; where the results need to be stored; or what target processes require these results; and so on.

In Chapter 1, we informally defined meta data as data, information about data, or more precisely as descriptions of information structures. Meta data is key to understanding what data means and how it is to be used. All the various software tools and products implementing the stages of any ISC rely on meta data to describe the data that they consume and transform. For a given product to properly operate on its data, that product must have a complete understanding of both the structure and semantic meaning of its data. This understanding is invariably provided by meta data. Meta data is a key input to the internal processing logic of the products and tools comprising an ISC. This product-internal logic uses meta data as the basis for making decisions on how to process the data. For a given collection of software products to effectively participate in an ISC and interoperate at the level of data, they must have a common understanding of the meta data describing that data. Put another way, each of the software products and tools comprising an ISC must be integrated at the meta data level before they can be effectively integrated at the data level.

Meta data-level integration, however, is difficult because most commercial products store meta data in widely varying formats. (The various software products and tools have different *implementation models*.) A given product's meta data is usually accessible to the rest of the world through some interface provided by the product. Just because meta data is *readily accessible* does not necessarily mean that it is *universally understandable*. The form and semantics of the meta data, as well as the interfaces providing access to it, are rarely uniform between products (even products manufactured by the same vendor) and are generally geared more toward the effective operation of each product, rather than toward integration with other products.

This diversity is largely the result of product development histories. Often, software products and tools are designed and built in relative isolation from one another. For example, an OLAP server produced by one vendor might be designed with an internal definition of meta data that is ideal for the server itself, but not necessarily adequate for the various reporting tools that need to work with the server. In other cases, vendors may have been reluctant to standardize on their meta data for fear of losing market share to competitors. When companies merge or acquire other companies, they find themselves having to support multiple product lines that, regardless of their similarities, support vastly different meta data structures.

In practice, tools with dissimilar meta data are integrated through the building of complex *meta data bridges*. A meta data bridge is a piece of software capable of translating meta data of one product into a format required by another product. Such a bridge needs to have detailed knowledge of the meta data structures and interfaces of each product that it attempts to integrate. Figure 2.3 illustrates several ISC components interconnected via meta data bridges. The hollow arrows illustrate the overall data flow, but each shaded arrow represents a distinct meta data bridge and its associated meta data flow.

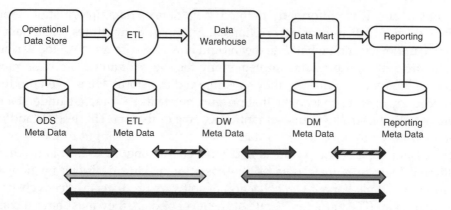

Figure 2.3 Meta-data-level integration using bridges.

This type of configuration is sometimes referred to as a *point-to-point meta data architecture*. Note that a separate bridge is required for each unique pair of tools being integrated. Furthermore, the bridge usually needs to be bidirectional (that is, capable of understanding meta data mappings in either direction). For example, moving data from a transaction system to a data warehouse requires a bridge that maps transactional meta data to dimensional meta data (for example, mapping a transaction table definition to a relational star-schema). Providing data warehouse users with the ability to drill-back to transactions requires a bridge that maps the dimensional meta data back to the transactional meta data. Each mapping is not necessarily an inverse of the other. Often, a certain amount of information loss occurs when translating from one form of meta data to another, and the bridge somehow needs to account for this. (Note that when a bidirectional bridge is implemented as a single software component, it still needs to define two distinct mappings; that is, two logically distinct, if not physically separate, meta data bridges are required, adding to the overall complexity of the bridging solution.)

Bridge building, whether performed by product vendors, third-party consultants, or the implementers of ISCs and data warehouses, is a very difficult and costly process. Bridges must have detailed knowledge of proprietary meta data models and interfaces, and knowledge of how the different models map to one another must be infused into the bridge. Furthermore, the processing logic comprising a particular bridge is not necessarily reusable in the construction of other bridges. Integrating software products in this manner diminishes the level of ROI of the data warehouse by adding considerably to its development and maintenance costs.

In spite of its cost and associated impact on ROI, we see that meta data integration is a prerequisite for effective data integration. In fact, an even broader issue is at hand here. Let's return to Figure 2.3 and consider the ISC environment as a whole, with its mixture of heterogeneous software products and tools. It becomes apparent that the meta data integration problem goes far beyond the simplistic, point-to-point integration of tools suggested earlier. The entire ISC must be integrated at the level of meta data, not just connections between tools comprising adjacent, or otherwise related, steps in the chain. For example, an analyst using a reporting tool at the end of the ISC should be capable of drilling down on some trend of interest to view the dimensional data revealing the trend. If necessary, the analyst then should be able to drill even further down, into the transactional data itself, to view the detailed business events ultimately comprising the trend. Being able to do this means that a single, unified description of all data flowing through the ISC needs to define the relationships and transformations between data elements and trace their lineage through the refinement process. This global meta data must be available to, and readily understood by, all software components comprising the ISC.

The need for a globally available and universally understood meta data definition is partially addressed through the use of a *meta data repository*. A meta data repository is a special-purpose database that stores, controls, and makes available to the rest of the environment all relevant meta data components. Figure 2.4 shows a meta data repository deployed in the ISC of Figure 2.3. Note that the various software products comprising the ISC retrieve global meta data from the central repository, rather than through point-to-point connections with other products. The repository contains a single definition of the total meta data defining the ISC, based on a single metamodel specific to the

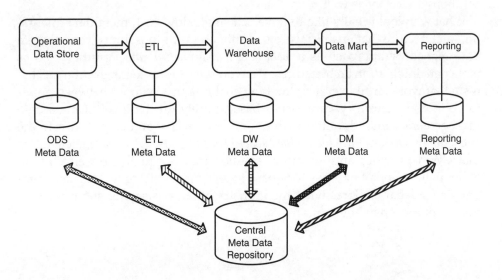

Figure 2.4 Adding a meta data repository to the information supply chain.

repository product itself. Each product must implement its own repository access layer (yet another form of bridge), which understands the repository-specific meta data structures (for example, interfaces and metamodel) and knows how to map these repository-specific structures to product-specific meta data structures. This type of configuration is sometimes referred to as a *hub-and-spoke meta data architecture.*

Although this approach mitigates the need to build many point-to-point bridges (as shown in Figure 2.3), the bridging problem has not been completely eliminated. A different access layer needs to be developed for each software product participating in the ISC (either by the product vendor, repository vendor, or third-party integrator), and each access layer is still specific to a particular repository product. Although this solution has reduced overall cost, it has not reduced cost to its lowest possible level, nor has it eliminated the vendor lock-in issue. The repository is yet one more tool that needs to be integrated with other products and tools deployed throughout the environment. Because the repository is built around its own proprietary metamodel, interfaces, and delivery services, a need exists to build meta data bridges (that is, the product-specific, repository access layers), although less so than in a point-to-point integration architecture. The cost of a meta data repository, whether purchased or custom built, and its integration with the rest of the environment additionally impacts the ROI of the overall ISC effort. Thus, an implementer of an ISC solution must weigh the cost incurred by one meta data integration strategy versus the other (for example, point-to-point versus a central meta data repository). Although point-to-point solutions are expensive because of the proliferation of product-wise bridges, meta data repository solutions are costly as well.

What we would really like to have is a single, low-cost, meta data integration architecture that enables us to use either a point-to-point or central meta data repository approach as a *meta data management strategy,* rather than as meta data integration architectures. We would like a single integration mechanism that works well in either situation, enabling us to choose between point-to-point and repository approaches based purely on the level of meta data management required, rather than on integration cost and complexity. In the subsequent section, *Introducing the Model-Driven Solution Approach,* we will see that CWM provides an integration solution that is equally cost-effective in either point-to-point or repository-based meta data environments. The accompanying sidebar explores what the industry at large is saying about the economics of meta data integration.

THE INDUSTRY PERSPECTIVE ON META DATA INTEGRATION AND ROI

The need for complete and relatively low-cost meta data integration in the data warehousing and business analysis environment is well recognized by industry experts and has been a topic of debate for a long time. Ralph Kimball in his seminal work, *The Data Warehouse Toolkit*, proclaimed rather ominously that there will never be a standard for meta data because of the reluctance of data warehousing tool vendors to agree on a standard. Contrary to Kimball's prediction, however, it appears highly likely that CWM will indeed become the universal meta data standard for data warehouse integration. The creators of CWM are confident that this is the case, not only because of the power and expressiveness of CWM, but also due to the compelling economic issues surrounding meta data integration. Data warehousing and business analysis product vendors can no longer afford to ignore this issue.

David Marco in *Building and Managing the Meta Data Repository: A Full Life Cycle Guide*, provides a thorough analysis of the economic aspects of meta data and its ultimate effect on ROI. He summarizes this in terms of a meta data ROI curve, in which the relative complexity of any meta data-intensive business process (that is, from simple data definition reporting all the way to meta data-driven systems) increases at a rate directly proportional to the value of that process to the business. This clearly underscores the need for effective meta data management and integration strategies and tools. Marco also states that the two greatest inhibitors to the deployment of wide-scale meta data integration are the lack of a commonly agreed upon model for meta data (an *industry standard metamodel*) and the lack of an open standard for interchange (based on XML). He predicts that when these mechanisms become widely available, a considerable amount of cohesion within the meta data integration market place will then take place.

Now, let's consider what some of the leading industry analysts have been saying about the issues of meta data and its ROI. As early as 1997, the META Group, in a report titled *DW Metadata Management: Bottom Up, Top Down* described the progression of meta data from its use in operational systems to its increasing importance to users of *decision-support systems* (DSS). The report describes how meta data discrepancies between tools force end-users to manage analysis-oriented meta data themselves, with little or no integration with the earlier stages of the ISC. Clearly, the need for users to regularly intervene manually in meta data management and integration (for example, through the creation and running of programmatic scripts) diminishes ROI. In fact, in any situation requiring regular manual intervention in an otherwise automated workflow, ROI is greatly diminished by the increase in operational costs.

(continues)

(Continued)

Several reports published by the Gartner Group provide a clear analysis of the data warehousing meta data integration issue and its impact on ROI. For example, the Gartner report "Data Warehousing Business Metadata Management Issues" emphasizes that sound meta data management strategy is a key determiner of data warehousing ROI and that meta data tools, and standards are only a part of a broader picture. This is certainly the case when using CWM to solve the meta data integration problem, and this topic is discussed further in the penultimate section of this chapter, *A Vision of Model-Based Meta Data Integration*, and in Chapter 6, "Developing Meta Data Solutions Using CWM." In a related report, *Data Warehousing Technical Meta Data Management Issues*, the technical meta data integration issue is directly addressed, citing differing vendor metamodels and interfaces as being a major inhibitor to the effective bridging of data warehousing tools and the capability of those tools to reuse meta data. (Note that the capability to reuse any available commodity generally enhances ROI, but the term reuse applied to meta data might seem a little odd. For our purposes, the term reuse means that meta data is defined only once and that this definition is shared as is, rather than being subjected to subsequent transformations or duplications. This definition corresponds to the concept of a shared, global view of meta data that's available to all components implementing the data warehouse. Hence, meta data reuse really means the capability to share and understand a single definition of the meta data). The report goes on to state that standards like CWM will help, but that a need exists to define a broader context for effectively managing meta data (see Chapter 6).

Yet another Gartner report, "Meta Data Management Alternatives for DWs and Data Marts," elaborates further on the need for standards. This report concludes that in the absence of an agreed-upon meta data standard, meta data reuse (that is, sharing) will remain limited and that meta data managers will continue to be plagued by a dependence on manual methods (further diminishing overall ROI).

Finally, the need for meta data integration standards, along with the pervasive use of XML as an interchange mechanism for meta data, is highlighted in two recent reports published by the META Group. *MetaData Maelstrom Sinks Standards and Repositories* emphasizes the need for vendors to address the ROI issue associated with meta data, claiming that the establishment of a meta data standard will greatly enhance ROI and reuse. Interestingly, the report also emphasizes the importance of an XML-based interchange mechanism as being key to the quest for improved meta data ROI.

The report, *21st Century Metadata: Mapping the Enterprise Genome*, likens meta data integration to a mapping of the genome of the enterprise, an intriguing analogy to current scientific research in DNA. An emphasis is placed on the need for a meta data standard and an XML-based interchange mechanism. Furthermore, the report describes the need for *ubiquitous meta data interchange* among information supply chain tools. (Note that this conclusion supports our observations in the previous section regarding the need for a global meta data definition accessible by all components of the ISC).

All of the evidence cited here clearly shows that industry leaders acknowledge that meta data integration is one of the leading problems facing the data warehousing and business analysis industry. Not only is the goal of providing a complete, standards-based meta data integration solution economically compelling, but it is also an intellectually challenging task.

Introducing the Model-Driven Solution Approach

In the previous sections, we provided a detailed description of the meta data integration problem in the context of data warehousing and business analysis. We used the metaphor of an *information supply chain* to describe how data flows between data warehousing and business analysis tools and explained why meta data integration is a key prerequisite to ensuring the effectiveness of this data flow. We also explained why achieving meta data integration between software tools is a difficult and costly undertaking, largely due to the dissimilar representations of tool-specific meta data. And, we elaborated on the economic justification for ensuring meta data integration in the ISC, demonstrating that there is a consensus amongst industry leaders that the economic underpinnings of the meta data integration problem are significant. They point toward the need for this problem to be solved through the use of meta data standards and low-cost, widely available interchange mediums, such as XML.

The following sections describe how the Object Management Group's Common Warehouse Metamodel resolves many of the difficulties associated with providing true meta data-level integration between software products and tools. The rationale behind the CWM solution is explained, and we will see why CWM is a critical component in providing low-cost and reusable solutions to the meta data integration problem, enabling us to build cost-effective information supply chains and ensuring high levels of ROI.

A Model-Based Approach to Meta Data

We had informally defined meta data as data or information describing other data; specifically, the business data processed by various software products, tools, applications, and databases. A given software product (for example, a relational database system) can perform operations on data effectively only if it has a precise definition of that data available. Meta data serves this purpose.

Several software products can be integrated effectively only if they have a common understanding of the data flowing among them. Meta data is used in this capacity, as well. The same meta data used internally by software products is also used as the basis for data integration between different products. This situation is problematic because considerable difficulty is involved in using product-internal meta data as the basis for the external integration of those products. As described previously, most products have differing or incompatible internal metamodels and proprietary interfaces exposing their meta data. CWM overcomes this fundamental problem.

For a given element of meta data to be an effective representation of the data it describes, it must describe its data precisely. Otherwise, no guarantee can be given that data operations based on that meta data will be performed correctly. Meta data does not usually describe all aspects of its data, only certain essential characteristics. For example, the meta data describing a numeric field in a record might define the field's position within the record and its type (for example, integer or real), but the meta data need not define the rules for adding two numeric values together. Presumably, an addition operation implemented within some software product already knows how to do this. All that's required by the addition operation is a limited amount of descriptive information about the data fields that are to be added together (for example, their location within the record and their numeric types). Meta data can generally afford to be abstract and concise. It need not describe all possible characteristics of the data, just the minimum information required by any operations to be performed on the data. What meta data does describe, however, it must describe precisely and unambiguously.

Often, the term *model* is used to describe such a precise, yet abstract, representation of something in the real world. For example, an architect might create a model of a house in the form of a blueprint. The blueprint precisely describes the house to be built but doesn't describe how to build the house (nor does it need to; the building contractor already knows how to do this). Nor does the blueprint describe all aspects of the house, only the minimal information that the contractor requires. Furthermore, separate blueprints may be used to provide different viewpoints on the same house. Each is used by a different type of contractor in the construction of the house (plumbing, electrical, and so on). Although the blueprint is an abstract description of the house, it must still be a precise description. Otherwise, the contractor may not be totally sure about how to build certain features of the house. Furthermore, to ensure that any contractor can understand it, the architect must draw the blueprint in accordance with well-established rules on the formation of blueprints (a limited collection of well-defined notational symbols, specific rules for combining or connecting these symbols, and so on). A model is an abstract and precise description of something, and in the interest of correctness, models must be constructed according to certain formal rules. Otherwise, we could build models that are nonsensical.

Given all of these considerations, it is now easy to see why meta data is essentially a formal model of its data (and, in an analogous manner, that data is also a formal model of some object in the real world). Meta data is an abstract description of data that describes data precisely. Meta data must also be formulated according to certain rules ensuring that it is correctly formed. This guarantees that any software product aware of the meta data description rules will always be able to correctly interpret meta data when performing operations on the corresponding data (assuming, of course, that the meta data is correctly formed).

Consider the simple relational table model shown in Figure 2.5. This simple model is expressed in the Unified Modeling Language (UML), which abstractly describes any relational table in terms of a named collection of columns. A relational table has a name. A column has a name and a data type. The data type is specified as a string whose value denotes the data type (for example, "integer"). A table may contain any number of columns, as indicated by the association line joining the table to the column. The '*' on the column end of the line denotes zero or more occurrences of column, and the black diamond and the '1' at the table end denotes a column as being owned by precisely one table.

Note that this relational table model does not describe any particular relational table, but rather describes *how relational tables are defined*. To specify an actual table, we need to create an *instance* of the table model. Figure 2.6 shows a UML *instance diagram* describing a simple relational table that stores data about products. The Product table consists of three columns: ID, which uniquely identifies each product; Name, which defines each product's name; and Color, which identifies the color of a particular product. The instance diagram represents an instance of the generic relational table model. Note that

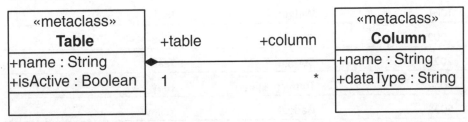

Figure 2.5   Simple relational table model.

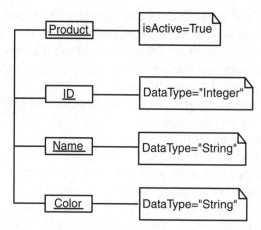

Figure 2.6 Product table instance.

the generic model prescribes that a table may have multiple columns, and the instance has three such columns. Each of the three columns has a name and a data type, as prescribed by the generic model. The Product table also has a name, as prescribed by the generic model.

The instance diagram in Figure 2.6 describes the structure of a particular relational table that could be implemented in a relational database management system. Table 2.1 shows an outline of that table and some possible data values as rows within the table. Following is a statement in the Structured Query Language Data Definition Language (SQL DDL) that when submitted to a relational database management system results in the actual construction of the Product table:

```
CREATE TABLE Product (
    ID              INTEGER NOT NULL,
    Name            CHARACTER NOT NULL,
    Color           CHARACTER NOT NULL
);
```

Table 2.1 Product Table and Its Data Values

PRODUCT ID	NAME	COLOR
1001	Widget	Red
2002	Gizmo	Blue
2022	Sproget	Teal
4034	Thingamagiger	Gray
5035	Gadget	Yellow

It should be clear from this example that the instance diagram of Figure 2.6 is a *model* of the Product table. Furthermore, the abstract relational table model in Figure 2.5 is a *model of the model* (that is, a *metamodel*) of the Product table. Also, note that the SQL DDL for building the Product table could easily be derived from the Product table model (for example, via a software process that reads the UML instance diagram and translates it into equivalent table creation statements in SQL DDL). When a relational database engine processes the SQL DDL statement, it generates internal meta data describing the Product table and stores this meta data in the relational database *catalog*, which is essentially a local repository of meta data describing all databases currently maintained by the relational database engine. The relational engine also allocates all of the necessary physical resources for actually implementing the table in the database and storing its data rows, indexes, and so on, as part of the table building process.

Users of various *data modeling tools* should be familiar with the scenario just described. Data modeling tools provide database architects or designers with the ability to visually define database schemas at various levels of abstraction, in the form of *entity-relationship diagrams*. In an entity-relationship diagram, an *entity* represents a type of object from the business domain being modeled (for example, Product entity, Customer entity, Account entity, and so on). Entities are connected via relationships similarly to the association connecting Table and Column in an abstract relational table model of Figure 2.5. Entity-relationship diagrams generally start off as logical models, capturing the basic entities and relationships from the business domain. At some point, when the logical model is reasonably complete, the logical entity-relationship diagram is transformed by the data modeler into a physical entity-relationship diagram, through the further specification of primary and foreign keys, data types, referential integrity constraints, and so on. The physical entity-relationship diagram is then directly translated into a collection of SQL DDL statements capable of building the corresponding physical database schema. This capability of a data modeling tool might be viewed largely as a matter of convenience; it makes it unnecessary for the database modeler to manually code the SQL DDL from the visual entity-relationship diagram. A much more profound implication is here: The entity-relationship diagram, like the Product table instance diagram in the previous example, effectively defines the meta data of the target information structures. The data modeling tool should be viewed not merely as a means of drawing entity-relationship models, but rather as a source of meta data, or perhaps even more profoundly as a *meta data authoring tool*.

We have demonstrated that a model expressed in a formal language, such as UML, can be used to define the meta data describing some information structure or schema. We have also demonstrated that this formal model can be translated (by some software process created specifically for this purpose) into an equivalent meta data definition that can be used to create an actual instance of the information structure itself. What is perhaps not immediately obvious is the fact that these various formal models, such as the instance diagram of Figure 2.6, are generally *platform-independent*. They do not exhibit physical features of the computing platform used to deploy the actual information structure, because formal modeling languages (such as UML or the various data modeling notations) are generally platform-independent specification languages. A collection of SQL DDL statements can be viewed as a *platform-specific model* because they specify the target information structure in the language of a particular computing platform (for example, a SQL-compliant relational database engine). The hypothetical translation process that converts a formal model, such as the UML instance diagram of Figure 2.6, into SQL DDL is said to *map* the platform-independent model to a platform-specific model, based on some set of formal *mapping rules* that the translation process *implements*.

Three very important conclusions can readily be drawn from the preceding observations:

- Any formal model of an information structure effectively *is* the meta data defining that information structure (recall that we have already established that meta data is essentially a formal model of the data that it describes).

- Meta data, when expressed as a formal and platform-independent model, can exist outside of, and independently of, any particular target platform.

- Meta data, when expressed as a formal and platform-independent model, can be translated to any of a number of different platform-specific models, each representing a different target platform (given, of course, appropriate sets of mapping rules and implementations of those rules).

These conclusions are important because they give us our first step toward solving the meta data integration problem for diverse software products and tools. We can see that one possible approach is to develop an *external representation of meta data*, which is not dependent upon any particular product or tool. Such a representation is based on formal and platform-independent models of information structures, described using an appropriate formal language, such as UML. A product uses such a formal model as the basis for its own meta data by invoking an appropriate *import mapping* process to translate the formal model into an instance of its own, product-specific meta data. Similarly, a product may expose its proprietary meta data to other products through an *export mapping* process that translates its internal meta data into a platform-independent, formal model.

How is this proposed solution any better than the meta data bridge solution described earlier? Recall that the main problem with meta data bridges is that each bridge must map between two proprietary, product-specific models. The bridge essentially needs to convert meta data from the format prescribed by one product's metamodel (the product's proprietary model of its own meta data) to that prescribed by the other product-specific metamodel. Now, if the metamodel itself is externalized and made independent of any particular implementation platform (that is, product), and the products interchanging meta data agree on this common, external metamodel, then the problem of translating between proprietary implementation models goes away.

As an example of this, consider once again the abstract relational table model in Figure 2.5, which is a metamodel of any relational table. Figure 2.7 shows another relational table model, that of an Account table. The Account table, like the Product table in Figure 2.6, is based on the same common metamodel. Any software process that understands the common metamodel defining relational tables in general can understand either of the Product or Account table models, both of which are instances of the same metamodel.

We've taken the use of formal models to represent meta data a step further, and we've hoisted the metamodel out of the products and into the external environment. The next question that arises is, "Is this approach too limiting?" The relational table metamodel of Figure 2.5 describes relational tables, but providing a common understanding of meta data requires that many more metamodels be externalized into the environment. To the extent that a metamodel provides an abstract description of objects in a particular domain of interest (for example, relational database schemas), we need to ensure that our metamodel is a reasonably complete representation of its domain. That is, we need to ensure that it is *semantically complete* or at least reasonably close to being so. To ensure that the metamodel is intelligible to all software products, we must form it according to certain agreed upon rules (that is, according to

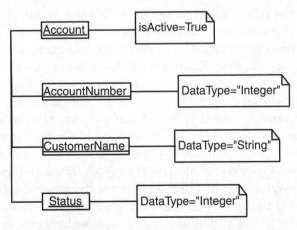

Figure 2.7   Account table instance.

the semantics of some formal language). In the example relational metamodel of Figure 2.5, the formal language used is UML.

This overall approach to meta data-level integration and interoperability can be described as a *model-based approach to meta data integration* or as a *model-driven architecture for meta data*. It consists fundamentally of the exchange of shared meta data between software products in the form of externalized meta data definitions expressed as formal and product-independent models. Software products and tools participating in this environment agree on the common metamodel defining the overall domain, enabling them to readily understand any instances of that metamodel (for example, any shared meta data that might be interchanged). Each product maps this shared meta data to its own internal meta data representations. This requires that the metamodel be a reasonably complete representation of its domain and that the metamodel further provide some means of extension, whereby any semantic gaps in the metamodel can be compensated for in a standard, agreed-upon manner by participating products.

The model-based approach to meta data integration eliminates or significantly reduces the cost and complexities associated with the traditional point-to-point meta data integration architectures based on meta data bridges. This approach also provides the same benefit to central repository-based, hub-and-spoke-style meta data architectures, as well. In point-to-point architectures, the model-based approach eliminates the need to build multiple meta data bridges, which interconnect each pair of product types that need to be integrated. Instead, each software product implements an *adapter* (a layer of software logic) that understands the common metamodel and the internal implementation metamodel of the product. The adapter is another form of a meta data bridge, but one that needs to be written only once for a given product, because all products agree on the common metamodel. This is in sharp contrast to the traditional meta data bridging approach, in which pair-wise bridges are built for every pair of product types that are to be integrated. The model-based solution clearly reduces the costs and complexities of building point-to-point meta data architectures, enhancing the overall ROI of the information supply chain or data warehouse effort. The use of a common metamodel eliminates the need to construct pair-wise meta data bridges and allows for a complete *semantic equivalence* (Gartner, 2000b) at the meta data level between the various products and tools comprising a typical ISC. Figure 2.8 shows a model-based, point-to-point meta data integration architecture.

In central repository-based hub-and-spoke meta data architectures, the repository generally takes on a new meaning as the central store for both the common metamodel definition and all of its various instances (models) used within the overall environment. The repository must implement a meta-model-aware adapter layer just like any other software product or tool participating in the architecture. The repository might implement its own internal metamodel and rely on its adapter layer to translate between shared instances

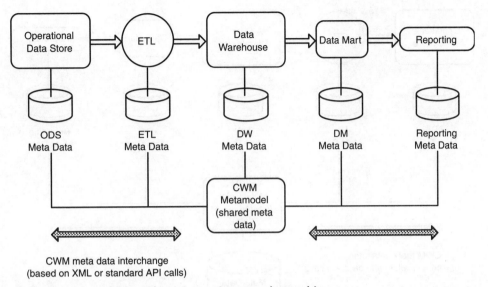

Figure 2.8   A model-based point-to-point meta data architecture.

of the common metamodel and its own metamodel, although it might be preferable for the repository to directly implemented some internal representation of the common metamodel. The metamodel-aware adapter associated with each product largely subsumes the repository access layer usually required in this type of meta data environment, further reducing the costs and complexities of building a central repository-based solution (see Figure 2.9).

Whether the *physical* meta data architecture consists of a point-to-point or hub-and-spoke configuration, the use of the model-based approach results in the creation of a *logical* hub-and-spoke architecture. In this case, the common metamodel defines the logical, central hub. Compare Figure 2.8 and Figure 2.9. Deciding which type of meta data architecture to implement in the model-based environment is less determined by integration issues and influenced more directly by overall meta data management issues and strategies, as it should be.

A Complete Model-Based Meta Data Integration Solution

We are now well on our way to being able to specify a complete solution for the meta data integration problem that overcomes many of the difficulties, costs, and impact on ROI, previously plaguing meta data integration efforts. This section defines the complete set of components comprising any model-based meta data integration architecture and delineates those features that are

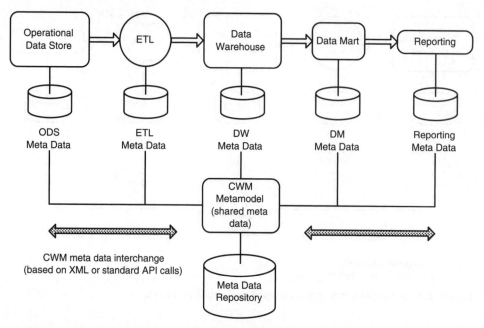

Figure 2.9 A model-based hub-and-spoke meta data architecture.

specific to the model-based integration mechanism itself from those aspects of the overall architecture that relate to management and policy decisions.

A complete model-based, meta data integration solution generally consists of the following components:

1. A formal language capable of specifying meta data in terms of shared, platform-independent models

2. A common metamodel defining the problem domain

3. A common interchange format for interchanging shared meta data

4. A common programming interface for meta data access

5. Standard mechanisms for extending the models

6. Standard mechanisms for extending the metamodel

7. Software adapters facilitating product-wise meta data import and export

8. A central meta data repository (an optional component of the architecture)

9. A comprehensive meta data management strategy

10. A comprehensive meta data technical architecture

Components 1 through 6 are the primary elements that must be provided by any model-based approach to meta data integration. We've already discussed the need for a formal and platform- and product-independent language for defining shared meta data models. We also discussed the need for a single metamodel that serves as the common semantic basis for the construction of those models. All components that participate in the overall meta data integration architecture (for example, software products and tools, applications, databases, and so on) must understand and agree on the common metamodel. Shared models interchanged between components are all instances of the common metamodel. The common metamodel is also platform- and product-independent. The metamodel must possess a sufficient level of semantics (*semantic coverage* or *semantic completeness*) to ensure that it can model almost all aspects of the problem domain. It must also have been formulated according to an established set of formal rules (*abstract language*) to ensure that the various software products and tools participating in the architecture are all capable of having a common understanding of the metamodel. The metamodel must have a consistent meaning to all products and tools that intend to use it as a mechanism for interpreting shared meta data.

Common interfaces supporting interchange and access to shared meta data must also be defined. We mentioned previously that two of the most significant inhibitors to meta data integration across the ISC are the lack of a standard metamodel and corresponding meta data interfaces. Furthermore, a common, stream-oriented interchange format is highly desirable, as well as a common application programming interface (API). Both types of interfaces can be derived via mapping rules based on the common metamodel. That is, the model-based solution should define a mapping from the common metamodel to both a stream-based interchange format and a programmatic interface expressed in some programming language. The stream-based interchange format is used for the bulk (coarse-grained) interchange of meta data. The programmatic interfaces facilitate fine-grained, programmatic access to meta data. Most products or tools participating in the model-based meta data integration architecture generally provide both, but the stream-based format is considered a minimal requirement.

The World Wide Web Consortium's (W3C) eXtensible Markup Language (XML) is currently the language of choice for interchanging data over the Web and in any inherently loosely coupled, distributed, asynchronous environment. XML documents are largely self-describing. XML allows for the definition of custom tags that are used to define elements within an XML document. In the world of model-based meta data integration, XML is similarly the meta data interchange medium of choice. Custom XML tags represent concepts defined by the metamodel (once again, a set of formal mapping rules are employed to associate metamodel elements with specific tags). The meta data itself is stored in the XML document in the form of element content. The following code illustrates a possible XML rendering of the Product table instance defined in Figure 2.6:

```
<?xml version="1.0"?>
<Table name="Product" IsActive="True">
```

```
<Column name="ID" dataType="Integer">
</Column>
<Column name="Name" dataType="String">
</Column>
<Column> name="Color" dataType="String">
</Column>
</Table>
```

In this case, the element content is meta data, and the tags defining the possible element types are *meta-meta data* (elements of the metamodel). Note that the metamodel itself can be rendered in XML. In this case, the tags would be defined according to the abstract language used to define the metamodel.

Having a common programmatic interface (or standard mappings from meta data elements to widely used programming languages) greatly simplifies the construction of programmatic clients that must access meta data from a particular product, tool, database, or other service. Programmatic meta data clients need to be coded against only one interface, regardless of the meta data provider implementing that interface. This greatly reduces costs, complexity, and overall application footprint for programmatic meta data clients.

Standard extension mechanisms for models, as well as the metamodel, must also be supported by the architecture. Although the metamodel, as an expression of a particular problem domain, needs to be as complete a description of that domain as possible, in some situations a need may exist to interchange meta data elements not directly accounted for in the metamodel. In this case, the metamodel may provide standard constructs for defining new elements. How these elements are to be interpreted is up to the tools participating in the interchange, as their semantic meaning cannot be inferred from the metamodel. In other situations, the metamodel may need to be extended to incorporate new domain concepts. We have mentioned that the metamodel must be formulated according to some formal or abstract language, although we have not yet defined what that abstract language is. Extending an existing metamodel with new domain concepts means that the abstract language itself must provide some sort of mechanism enabling us to do this. Note that custom extensions to a metamodel may inhibit integration to the extent that any products participating in the architecture that are affected by such extensions need to made aware of the fact that these extensions have been added to the basic metamodel.

Product-specific adapters and meta data repositories (components 7 and 8) fall within the realm of the implementation (*realization*) of the overall model-based meta data integration architecture. As mentioned, adapters provide the basic mechanism whereby a given software product, application, tool, or database *plugs in* to the meta data architecture. Each adapter is specific to a particular product and contains logic for mapping the common metamodel to the product's internal metamodel. An adapter is the means by which a product exports its meta data in the form of standard models to the environment, as well as the means by which a product may import shared models from the environment.

A meta data repository is a specialized store for maintaining global, shared meta data. In the model-based meta data integration architecture, the repository serves as a central location for the storing and management of both the common metamodel and its model instances. The repository also facilitates the publishing of the various models by making models available to the environment at large and by providing them to any specific tools or products requesting them. The repository usually provides a number of critical services to authors and modifiers of meta data, such as multiuser access control, security, and versioning. The use of a meta data repository may or may not be employed by the solution architecture, depending upon the requirements of the overall meta data management strategy.

Meta data management strategy (component 9) refers to an organization's policy regarding how its meta data is to be managed, controlled, and used. We will say more about meta data strategies in Chapter 6, "Developing Meta Data Solutions Using CWM." For now, note that a meta data management strategy is not a component of the model-based meta data integration approach, although the use of a model-based approach to meta data integration certainly has a profound affect on the overall meta data strategy and how it is formulated. Using a model-based approach to meta data integration without having a sound, overall meta data management strategy in place can greatly diminish the probability of success of the ISC effort. This is in spite of the enormous benefits provided by the model-based approached (see Gartner, July 2000; Gartner, 1999; and Marco, 2000 on the related topic of *data stewardship* and meta data management strategies).

The meta data management strategy determines, amongst other things, the overall *workflow* of meta data throughout the environment. For example, the meta data management strategy generally determines which products or tools are responsible for authoring meta data; which are responsible for publishing, staging, controlling, updating, and managing existing meta data; and which are read-only consumers of shared meta data. This strategy ultimately determines the overall meta data technical architecture, which follows directly from the meta data management strategy, as well as the tools selected for implementing the meta data integration architecture.

The meta data technical architecture (component 10) defines how the meta data management strategy is physically realized. It defines the specific meta data integration and interconnection topology, such as point-to-point, hub-and-spoke, or federated network. The architecture also defines the distribution of various meta data services to specific points in the topology. For example, the model-based approach to meta data integration invariably leads to a logical (if not physical) hub-and-spoke architecture, in which the logical hub consists of the common metamodel. If it is decided that the common metamodel is to be published and managed by a repository, the deployed repository constitutes a physical hub in the overall architecture. If a central repository is not to be deployed, the architecture must somehow account for repository-like services and where they are realized within the architecture. For example, if a particular tool requires a particular model, where does it go to get it? How does it know where to go? Is there, for instance, a central directory service that can be invoked for finding where particular models are stored? Note that meta data not only needs to globally accessible and universally understandable throughout our model-based architecture, but it needs to *locatable*, as well.

In general, the meta data technical architecture is physically implemented by a number of key software components, including all of the various product-specific adapters and the meta data repository (if we chose to include one in the overall architecture). Furthermore, a need exists to implement an overall control framework capable of realizing the workflow through the architecture, while providing other important functions, such the directory services component alluded to previously.

CWM As a Model-Based Approach to Meta Data Integration

The CWM is an open industry standard of the OMG for integrating data warehousing and business analysis tools, based on the use of shared meta data. In the previous sections, we described the general characteristics of a model-based approach to meta data integration and interoperability. In this section, we provide an overview of CWM as a realization of the model-based meta data integration paradigm.

CWM Overview

CWM is a complete metamodel representing the data warehousing and business analysis problem domain. As a metamodel, CWM provides both the syntax and semantics required to construct meta data (for example, models or instances of the metamodel) describing all of the components of a complete ISC.

CWM actually is comprised of a number of different but closely related metamodels. Each metamodel represents some subdomain of the ISC environment. A block diagram describing the overall organization of CWM is shown in Figure 2.10. Each block represents a constituent metamodel, or *package*, of CWM and corresponds to an important functional area of a typical ISC. A given model derived from one of the CWM packages (for example, an instance of one of the constituent metamodels) defines a piece of meta data that in turn describes some data within the corresponding functional area. For

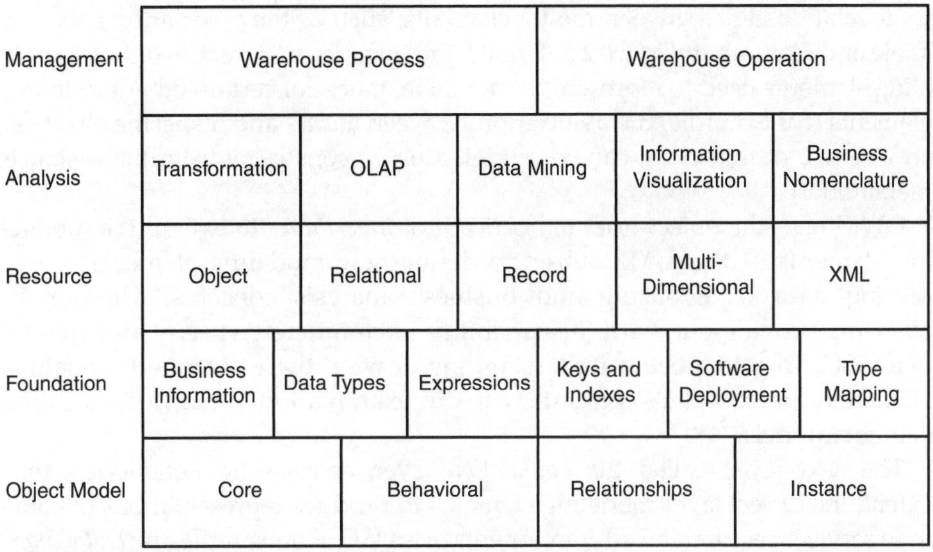

Management	Warehouse Process			Warehouse Operation	
Analysis	Transformation	OLAP	Data Mining	Information Visualization	Business Nomenclature
Resource	Object	Relational	Record	Multi-Dimensional	XML
Foundation	Business Information	Data Types	Expressions	Keys and Indexes	Software Deployment	Type Mapping
Object Model	Core	Behavioral	Relationships	Instance

Figure 2.10   CWM metamodel layering.

example, a model derived from the relational metamodel is meta data describing some instance of relational data (that is, a collection of rows from our Product table). Note that whether or not this data actually exists out there in the real world doesn't really matter. The key point here is that regardless of whether or not the data exists right now or at some future point in time, we can still *describe it*, because models derived from CWM exist independently of any particular software product, technology, or platform.

We stated previously that a model-based meta data integration architecture requires a formal language capable of representing meta data in terms of shared, platform-independent models. In CWM, this language is UML (actually, a very specific subset of the UML). UML is an OMG standard language for specifying abstract models of discrete systems (Booch et al., 1999; Rumbaugh et al., 1999). CWM is expressed in UML. While UML is the notational basis for the definition of CWM, CWM also *extends* a subset of the UML language to include data warehousing and business analysis domain concepts. CWM relies on the expressiveness and power of UML as a means of defining complex meta data structures and relationships.

Note the lowest layer in the CWM block diagram of Figure 2.10, referred to as the *Object* layer. This UML subset layer is used by CWM as its base metamodel. The Object layer consists of four metamodels: *Core, Behavioral, Relationships*, and *Instance*. The Core metamodel defines the most basic, static modeling elements residing within the core of the UML language. The Behavioral metamodel extends those static structures to define behavioral things, such as operations and procedures. The Relationships metamodel defines the basic relationships between model elements, such as the association between Table and Column in Figure 2.5. Finally, the Instance metamodel defines modeling elements used to represent the actual instances of certain other modeling elements (for example, the association between a *class* and a specific *object*, as an instance of that class, can be modeled using constructs from the Instance metamodel).

CWM uses the object-oriented concept of *inheritance* to extend the modeling elements of this UML subset to define new modeling elements representing data warehousing and business analysis concepts. These new elements provide one with the capability to completely specify an instance of an ISC. To gain a better understanding of what these extended modeling elements consist of, let's continue with our examination of the various CWM submetamodels.

The next layer, called the *Foundation* layer, consists of metamodels that extend the Object layer modeling elements to produce representations of common services required by all components of an ISC. For example, the *Data Types* metamodel extends certain modeling elements in the Object layer to define new elements representing basic data types that we must be able to express in our meta data. *Type Mapping* defines new modeling elements that enable us to create models of mappings between dissimilar type systems (obviously necessary for ensuring interoperability between dissimilar software tools and platforms). The *Keys Indexes* metamodel similarly builds upon the basic modeling elements defined by the Object layer to define the abstract concepts of unique and foreign keys, as well as ordering constraints imposed on data sets. These concepts are fundamentally important to building models of relational database structures, but the notion of a unique key is not limited to a relational database. It is also important to record-oriented and multidimensional databases (for example, an OLAP dimension can define a unique key).

The *Business Information* metamodel defines elements that support the modeling of basic business information pertaining to the environment (for example, contact names and descriptions of modeling element instances). *Software Deployment* facilitates the modeling of component-oriented applications and their deployment across nodes in a distributed computing platform, and *Expressions* defines elements used to construct explicit expression structures (as expression trees) in a standard and interchangeable way. The key point to this layer is that, by defining these concepts at a very abstract level of the CWM architecture, we ensure that these concepts are defined only once and that they can be reused in more specific contexts.

The next layer of CWM, *Resource*, defines metamodels of the various types of data resources comprising an information supply chain. The *Relational*, *Record*, *Multidimensional*, and *XML* metamodels extend both the Object and Foundation layers to define new modeling elements used to construct meta data defining relational databases, record-oriented databases, multidimensional servers, and XML document-based data resources. Note that object-oriented databases are not explicitly represented, because the Object layer as a subset of UML is replete with object-oriented modeling concepts. We can use CWM to define any conceivable meta data representing the various types of data resources that need to be managed by a data warehouse or ISC.

Business analysis concepts, the real heart and purpose of the data warehouse and ISC, are represented by metamodels comprising the fourth layer of CWM, the *Analysis* layer. Perhaps one of the most important metamodels in the Analysis layer is the *Transformation* metamodel. This metamodel defines modeling elements that can be used to specify source and target mappings and transformations between data resource models (instances of the Resource layer metamodels) as well as source and target mappings and transformations between data resources models and any of the various *analysis models*. These mappings often cross one or more levels of abstraction. For example, a purely logical OLAP model satisfying some business analysis requirement might be formulated using the OLAP metamodel. Similarly, a physical model of a relational *star-schema* might be specified using the Relational metamodel. The two models, logical and physical, then are linked together using instances of transformation mappings. The dimensional tables of the star-schema relational database are *semantically identified* as the *physical implementations* of *logical dimension* by virtue of this semantic mapping.

The Analysis layer provides additional metamodels that support the modeling of analysis-oriented meta data: *data mining*, *business nomenclature*, and *information visualization*. Data mining defines modeling elements used to specify meta data associated with various data mining tools that are often applied against the various data resources to extract important patterns and trends from the data. Business nomenclature allows for the construction of meta data defining and relating taxonomies of business terms and concepts. Elements defined by the Visualization metamodel enable the construction of meta data that is relevant to advanced reporting and visualization tools. Collectively, these metamodels provide the necessary semantic constructs required to build meta data supporting the analysis phases of the ISC (see Figure 2.1).

Finally, the *Management* layer defines two metamodels that are critical to defining meta data describing the ISC processing as a whole. The *Warehouse Process* metamodel enables us to model specific warehouse processes, such as ETL processes. *Warehouse Operation* defines modeling elements that are used to construct meta data defining the specific, periodic, and routine operations, such as scheduled events and their interdependencies. This meta data is of interest to ETL tools, time-dependent schedulers, and other warehouse management tools.

We've shown that CWM provides the semantically replete, common metamodel describing the problem domain that a model-based, meta data integration architecture for data warehousing and business analysis would require. If the various software products, tools, applications, and databases used in the construction of an ISC agree on the CWM metamodel, all are fundamentally capable of understanding the same instances of the CWM metamodel (models or meta data). Meta data can readily be interchanged (shared or reused) between the software components comprising the ISC. In fact, the collection of metamodels provided by CWM is comprehensive enough to model an entire data warehouse and ISC environment. A complete model of an entire ISC, from front-end data resources, to transformation and cleansing, to end-user analysis, to data warehouse management, can be constructed using the CWM metamodel. Such a model is essentially a top-to-bottom *slice* through the layered CWM metamodel depicted in Figure 2.10.

This ISC model can be made available to the entire environment (for example, via either a meta data repository or through point-wise interchange) and consumed by CWM-aware tools comprising the ISC. Each tool consumes those portions of the shared, global model that are relevant to its operations. A relational server would read that portion of the ISC model defining the relational schema of the data warehouse and use this submodel to build its internal catalog. Similarly, an OLAP server would extract an OLAP schema, along with transformation mappings back to the relational database schema, and use this particular submodel as the basis for constructing its internal multidimensional structures and data resource links. Therefore, from a single, model-based definition, an entire ISC could be generated (assuming that the various software tools implementing the ISC are all CWM-aware).

We also stated earlier that the common metamodel, serving as the heart of the model-based meta data integration approach, must be formulated according to certain formal rules (an abstract language) to ensure that all software tools will interpret the common metamodel in the same, intended manner. In the case of CWM, the OMG's Meta Object Facility (MOF) provides this required set of formal rules. MOF is an OMG standard defining a common, abstract language for the specification of metamodels. MOF is essentially a meta-metamodel, or model of the metamodel (sometimes called an *ontology*). It defines the essential elements, syntax, and structure of metamodels that are used to construct models of discrete systems. MOF serves as the common model of both CWM and UML. The power of MOF is that it enables otherwise dissimilar metamodels (representing different domains) to be used in an interoperable manner. MOF-aware applications may not have any knowledge of the domain-specific interfaces of some model instance but can still read and update that model using the generic operations of the reflective interfaces.

MOF semantics generally define certain meta data repository services that support model construction, discovery, traversal, and update. In particular, MOF defines *model life cycle* semantics that define effective meta data authoring and publishing functions, especially if combined with support for visual modeling (for example, a UML-oriented modeling tool). For example, newly developed metamodels can be persisted in the MOF repository and combined with other, existing metamodels. A MOF-compliant repository provides a number of important meta data services that go well beyond the construction and serving of meta data (for example, persistence, versioning, and directory services).

The model-based approach to meta data integration also requires a common interchange format for exchanging instances of shared meta data, as well as a common programming interface for meta data access. We had previously discussed the advantages of using the XML for this purpose, and this viewpoint is supported by much of the industry and advocated by leading meta data experts. The XML interchange encoding used by CWM is XMI, an OMG standard that defines a formal mapping of MOF-compliant metamodels, such as CWM to XML. XMI defines precisely how XML tags are to be used to store CWM metamodel instances in XML documents. The CWM metamodel is used to define a collection of XML tags expressed in the form of an XML Document Type Definition (DTD). CWM meta data (for example, instances of the CWM metamodel) then are serialized in XML documents. Each instance of meta data is stored as XML element content, delimited by appropriate metamodel tags.

XMI solves many of the difficult problems encountered when trying to use a tag-based language to represent objects and their associations. Furthermore, the fact that XMI is just a way of using XML means that both tags and the items the tags describe (element content) can be packaged together in the same document, enabling applications to readily understand the document content. Communication of content is both self-describing and inherently asynchronous, which is why XMI and XML-based interchange is so important in distributed and heterogeneous environments.

Programmatic access to CWM-enabled meta data resources is defined via standard mappings from MOF-compliant metamodels to various programming languages. The MOF specification, in particular, defines a mapping from any MOF-compliant metamodel, such as CWM, to the OMG's IDL, a language-neutral notation for specifying programmatic interfaces. The CWM specification includes the complete IDL definition for CWM. Defining a programmatic interface in some programming language of choice (for example, Java or C++) requires compiling the CWM IDL into interface definitions expressed in the syntax of the target language, using an appropriate IDL compiler for the target language.

Finally, we stated that a model-based, meta data integration solution must also provide some standard means of extending models, which is necessary to define highly product-specific meta data not accounted for by CWM. It is also necessary to be able to extend to the metamodel to include new metamodels representing additional subdomains that we might later want to include in our overall ISC solution. Because CWM is based on UML, we can rely on standard UML extension mechanisms to extend our models. These standard UML extension mechanisms consist of the modeling elements *Tagged Value*, *Stereotype*, and *Constraint*. These modeling elements are defined within the Core metamodel of the CWM Object layer. Extending the CWM metamodel requires defining a new metamodel representing some new subdomain. For example, suppose that a user of a CWM-aware data warehouse wanted to add support for *Customer Relationship Management* (CRM) tools. The user creates a CRM metamodel, preferably using a CWM-enabled, visual modeling tool that supports the automatic translation of UML models into CWM metamodels. This metamodel is combined with the definition of the core CWM metamodel currently understood by the environment (that is, via the central repository) and then publishes this new, extended CWM metamodel to the environment. Any CWM-aware CRM tools may now be integrated into the environment and can participate in interchanges of CRM meta data.

We have demonstrated throughout this subsection that CWM satisfies all of the model-specific characteristics of the model-based meta data integration approach. Much of the material described here is discussed in greater detail in subsequent chapters. The OMG foundation technologies leveraged by CWM (for example, UML, MOF, and XMI) are given a more thorough treatment in Chapter 3, "Foundation Technologies," and Chapter 4, "An Architectural Overview of CWM," and Chapters 5, 6, and 7 provide detailed examples of both using and extending CWM to provide meta data-level interoperability in data warehousing and business analysis environments. The next subsection describes those aspects of model-based meta data integration not directly provided by CWM.

What CWM Does Not Provide

CWM addresses all of the model-oriented aspects of model-based meta data integration, but certain other aspects of meta data integration are beyond the scope of CWM. These issues must be addressed, however, for a CWM-based solution to be effective.

CWM does not prescribe any implementation architecture.   CWM is a model of *usage*, not a model of implementation. As a usage model, the various CWM modeling elements are ultimately used to define *standard interfaces* (either in terms of XML or in the form of programmatic interfaces) for accessing the meta data instances they represent. How meta data is stored in a software product and how it is served to a client via one of these standard interfaces is up to the product implementation and is not prescribed by CWM. Participation in a CWM-aware environment does not require that a product or tool rearchitect internal meta data models or representations to conform to the CWM metamodel. Similarly, the design and implementation of the software adapters described earlier, which facilitate meta data import and export, are beyond the scope of CWM.

CWM does not define any repository architecture.   However, CWM's derivation from the MOF does imply that a CWM-compliant meta data repository must support certain meta data services required by all MOF-compliant repositories, in addition to the standard interfaces (XML and programmatic APIs) used to access CWM-compliant meta data. A number of important, repository-oriented services, such as versioning of models, persistence, and access control are not addressed specifically by CWM, because these services are highly dependent on the underlying technology platform, and CWM strives to be strictly technology-neutral.

CWM does not define a strategy for meta data management.   A coherent meta data strategy is key to the successful application of any meta data integration solution, whether CWM-based or not. An overall meta data management strategy, however, is not defined by CWM. (The use of CWM will have certain implications for the strategy.) Chapter 6, "Developing Meta Data Solutions Using CWM," explores meta data strategies and how they relate to CWM in greater detail.

CWM does not define meta data integration architecture.   The meta data architecture generally follows directly from the meta data management strategy. (It is a *realization* of the overall strategy). We have discussed the various interconnection topologies associated with meta data integration architectures (for example, point-to-point and hub-and-spoke). We've also demonstrated that CWM simplifies the application of these various topologies. (CWM is equally effective whether used to implement a point-to-point interconnection or a hub-and-spoke architecture). Selection of a particular interconnection topology is now driven more by meta data management considerations, rather than by meta data integration issues. These issues are discussed in detail in Chapter 6.

A Vision of Model-Based Meta Data Integration

Now that we've investigated CWM within the overall context of model-based meta data integration, let's step back and look at the some of the more profound and far-reaching ramifications of this general approach to meta data integration. We had stated previously that in the model-based approach, we achieve effective meta data integration through the exchange of shared, product- and platform-independent models. These models are based on a common meta-model and that common meta data is based on a well-defined abstract language, which in the case of CWM is provided by the OMG MOF. Software products and tools implement adapters that provide the capability to translate between the various shared models and their private, internal meta data definitions. In our world, the shared models *are* the meta data that drive our various software products and tools.

What is most significant about this approach is the complete independence of the system specification from any implementation technology or platform. The complete system definition (model) exists independently of any implementation model and may include formal mappings to many possible platform infrastructures. Meta data now exists externally to, and independently of, any particular software product, technology, or platform. It becomes an *information resource* in its own right.

Thus, interoperability between heterogeneous software components in the model-driven environment is ultimately achieved via ubiquitous, shared models, and the overall strategy for sharing and understanding those models consists of enabling software components to understand the common metamodel describing those models. The automated development, publishing, management, and interpretation of models are the steps that drive the overall model sharing process. This means that many heterogeneous applications, software tools, databases, and other components should ultimately be capable of plugging into the environment and discovering the various models describing the environment at large. Similarly, a component or product introduced to this environment should also be capable of publishing its own meta data (in the form of yet another shared model) to the rest of the environment. This scenario is illustrated in Figure 2.11.

Having an abundance of shared, descriptive, readily understandable, and easily locatable meta data (*ubiquitous meta data*, as described in Gartner, January 2000b) facilitates software component interoperability in a number of very specific ways, including.

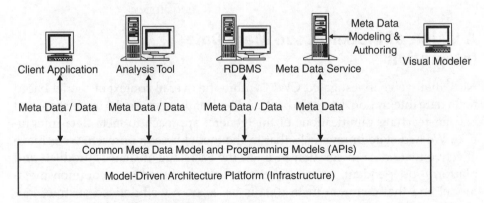

Figure 2.11 A meta data-driven environment.

1. Data interchange, transformation, and type mapping between dissimilar data resources can be driven by formal, product-independent meta data descriptions of the transformations, data types, and type-system mappings.

2. Schema generation can be based on shared meta data descriptions of common schema elements. For example, both a relational database and an OLAP server can build their internal representations of a dimensional model, according to a standard, meta data definition of a dimension that has been published to the environment. Having common meta data definitions facilitates data interchange between various subsystems, because there is a common understanding of what the data means.

3. Business analysis and visualization and reporting functions can use meta data in the processing and formatting of data for analysis and display purposes. Meta data descriptions confer the *higher level of meaning* on data items that analysts and reporting users need to make sense of data points and results (for example, definitions of common business terms, glossaries, taxonomies, nomenclatures, and so on, are all a part of the shared meta data).

4. Software components with no prior knowledge of each other's capabilities, interfaces, and data representations can interoperate once they've established a meta data *handshake*, in which each exposes its features and assesses those of the other. Note that this exchange of knowledge does not always need to be complete, but to the extent that components can make sense of each other's capabilities, they can interact with one another. In the absence of specific knowledge, components might rely on standard defaults or might be able to refer to some other sources of information to fill the knowledge gaps.

5. System architecture and behavior becomes more dynamic in nature. Publishing a new version of a model in a repository causes all software systems in the environment to automatically adjust their own behaviors to reflect the changes. Meta data is updated while the system is executing, and the resulting changes to system structure and behavior take effect as soon as the running system is ready to expose those changes. Nonprogrammers can modify system structure and behavior by modifying system models.

As stated previously, the model-based approach does not prescribe any implementation architecture. It does not require that the various internal representations of meta data within applications, tools, and databases be modified to correspond to the common metamodel. Product-specific internals and programming models remain as they are, and no need exists to re-engineer product internals to accommodate the model-based integration approach. Only the one-time construction of a product-specific adapter (for each product type) is necessary. This ensures that both the efficacy and cost-effectiveness of meta data integration, enhancing the economic returns on any data warehousing and business analysis effort.

Summary

In this chapter, we thoroughly examined the need for comprehensive meta data integration in the data warehousing and business analysis environments. We used the metaphor of the information supply chain to describe the movement of data through this environment and described why effective meta data integration between software products and tools supporting this environment was critical to ensuring that the supply chain flows smoothly.

We determined that a lack of meta data standards (that is, in terms of a commonly agreed-upon metamodel and an associated interchange format and programmatic interfaces) greatly inhibits meta data integration across the ISC. We concluded that this inability to integrate ISC tools and to reuse (share) meta data in a standard way has a major impact on the economic ROI of data warehousing and business analysis efforts. In fact, we might even conclude that meta data integration (or the lack thereof) is perhaps the single greatest economic issue in the deployment of data warehousing and business analysis solutions.

The Object Management Group's Common Warehouse Metamodel standard was described in detail, and we discussed how CWM is used in realizing completely integrated information supply chains comprised of multivendor software products and tools. This enhances the overall value-proposition for the ISC implementation effort (reducing integration costs and allowing for an optimal mixture of low-cost and best-of-breed tools). We showed that CWM satisfies the model-oriented requirements of a model-based approach to meta data integration. And, we delved considerably into the underlying OMG technologies for metamodeling and meta data interchange and interoperability that CWM leverages.

Finally, we provided a vision of what the model-based approach to meta data integration may bring in the near-term. We described the possibility of having abundant, shared meta data external to tools and products that could be readily leveraged by data warehouse components, providing nearly seamless interoperability and dynamic supply chain architectures.

CHAPTER

3

Foundation Technologies

The goal of CWM is to standardize the interchange format of shared meta data for data warehousing and business intelligence and to standardize the programming language API for accessing such meta data. To achieve this goal in an effective and consistent manner, CWM uses a model-driven approach that consists of the following steps:

1. Define the model of shared meta data for CWM (that is, the CWM metamodel) in Unified Modeling Language (UML).

2. Generate the specification of the interchange format for CWM meta data in eXtensible Markup Language (XML).

3. Generate the specification of the programming language API for accessing CWM meta data in CORBA Interface Definition Language (IDL).

Steps 2 and 3 are made possible using the OMG Meta Object Facility (MOF). In particular, Step 2 relies on XMI (XML Meta data Interchange), and Step 3 relies on the MOF to IDL Mapping.

Java has been the most widely used implementation platform for CWM and, therefore, is also a key foundation technology for CWM. In the following, we give an overview of these foundation technologies: UML, XML, MOF, and XMI. We will not discuss CORBA IDL or Java because they have been in existence for some time and are well known.

Unified Modeling Language (UML)

UML is a language for specifying, visualizing, constructing, and documenting the artifacts of systems, particularly software systems. Before UML, more than 50 object-oriented modeling languages existed. Among these, the most prominent ones included Grady Booch's Booch Method, Ivar Jacobson's Object-Oriented Software Engineering (OOSE), and Jim Rumbaugh's Object Modeling Technique (OMT). In 1996, these three modeling languages were unified and published as UML 0.9. A revised version, UML 1.1, was adopted by the OMG as a standard in November 1997 (Rumbaugh et al., 1999).

CWM 1.0 is based on UML 1.3, which was adopted by the OMG in June 1999. The UML 1.3 specification consists of the following parts:

UML Semantics. Defines the semantics of the UML metamodel. The UML metamodel is layered architecturally and organized by packages. Within each package, the model elements are defined in terms of abstract syntax (using class diagrams), well-formedness rules (in OCL, see the following section), and semantics (in English).

UML Notation Guide. Specifies the graphic syntax (for example, class diagram) for expressing the semantics of the UML metamodel.

Object Constraint Language Specification. Defines the Object Constraint Language (OCL) syntax, semantics, and grammar. OCL is a formal language for expressing constraints (Warmer and Kleppe, 1999).

UML XMI DTD Specification. Uses XML DTD to define a mechanism for interchanging UML models that conform to the UML metamodel.

UML CORBAfacility Interface Definition. Uses IDL to specify a repository that enables the creation, storage, and manipulation of UML models.

UML Standard Profiles. Defines the UML Profile for Software Development Processes and the UML Profile for Business Modeling.

CWM 1.0 depends only on the first three parts of the UML 1.3 specification.

Building Blocks and Well-Formedness Rules

UML provides an object-oriented modeling language that consists of building blocks and well-formedness rules. The basic building blocks of UML are as follows:

Model elements.   Common object-oriented concepts such as classes, objects, interfaces, components, use cases, and so on.

Relationships.   Connections among model elements such as associations, generalization, dependencies, and so on.

Diagrams.   Groups of graphic symbols that can be used to represent model elements and their relationships, such as class diagrams, object diagrams, use case diagrams, and so on.

Simple building blocks can be used together to construct large, complex models as illustrated in Figure 3.1, which shows a class diagram representing a model of carbon-hydrogen compounds. In the model, a chemical element is represented as a UML class. Because both carbon and hydrogen are chemical elements, they are represented as UML classes as well, specifically as a specialization of the class that represents the chemical element. The bonding between carbon and hydrogen is represented as a UML association, with a special label <<covalent>>. The two ends of the covalent bond are represented as UML *Association Ends* and are marked with role names "C" and "H" (for carbon and hydrogen, respectively). The bonding between carbon and carbon is represented in a similar fashion.

Figure 3.2 shows an object diagram representing a specific instance of the model of a carbon-hydrogen compound, which represents the C_2H_6 molecule. In the diagram are two instances of the Carbon class with both instances linked together. The link is an instance of the <<covalent>> association between Carbon classes. Six instances of the Hydrogen class, with three instances each, are linked to an instance of the Carbon class. The link is an instance of the <<covalent>> association between the Carbon class and the Hydrogen class.

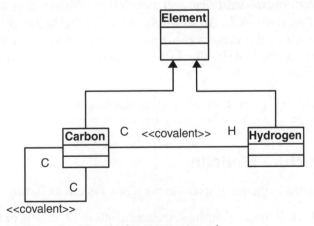

Figure 3.1   Class diagram: Carbon-hydrogen compounds.

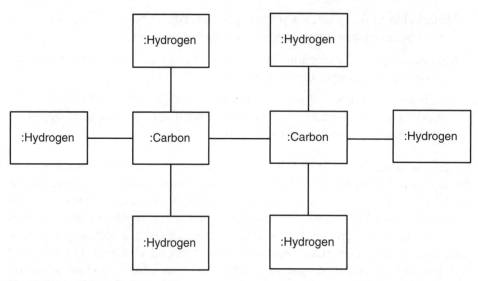

Figure 3.2   Object diagram: C_2H_6.

Well-formedness rules can be used to ensure that a model or model fragment adheres to all syntactic and semantic rules that apply to it. As an example of syntactic rules, a class is drawn as a solid-outline rectangle with three compartments separated by horizontal lines. The top compartment contains the class name and the other compartments contain attributes and operations, respectively. Only the top compartment is required; either or both of the attribute and operation compartments may be suppressed, as is the case in Figure 3.1. Also shown is an example of syntactic guidelines: Class names begin with an uppercase letter.

Some semantic rules can be expressed using graphic notations. These include scope, visibility, and multiplicity. We will see examples of these when we discuss attributes, operations, and associations. Most semantic rules can be expressed using only OCL. An example is the following semantic constraint on a concrete class: If a class is concrete, all the operations of the class must have a realizing method in the full descriptor. In OCL, this constraint is expressed as follows:

```
not self.isAbstract implies self.allOperations->
forAll(op | self.allMethods->exists(m | m.specification->includes(op)))
```

Static Structure Modeling

UML can be used to model different aspects of a system including the following:

Structural modeling.   Emphasizes the structure of objects of the system, including their classes, relationships, attributes, and operations. Structural modeling consists of static structure modeling using class diagrams and object diagrams, and implementation modeling using component diagrams and deployment diagrams.

Use case modeling. Emphasizes the functionality of the system as it appears to outside users. A use case model partitions system functionality into transactions (use cases) that are meaningful to users (actors).

Behavioral modeling. Emphasizes the behavior of objects of the system, including their interactions, events, and control and data flow. Behavioral modeling consists of interaction modeling using sequence diagrams and collaboration diagrams, event modeling using state chart diagrams, and control and data flow modeling using activity diagrams.

Among these, only the static structure modeling aspect is needed for modeling meta data.

The core elements of static structures are classes, objects, attributes, and operations. A *class* is a description of a set of objects that share the same attributes, operations, and semantics. All *objects* are instances of a class. A class has attributes that describe the characteristics of the objects. A class also may have operations that manipulate the attributes and perform other actions. An *attribute* has a name and type, which can be a primitive type or class. An attribute can have different scope—*class-scope* or instance-scope—and different visibility—public (+), protected (#), or private (-). An *operation* has a name, type, and zero or more parameters. Similar to attributes, an operation can have different scope—*class-scope* or instance-scope—and different visibility—public (+), protected (#), or private (-). These core elements are illustrated in Figure 3.3, which shows a Window class represented in varying levels of

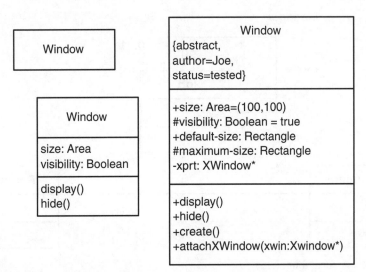

Figure 3.3 Class diagrams: Window.

detail: The first class diagram shows only the class name; the second class diagram also shows the public and protected attributes and operations; and the third class diagram shows all attributes and operations as well as the class name with annotations.

The core relationships of static structures include the following—association, aggregation, generalization, dependency, and refinement. *Association* is a relationship between two or more classes, which involves connections among their objects. An association normally is bidirectional but may be unidirectional. It has multiplicity at both ends, which expresses how many objects can be linked—zero-to-one (0..1), one-to-one (1..1), zero-to-many (0..* or *), or one-to-many (1..*). *Aggregation* is a special form of association that specifies a whole-part relationship between the aggregate (whole) and the component (part). An aggregation may be *shared*, in which case the parts may be parts in any wholes, or the aggregation may be a *Composition*, in which case the whole owns the parts, and the multiplicity on the whole must be zero-to-one. *Generalization* is a taxonomic relationship between a more general and a more specific element. An instance of the more specific element may be used wherever the more general element is allowed. *Dependency* is a relationship between two elements in which a change to one element (the independent element) will affect the other element (the dependent element). *Realization* is a relationship between a specification and its implementation. Examples of associations are shown in Figure 3.4. An association named Job exists between the Person class and Company class, with role names employee and employer, respectively. The Job association has an associated class by the same name, which is used to describe its characteristics. The Job class is related to itself by an association

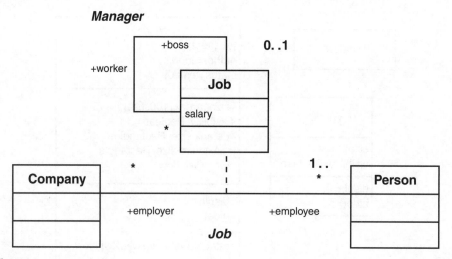

Figure 3.4 Associations.

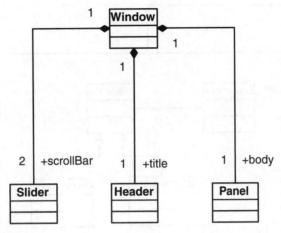

Figure 3.5 Compositions.

named Manages, with role names boss and worker. Examples of Compositions are shown in Figure 3.5. The Window class owns the Slider, Header, and Panel classes.

Model Management

UML uses *package* as the mechanism for organizing model elements into semantically related groups. A package owns its model elements, and a model element cannot be owned by more than one package. A package can import model elements from other packages, which means that the public contents of the target package are added to the namespace of the source package. A package can have different visibility—public (+), protected (#), or private (-). Figure 3.6 shows a Warehouse package owning four classes and an association.

Extensible Markup Language (XML)

XML is a language for defining markup languages (for example, HTML). It describes a class of data objects, XML documents, that are written using these markup languages and describes the behavior of computer programs that process them. XML is designed for use over the Internet. XML documents are formal and concise (that is, machine-processable) and reasonably clear (human-legible). They are also easy to create and process. Therefore, since its birth in 1998, XML has rapidly become the universal format for data interchange and application interchange.

CWM 1.0 is based on XML 1.0, which was adopted by the W3C in February 1999. The XML 1.0 specification consists of the following parts:

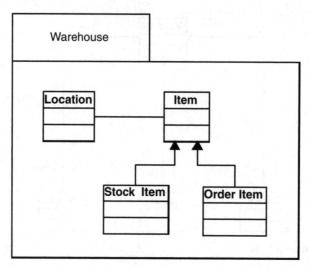

Figure 3.6   Package.

XML document definition.   Defines the logical and physical structures of an XML document

Document Type Definition (DTD) definition.   Defines the grammar rules that can be used to define document markups

XML Document

An XML document has both a logical and a physical structure. Physically, the document is composed of units called *entities*. A document begins in a document (or root) entity. Logically, the document is composed of elements, declarations, comments, character references, and processing instructions. All of these are indicated in the document by explicit markups. An XML document must be well formed—that is, the logical and physical structures must meet the well-formedness constraints defined in the XML 1.0 specification. (They must nest properly.)

Each XML document contains one or more *elements*, which are either delimited by start-tags and end-tags, or, for empty elements, by an empty-element tag. Each element has a type, identified by name, and may have a set of attributes. Each *attribute* has a name and a value. The text between the start-tag and end-tag is called the *content*. The content of an element may consist of other (child) elements, character data optionally interspersed with child elements, or nothing. The following is an example of a Window element with two attributes (size and visibility) and an empty content:

```
<Window size="(100, 100)" visibility="true"/>
```

XML documents normally begin with an *XML declaration* that specifies the version of XML being used. For example,

```
<?xml version="1.0">
```

This generally is followed by a *document type declaration,* appearing before the first element in the document, which contains or points to markup declarations that provide a grammar for a class of documents (known as a document type definition to be discussed in the next section). Comments may appear anywhere in an XML document outside other markup; they are not part of the document's character data. An example of a comment follows:

```
<!- An Instance of Window ->
```

Figure 3.7 shows a complete, well-formed XML document that contains the markups we just described. The document can be used to interchange an instance of the Window class represented in Figure 3.3.

DTD

An XML document, in addition to being well formed, may also be valid if it meets validity constraints defined in the XML 1.0 specification. These validity constraints generally are defined in reference to the document type declaration that contains or references a DTD. The DTD for a document consists of both the internal subset of markup declarations contained within the document and the external subset referenced by the document. A markup declaration is an element type declaration, an attribute-list declaration, an entity declaration, or a notation declaration.

The element type and attribute-list declarations constrain the element structure of an XML document. The element type declaration constrains the element's content. An element type may have empty content, any content, mixed content, or element content. An element type has empty content when elements of that type have no content (character data or child elements). An element type has any content when elements of that type may contain any child elements. An element type has mixed content when elements of that type may contain character data, optionally interspersed with child elements. In this case, the types of child elements may be constrained but not their order or

```
<?xml version="1.0"?>
<!- A Instance of Window ->
<Window size="(200, 200)" visibility="true"/>
```

Figure 3.7 A well-formed XML document.

their number of occurrences. An element type has element content when elements of that type must contain only child elements. In this case, the constraint includes a content model governing the allowed types of the child elements and the order in which they are allowed to appear. The following shows examples of element type declarations with, respectively, empty-content, any-content, mixed-content, and element-content models:

```
<!ELEMENT br EMPTY>
<!ELEMENT list ANY>
<!ELEMENT para (#PCDATA)>
<!ELEMENT section (para, br, list?)>
```

The *attribute-list declaration* specifies the name, data type, and default value (if any) of each attribute associated with a given element type. When more than one attribute-list declaration is provided for a given element type, the contents of all those provided are merged. When more than one definition is provided for the same attribute of a given element type, the first declaration is binding, and later declarations are ignored. Attribute types are of three kinds: A string type, a set of tokenized types (for example, ID and IDREF), and enumerated types. An attribute default provides information on whether the attribute's presence is required in a document, and if not, how an XML processor should handle the attribute if it is absent in a document. The following shows examples of attribute-list declarations:

```
<!ATTLIST section
     id   ID    #REQUIRED
     name CDATA #IMPLIED>
<!ATTLIST list
     type (bullet|ordered) "bullet">
```

Figure 3.8 shows the same XML document as in Figure 3.7, but it now references a DTD and is valid against the DTD. The DTD defines the class of XML documents that can be used to interchange an instance of the Window class represented in Figure 3.3.

XML Namespaces

An XML document is likely to contain elements and attributes that are defined for and used by multiple software systems. Such documents, containing multiple markup vocabularies, pose problems of recognition and collision. Software systems need to be able to recognize the elements and attributes that they are designed to process, even in the face of collisions occurring when

```
window.xml:


<?xml version="1.0"?>
<!- A Instance of Window ->
<!DOCTYPE Window SYSTEM "window.dtd">
<Window size="(200, 200)" visibility="true"/>




window.dtd:


<!ELEMENT Window EMPTY>
<!ATTLIST Window
     size CDATA "(100, 100)"
     visibility (true|false) "true">
```

Figure 3.8 A valid XML document and its DTD.

markup intended for some other software systems uses the same element type or attribute name. XML namespaces provide the mechanism for element types and attributes to have universal names, whose scope extends beyond their containing document.

Names from XML namespaces may appear as qualified names, which contain a single colon, separating the name into a namespace prefix and a local part. The prefix, which is mapped to a URI reference, selects a namespace. The combination of the universally managed URI namespace and the document's own namespace produces identifiers that are universally unique. Namespaces may be declared as default (that is, without a prefix) and overridden, as shown in the following example:

```
<?xml version="1.0"?>
<!- the initial default namespace is "books" ->
<book xmlns='urn"loc.gov.books'
     xmlns:isbn='urn:ISBN:0-395-36341-6'>
   <title>Client/Server Data Access with Java and XML</title>
   <isbn:number>0-471-24577-1</isbn:number>
   <notes>
       <!- the local default namespace is "HTML" ->
       <p xmlns='urn:w3.org-ns:HTML'>
           This is a new book of great value to DBUniverse attendees!
       </p>
   </notes>
</book>
```

Meta Object Framework (MOF)

MOF is a model-driven, distributed object framework for specifying, constructing, managing, interchanging, and integrating meta data in software systems. The aim of the framework is to support any kind of meta data and to allow new kinds of meta data to be added as required. In order to achieve this, MOF uses a four-layer meta data architecture, the so-called OMG Meta Data Architecture, as shown in Table 3.1. This architecture treats meta data (M1) as data (M0) and formally models each distinct type of meta data. These formal models, the so-called metamodels (M2), are expressed using the meta-modeling constructs provided by a single meta-metamodel (M3), which is called the MOF Model. Figure 3.9 shows an example of the OMG Meta Data Architecture, which further illustrates the relationships between the MOF Model (the meta-metamodel), the UML metamodel (an example of a metamodel), a user model (an example of model or meta data), and user objects (examples of object or data).

CWM 1.0 is based on MOF 1.3, which was adopted by the OMG in September 1999. The MOF 1.3 specification consists of the following parts:

The MOF Model. Defines the modeling elements, including the rules for their use, which can be used to construct metamodels

MOF reflective interfaces. Allows a program to create, update, access, navigate, and invoke operations on meta data without using metamodel specific interfaces

MOF to IDL mapping. Defines the standard mapping from a metamodel defined using the MOF Model onto CORBA IDL, thus allowing the automatic generation of metamodel specific interfaces for accessing and manipulating meta data

Table 3.1 OMG Meta Data Architecture

META-LEVEL	MOF TERMS	EXAMPLES
M3	Meta-metamodel	MOF Model
M2	Metamodel, Meta-meta data	UML Metamodel, **CWM Metamodel**
M1	Model	UML models
M0	Object, data	Modeled systems, **Warehouse/BI data**

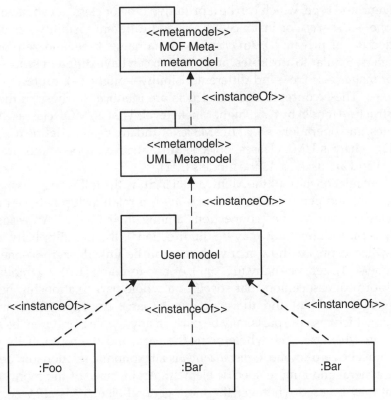

Figure 3.9   OMG meta data architecture: An example.

The MOF Model

The MOF Model is based on the concepts and constructs of UML, particularly its static structure model and model management. As such, the MOF Model does not define its own graphical notation or constraint language but uses the UML notation and OCL for such purposes, respectively. Like the UML meta-model, the MOF Model is layered architecturally and organized by packages. Within each package, the model elements are defined in terms of abstract syntax (using class diagrams), well-formedness rules (in OCL), and semantics (in English).

The core elements of the MOF Model are classes, objects, attributes, and operations. A *class* is a description of a set of objects that share the same attributes, operations, and semantics. All *objects* are instances of a class. A class has attributes that describe the characteristics of the objects. A class also may have operations that manipulate the attributes and perform other actions. An *attribute* has a name and type, which can be a primitive type or class. It can have different scope—*class-scope* or instance-scope—and different visibility—public (+), protected (#), or private (-). An *operation* has a name, type, and zero or more parameters. Similar to attributes, an operation can have different scope—*class-scope* or instance-scope—and different visibility—public (+), protected (#), or private (-). These concepts and constructs are identical to those in the UML static structure model but at a higher meta level. That is, MOF classes, objects, attributes, and operations are at the M3 level and are used to define metamodels (M2); whereas UML classes, objects, attributes, and operations are at the M2 level and are used to define models (M1).

The core relationships of the MOF Model include the following—association, aggregation, and generalization. *Association* is a relationship between two or more classes that involves connections among their objects. An association usually is bidirectional but may be unidirectional. It has multiplicity at both ends, which expresses how many objects can be linked—zero-to-one (0..1), one-toone (1..1), zero-to-many (0..* or *), or one-to-many (1..*). *Aggregation* is a special form of association that specifies a whole-part relationship between the aggregate (whole) and the component (part). An aggregation may be *shared*, in which case the parts may be parts in any wholes, or it may be a *Composition*, in which case the whole owns the parts and the multiplicity on the whole must be zero-to-one. *Generalization* is a taxonomic relationship between a more general and a more specific element. An instance of the more specific element may be used wherever the more general element is allowed. These concepts and constructs again are identical to those in the UML static structure model but at a higher meta level. That is, MOF associations, aggregations, and generalizations are at the M3 level and are used to define metamodels (M2); whereas UML associations, aggregations, and generalizations are at the M2 level and are used to define models (M1).

MOF uses *package* as the mechanism for organizing model elements into semantically related groups. A package owns its model elements, and a model element cannot be owned by more than one package. A package can import model elements from other packages, which means that the public contents of the target package are added to the namespace of the source package. A package can have different visibility—public (+), protected (#), or private (-). This mechanism is identical to that used in UML model management.

Although the MOF Model is identical to the UML static structure model and model management in most concepts and constructs, major differences do exist. First, an MOF association is restricted to be binary; it is defined between two classes and it has two association ends. Each association end has a name, type, and multiplicity. Second, an MOF association cannot have an attached class (the *association class* in UML, refer to Figure 3.4). Third, an MOF class can have references. A reference defines the class's knowledge of, and access to, links that are instances of an association. A reference has a name, and the referenced AssociationEnd. Figure 3.10 shows a simple MOF metamodel of a relational database that consists of Schema, Table, and Column, with binary associations and references.

Meta Objects and Interfaces

Various kinds of meta objects represent meta data in MOF for access and manipulation. Both the reflective interfaces and the MOF to IDL mapping share a common, object-oriented model of meta data with five kinds of M1-level meta objects: Instance object, ClassProxy object, Association object, Package object, and PackageFactory object. These objects and their relationships among each other are shown in Figure 3.11.

The instances of an M2-level package are represented as *Package* objects. A package object provides access to a collection of meta objects described by a metamodel. In particular, there are the following:

- One package attribute for each M2-level package nested or clustered by the Package
- One class proxy attribute for each M2-level class in the package
- One association attribute for each M2-level association in the package

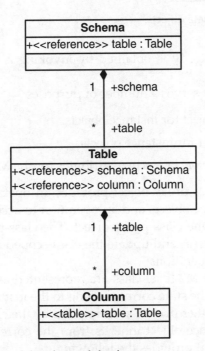

Figure 3.10 MOF metamodel: Relational database.

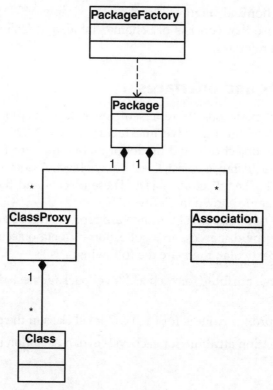

Figure 3.11 M1-level meta objects.

A package object typically is obtained by invoking a create operation on a *PackageFactory* object.

A class proxy object serves a number of purposes:

- It is a Factory object for instance objects.
- It is the container for instance objects.
- It holds the state of class-scope attributes for the M2-level class.

The interface of a class proxy object provides an operation that enables the client to create Instance objects and an operation to access the set of Instance objects contained by the class proxy object. The class-proxy object also provides operations to access and update the class-scoped attributes state and to invoke class-scoped operations.

The instances of an M2-level class are represented as Instance objects. An instance object holds the state corresponding to the instance-scoped attributes of the class and any other private state implied by the class specification. The interface for an Instance object inherits from the corresponding ClassProxy interface. In addition, it provides the following:

- Operations to access and update the instance-scoped attributes
- Operations to invoke the instance-scoped operations
- Operations to access and update associations via References
- Operations that support object identity for the instance
- An operation for deleting the instance object

The instances (links) of M2-level associations are not represented as meta objects. Instead, an M1-level *Association* object holds a collection of links (that is, the link set) corresponding to an M2-level association. The interface of an association object provides the following:

- Operations for querying the link set
- Operations for adding, modifying, and removing links from the set
- An operation that returns the entire link set

MOF Reflective Interfaces

The MOF reflective interfaces allow a program to do the following:

- Create, update, access, navigate, and invoke operations on M1-level instance objects
- Query and update links using M1-level Association objects
- Navigate an M1-level package structure

These operations can be performed without using metamodel specific interfaces. These interfaces, therefore, can be used for general-purpose (metamodel independent) access and manipulation of M1-level meta objects. They also can be used for interoperability across metamodels.

The MOF reflective interfaces include four abstract interfaces:

RefBaseObject. Provides common operations for all M1-level meta objects

RefObject. Provides common operations for M1-level instance objects and class proxy objects

RefAssociation. Provides common operations for M1-level association objects

RefPackage. Provides common operations for M1-level package objects

RefObject, RefAssociation, and RefPackage all inherit from RefBaseObject and, therefore, support the operations provided by RefBaseObject.

```
interface RefBaseObject {
    string ref_mof_id ();
    DesignatorType ref_meta_object ();
    boolean ref_itself (in RefBaseObject other_object);
    RefPackage ref_iddediate_package ();
    RefPackage ref_outermost_package ();
    void ref_delete() raises (MOFError);
}
```

Figure 3.12 RefBaseObject.

RefBaseObject provides every M1-level object with the following operations (see Figure 3.12 for its representation in CORBA IDL):

mofId.   Returns this object's permanent unique identifier string

metaObject.   Returns the object that describes this object

itself.   Tests whether this object and the other supplier object are the same

immediatePackage.   Returns the RefPackage object for the package that immediately contains this object

outermostPackage.   Returns the RefPackage object for the package that ultimately contains this object

delete.   Destroys this object, including the objects it contains directly or transitively

RefObject provides every M1-level instance object and class proxy object with the following operations (see Figure 3.13 for its representation in CORBA IDL):

isInstanceOf.   Tests whether this object is an instance of the supplier class

createInstance.   Creates an instance of the class for this object's most derived interface

allObjects.   Return the set of all instances in the current extent whose type is given by this object's class

setValue.   Assigns a new value to an attribute or reference

value.   Returns the current value of an attribute or reference

unsetValue.   Resets an optional attribute or reference to contain no element

addValue, addValueAt, addValueBefore.   Adds a new element to the current value of a multivalued attribute or reference

modifyValue, modifyValueAt.   Replaces one element of a multivalued attribute or reference with a new value

```
interface RefObject : RefBaseObject {
    boolean ref_is_instance_of (in DesignatorType some_class,
        in boolean consider_subtypes);
    RefObject ref_create_instance (in ValueTypeList args)
        raises (MofError);
    RefObjectSet ref_all_objects (in boolean include_subtypes);
    void ref_set_value (in DesignatorType feature,
        in ValueType new_value) raises (MofError);
    ValueType ref_value (in designatorType feature)
        raises (NotSet, MofError);
    void ref_unset_value() raises (MofError);
    void ref_add_value (in DesignatorType feature,
        in ValueType new_element) raises (Moferror);
    void ref_add_value_at (in DesignatorType feature,
        in ValueType new_element, in unsigned long position)
        raises (Moferror);
    void ref_add_value_before (in DesignatorType feature,
        in ValueType new_element, in ValueType before_element)
        raises (Moferror);
    void ref_modify_value (in DesignatorType feature,
        in ValueType new_element, in ValueType old_element)
        raises (NotFound, MofError);
    void ref_modify_value_at (in DesignatorType feature,
        in ValueType new_element, in unsigned long position)
        raises (NotFound, MofError);
    void ref_remove_value (in DesignatorType feature,
        in ValueType old_element) raises (NotFound, MofError);
    void ref_remove_value_at (in DesignatorType feature,
        in unsigned long position) raises (NotFound, MofError);
    RefObject ref_immediate_composite ();
    RefObject ref_outermost_composite ();
    ValueType ref_invoke_operation (
        in DesignatorType requested_operation,
        inout ValueTypeList args) raises (OtherException, MofError);
}
```

Figure 3.13 RefObject.

removeValue, removeValueAt.   Removes an element of a multivalued attribute or reference

immediateComposite.   Returns the immediate composite object for this object

outermostComposite.   Returns the outermost composite object for this object

invokeOperation.   Invokes a metamodel defined operation on this object

```
interface RefAssociation : RefBaseObject {
    LinkSet ref_all_links ();
    boolean ref_link_exists (in Link some_link) raises (MofError);
    RefObjectUList ref_query (in DesignatorType query_end,
        in RefObject query_object) raises (MofError);
    void ref_add_link (in Link new_link) raises (MofError);
    void ref_add_link_before (in Link new_link,
        in DesignatorType position_end,
        in RefObject before) raises (NotFound, MofError);
    void ref_modify_link (in Link old_link,
        in DesignatorType position_end,
        in RefObject new_object) raises (NotFound, MofError);
    void ref_remove_link (in Link old_link)
        raises (NotFound, MofError);
}
```

Figure 3.14   RefAssociation.

RefAssociation provides every M1-level association object with the following operations (see Figure 3.14 for its representation in CORBA IDL):

allLinks.   Returns all links in the link set for this association object

LinkExists.   Tests whether the supplied link is a member of the link set of this association object

Query.   Returns a list containing all instance objects that are linked to the supplier queryObject by links within the extent of this association object

addLink, addLinkBefore.   Adds a new link to the link set of this association object

ModifyLink.   Updates a link in the link set of this association object by replacing the Instance object at positionEnd

RemoveLink.   Removes a link from the link set of this association object

RefPackage provides every M1-level package object with the following operations (see Figure 3.15 for its representation in CORBA IDL):

classRef.   Returns the ClassProxy object for a given class

associationRef.   Returns the Association object for a given association

packageRef.   Returns the package object for a supplied package, which must be either nested or clustered within the package for this package object

```
interface RefPackage : RefBaseObject {
    RefObject ref_class_ref (in DesignatorType type)
        raises (MofError);
    RefAssociation ref_association_ref (
        in DesignatorType association) raises (MofError);
    RefPackage ref_package_ref (in DesignatorType package)
        raises (InvalidDesignator);
}
```

Figure 3.15 RefPackage.

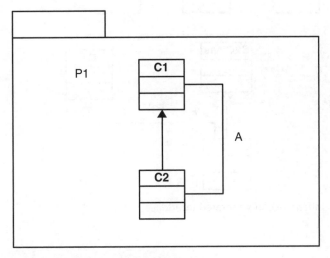

Figure 3.16 Example of a metamodel definition.

MOF to IDL Mapping

The MOF to IDL mapping defines the standard mapping from a metamodel defined using the MOF Model onto CORBA IDL. The resulting interfaces enable a user to create, access, and update instances of the metamodel (that is, M1-level meta objects) using CORBA client programs. The following describes the patterns of interface inheritance in the CORBA IDL generated by the MOF to IDL mapping. First, Figure 3.16 shows an example metamodel that consists of a package P1. The package P1 contains classes C1 and C2, where C2 is a subclass of C1, and an association A that connects C1 and C2. Figure 3.17 shows the inheritance graph for the generated interfaces that correspond to the example metamodel. The root of the inheritance graph is the group of four interfaces that make up the MOF reflective interfaces. The inheritance patterns are as follows:

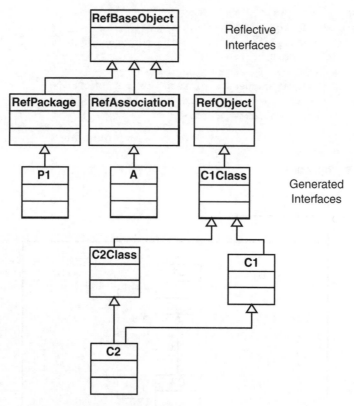

Figure 3.17 Inheritance in generated interfaces.

- All package object interfaces inherit (directly or indirectly) from RefPackage.

- All association object interfaces inherit from RefAssociation.

- All class proxy interfaces inherit (directly or indirectly) from RefObject.

- All instance object interfaces inherit from the corresponding class proxy interfaces.

- When an M2-level package P2 inherits from another package P1, the corresponding interface P2 inherits from the corresponding P1.

- When an M2-level class C2 inherits from another class C1:

- The class proxy interface for C2 inherits from the class proxy interface for C1.

- The Instance object interface for C2 inherits from the Instance object interface for C1.

Because all generated interfaces inherit from the corresponding MOF reflective interfaces, all general-purpose meta object operations provided by MOF reflective interfaces are available for use from metamodel specific, generated interfaces.

As shown in Figure 3.16 and Figure 3.17, the MOF IDL mapping rules are defined under the assumption that a top-level (that is, un-nested) M2 package and its contents are mapped onto CORBA IDL as a single unit. The mapping rules are defined in terms of IDL templates. Each template describes the maximum IDL that could be generated when mapping MOF Model constructs. In any specific case, the actual IDL generated will depend on the properties of the corresponding MOF model construct. The mapping for MOF Model constructs is as follows:

Package.   Each M2-level package maps onto a CORBA IDL module that contains the IDL for all of the package's contained elements, including packages, classes, associations, constants, exceptions, DataTypes, and constraints. The module also contains the IDL for M1-level package and package factory objects. A package factory interface is generated for top-level M2 package packages only.

Class.   Each M2-level class (for example, C1) maps onto two CORBA IDL interfaces:

■ The C1Class interface represents the class proxy object. It contains the IDL for all of the class's contained elements, including constants, exceptions, data types, and constraints. It has IDL attributes and operations for each class-scope M2-level attribute and operation defined for the class. It also has a factory operation for C1 instances and IDL sequence attributes giving all C1! subtype instances.

■ The C1 interface represents the instance objects of the class. It has IDL attributes and operations for each instance-scope M2-level attribute and operation and each reference defined for the class. The C1 interface inherits the C1Class interface.

Association.   Each M2-level association maps onto a CORBA IDL interface. It has operations for querying and updating the links belonging to an association object. The links are represented as a CORBA struct with two fields.

XML Meta Data Interchange (XMI)

XMI is an XML language for interchanging meta data in software systems. XMI integrates the three foundation technologies discussed previously: UML,

MOF, and XML. UML defines a rich, object-oriented modeling language that is supported by a wide range of graphical notations. XML provides a universal format for interchanging meta data (and data). MOF defines an extensible framework for defining models for meta data (using the UML notation) and providing tools with programmatic interfaces to create, update, access, and navigate meta data. XMI allows MOF meta data, that is meta data that conforms to an MOF (based) metamodel, to be interchanged as streams or files with a standard format based on XML.

XMI supports the interchange of complete meta data or meta data fragments, as well as tool-specific extension meta data. Each XML document that contains meta data conforming to XMI contains XML elements that are required by XMI, XML elements that contain meta data conforming to a MOF metamodel, and, optionally, XML elements that contain meta data that represent extensions of the metamodel. Metamodels are explicitly identified in XML elements required by XMI. The XML Namespace mechanism allows XMI to use multiple metamodels at the same time in an XML document.

CWM 1.0 is based on XMI 1.1, which was adopted by the OMG in October 1999. The XMI 1.1 specification consists of the following parts:

XML DTD production.   Rules for transforming MOF metamodels into XML DTDs

XML DTD design principles.   For producing XML DTDs

XML document production.   Rules for encoding and decoding MOF meta data in XML documents

XML generation principles.   For producing XML documents

Essentially, XMI is a pair of parallel mappings between MOF metamodels and XML DTDs and between MOF meta data and XML documents.

XML DTD Production

An XML DTD provides a means by which an XML processor can validate the syntax and the structural semantics of an XML document. XMI provides rules by which a DTD can be generated for any MOF metamodel. However, the use of DTD is optional; an XML document need not reference a DTD, even if one exists. Performing XML validation on the XML document containing MOF meta data can be advantageous. If a DTD is referenced in the XML document, any XML processor can perform some verification, relieving meta data import and export tools of the burden of performing these checks.

XML validation can determine whether the XML elements required by XMI are present in the XML document containing MOF meta data, whether XML attributes required in these XML elements have values for them, and whether some of the values are correct. XML validation also can perform some verification that the meta data conforms to a metamodel. However, although some checking can be done, you cannot rely solely on XML validation to verify that the meta data satisfies all of a metamodel's semantic constraints. Finally, XML validation can be used to validate extensions to the metamodel, because extensions must be represented as elements declared in the DTD.

Every XMI DTD, that is an XML DTD produced using rules defined by XMI, consists of the following declarations:

- The required XMI declarations
- Declarations for a specific metamodel
- Declarations for differences
- Declarations for extensions

XMI requires that a number of XML element declarations be included in the DTD, which enables XML validation. Some of these XML elements contain information about the meta data to be interchanged—for example, the identity of the metamodel associated with the meta data, the time the meta data was generated, the tool that generated the meta data, whether the meta data has been verified, and so on. All elements defined by XMI have the prefix *XMI* to avoid name conflicts with XML elements that would be part of a metamodel. In addition to required XML element declarations, some attributes must be defined according to XMI. Every XML element that corresponds to a metamodel class must have attributes that enable the XML element to act as a proxy for a local or remote XML element. These attributes are used to associate an XML element with another XML element. Most of the XML attributes defined by XMI have the prefix *xmi*; however, the XML attributes of XMI elements defined by XMI do not, in general, have this prefix. The required XMI attributes are shown in Table 3.2. The required common XMI elements are shown in Table 3.3.

Table 3.2 Required XMI Attributes

XMI ATTRIBUTE	DESCRIPTION
xmi.id	A locally unique identifier for an XML element
xmi.label	A string label identifying an XML element
xmi.uuid	A globally unique identifier for an XML element
Href	Simple Xlink, can be used to reference XML elements whose xmi.id, xmi.label, or xmi.uuid attributes are set to particular values.
xmi.idref	Allows an XML element to refer to another XML element within the same document whose xmi.id is set to a particular value

Table 3.3 Common XMI Elements

XMI ELEMENT	DESCRIPTION
XMI	The top level XML element for each XMI document
XMI.header	Contains XML elements, which identify the model, metamodel, and meta-metamodel for the meta data, as well as an optional XML element containing various items
XMI.content	Contains the actual meta data being interchanged. It may represent instance (M0), model (M1), or metamodel (M2) information.
XMI.extensions	Contains XML elements, which contain meta data that is an extension of the metamodel
XMI.extension	Contains XML elements, which also contain meta data that is an extension of the metamodel. It can be included directly in XML elements in the content section of an XMI document to associate the extension with a particular XML element.
XMI.documentation	Contains information about the meta data being interchanged, including XMI.owner, XMI.contact, XMI.longDescription, XMI.shortDescription, XMI.exporter, XMI.exporterVersion, and XMI.notice
XMI.owner	Contains information about the owner of the meta data
XMI.contact	Contains information about a contact person for the meta data
XMI.longDescription	Contains long descriptions of the meta data
XMI.shortDescription	Contains short descriptions of the meta data
XMI.exporter	Contains information about the exporter tool, which created the meta data
XMI.exporterVersion	Contains information about the version of the exporter tool, which created the meta data
XMI.notice	Contains copyright or other legal notices regarding the meta data
XMI.model	Identifies the model to which the instance data (M0) being interchanged conforms
XMI.metamodel	Identifies the metamodel to which the model data (M1) being interchanged conforms
XMI.metametamodel	Identifies the meta-metamodel to which the metamodel data (M2) being interchanged conforms
XMI.import	Identifies additional documents that are needed to process the current document

Table 3.3   Continued

XMI ELEMENT	DESCRIPTION
XMI.difference	Contains XML elements representing differences to base meta data
XMI.delete	Represents a deletion to base meta data. It must be within an XMI.difference XML element.
XMI.add	Represents an addition to base meta data. It must be within an XMI.difference XML element.
XMI.replace	Represents a replacement of base meta data with other meta data. It must be within an XMI.difference XML element.
XMI.reference	Allows references to other XML elements within an attribute of type string or an XMI.any element, which represents a data type that is not defined in the metamodel

Every metamodel (M2) class is represented in the DTD by an XML element whose name is the Class name. The element definition lists the attributes of the class; references to association ends relating to the class; and the classes that this class contains, either explicitly or through Composition associations. Every attribute of a metamodel class is represented in the DTD by an XML element whose name is the attribute name. In addition, attributes that have primitive or enumeration data types are represented in the DTD by an XML attribute declaration. The XML elements representing attributes are included in the content model of the XML element corresponding to the metamodel class. Each association (both with and without containment) between metamodel classes is represented by two XML elements that represent the roles of the association ends. The multiplicities of the association ends are not included in the DTD. The content model of the XML element that represents the Container class has an XML element with the name of the role at the association end. The XML element representing the role has a content model that allows XML elements representing the associated class and any of its subclasses to be included. The mapping between MOF constructs and XML constructs is shown in Table 3.4.

Every XMI DTD contains a mechanism for extending a metamodel class. Any number of *XMI.extension* elements may be included in the content model of any class. These extension elements have a content model of ANY, allowing considerable freedom in the nature of the extensions. In addition, the top-level XMI element may contain zero or more *XMI.extensions* elements, which provide for the inclusion of any new information. Tools that rely on XMI are expected to store the extension information and to export it again to enable round trip engineering, even though it is unlikely that they will be able to process it further.

Table 3.4 Mapping between MOF and XML Constructs

MOF CONSTRUCT	XML CONSTRUCT
Class	XML element, ID attribute
Basic attribute	XML attribute, CDATA
Object-typed attribute	XML element
Containment	XML element
Reference	XML IDREF attribute

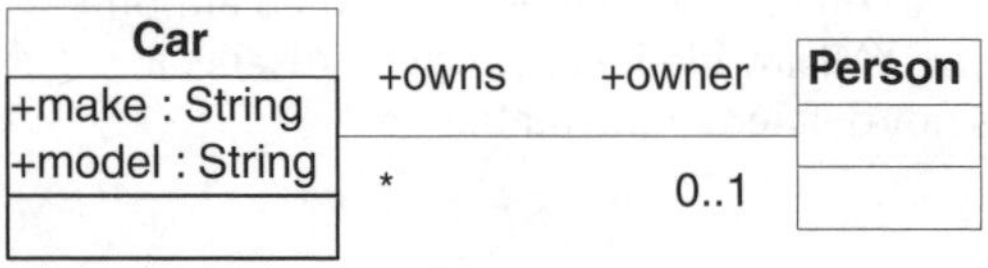

Figure 3.18 UML model: Car.

XML Document Generation

XMI defines the manner in which meta data will be represented as an XML document. Every *XMI document*, that is an XML document generated using rules defined by XMI, consists of the following declarations:

- An XML declaration; example: <? XML version="1.0"?>
- Any valid XML processing instructions
- An optional external DTD declaration with an optional internal DTD declaration; example: <!DOCTYPE XMI SYSTEM http://www.xmi.org/xmi.dtd>

XMI imposes no ordering requirements beyond those defined by XML. The top element of the XMI document is the XMI element.

Figure 3.18 shows a simple UML model (M1) of a Car that is owned by a Person. The XML document generated for interchanging the model information is shown in Figure 3.19. UML 1.3 is the metamodel to which the model data (M1) being interchanged conforms.

```
<XMI xmi.version="1.1" xmlns:uml="org.omg/uml1.3">
    <XMI.header>
        <XMI.documentation>
            A UML model of car.
        </XMI.documentation>
        <XMI.metamodel xmi.name="UML" xmi.version="1.3" />
        <XMI.model name="CarModel" version="1.0" />
    </XMI.header>
    <XMI.content>
        <Class xmi.id="C1">
            <name>Car</name>
            <Classifier.feature>
                <Attribute name="make"/>
                <Attribute name="model"/>
            </Classifier.feature>
        </Class>
        <Class xmi.id="C2">
            <name>Person</name>
        </Class>
        <Association>
            <Association.connection>
                <AssociationEnd name="owner">
                    <AssociationEnd.type>
                        <Class xmi.idref="C2" />
                    </AssociationEnd.type>
                </AssociationEnd>
                <AssociationEnd name="owns">
                    <AssociationEnd.type>
                        <Class xmi.idref="C1" />
                    </AssociationEnd.type>
                </AssociationEnd>
            </Association.connection>
        </Association>
    </XMI.content>
</XMI>
```

Figure 3.19   CarModel.xml.

Summary

In this chapter, we provided an overview of CWM as a model-driven approach to meta data integration, in which a model of shared meta data is formulated and then translated into specifications for both interchange and programmatic access. The notion of a model-driven approach was first alluded to in Chapter 2, and in this chapter, we've delved specifically into the modeling technologies that constitute the underpinnings of CWM. We've shown that CWM is firmly grounded in the OMG's standard metamodeling architecture, generally consisting of UML, MOF, and XMI (XMI, of course, is a way of using XML, a standard of the W3C, for meta data interchange).

We provided an example of using UML to create a static model of a small, discrete system (a simple molecular compound), and we discussed the fundamental components of UML class diagrams, such as Classes, Associations, Features (i.e., Operations and Attributes), and Packages. We discussed XML and its three major components: The XML Document, the Document Type Definition (DTD), and XML Namespaces. We described how an XML Document is essentially a structured text document consisting of elements based on tags defined by DTDs, and we described what it means for an XML Document to be both well formed and valid. We also described how XML element types and attributes are guaranteed to be unique through the use of XML Namespaces.

The OMG's MOF was presented as the generic object framework for the specification of metamodels. The four-layer *modeling stack* (M0 through M3) was discussed, along with the MOF Model and Reflective interfaces. We described how the MOF ultimately provides the basis for the construction and specification of interoperable metamodels and their associated interfaces. CWM is a prime example of a MOF-compliant metamodel.

Finally, we discussed how XMI unifies the UML, MOF, and XML technologies by providing a standard language for interchanging meta data based on MOF-compliant metamodels (such as CWM), in a self-describing and asynchronous manner. We saw that XMI defines rules for mapping MOF-compliant metamodels to XML DTDs, and for mapping instances of those metamodels (meta data) to XML Documents. The result is that an XMI representation of meta data can always be validated against the DTD representation of the metamodel.

Chapter 4, "An Architectural Overview of CWM," examines CWM's own layered architecture in considerable detail. In particular, Chapter 4 "re-casts" the OMG modeling concepts presented in this chapter in terms of the roles they play in defining the architecture of CWM. Note that, although the OMG modeling concepts may be a little difficult to get through, they are certainly worth understanding (at least, at a general level), in order to appreciate, as fully as possible, how the OMG concepts are leveraged in the architecture of CWM.

An Architectural Overview of CWM

For most of us, *architecture* implies a recognizable style of building construction. For example, we often speak of the architecture of a particular building whose style we either like or dislike. We give names to building styles that are reminiscent of other times and places: The state capitol has a *Colonial* architecture; those columns down at the courthouse are *Greek*.

In the everyday world, architecture serves two masters—art and engineering. We require our buildings to be pleasing in appearance without sacrificing our ability to live and work in them, and we often have many opinions about how well this tradeoff is accomplished. A building that is attractive to the eye but difficult to move around in is a continuing annoyance to its occupants. A well laid-out building whose exterior clashes with its surroundings is considered ugly. We might say that a successful building is both attractive and useful.

Architecture describes both the materials from which a building is made—the kinds of bricks, mortar, and wiring used in construction—and the ways in which these materials are organized—the building's blueprint. For example, the foundation walls are six-inches thick; the bricks are a nonstructural, exterior façade; and so on. This building architectural metaphor is a convenient way to help us understand how the CWM is constructed.

When transferred to the realm of computers, the notion of architecture retains strong similarities with building construction. Computer hardware and software systems are said to have architectures that describe the parts (the bricks) from which they are made and how those parts are arranged (a blueprint showing how the bricks are arranged). Computer architectures are also given recognizable names—computer hardware might have a *parallel* architecture; a large software system might have a *component* architecture.

This chapter is a parts list and a set of blueprints for the CWM. It describes the CWM's bricks (*classes*), how specific classes are interconnected with a kind of mortar (*associations*), and how classes and associations are collected into usable groups (*packages*).

How CWM Extends the OMG Architecture

At its core, the CWM is a set of extensions to the OMG metamodel architecture that customize it for the needs and purposes of the data warehousing and business intelligence domains. As such, it also has an architecture that describes the parts from which it is constructed and how those parts are arranged. Although the terminology of metamodel architectures is still relatively immature, the CWM has a modular, or *package*, architecture built on an *object-oriented* foundation (that is, the OMG metamodel architecture).

Because the CWM is a metamodel, our building construction metaphor needs to be modified to better reflect reality. The preceding discussion implied that the CWM was somewhat like a parts list and blueprint for constructing a building. However, in the OMG context, this characterization would not be correct. A building's parts list and blueprint (collectively, its *plans*) are M1 level objects in the OMG metamodel architecture because they describe a specific building, and the individual bricks in our building are M0 level objects because they are discrete physical objects.

The CWM, in contrast, is defined at a higher abstraction level than a set of construction plans. In our construction metaphor, the CWM corresponds more closely to a filing cabinet full of plans for many buildings. The drawers in this filing cabinet contain collections of plans for specific kinds of buildings. All the plans in one drawer are similar in some important way, which distinguishes them *as a group* from the contents of the other drawers. For example, the first drawer might be labeled "Office Buildings," the second "Single Family Residences," the third "Multi-Unit Dwellings," and so on. The plans for both the "Acme Business Tower" and "Consolidated Quantum Plaza" buildings could be found in the first drawer because they are both office buildings. In contrast, the plans for the "Seaside Arms Apartments" would be found in the drawer labeled "Multi-Unit Dwellings."

The CWM's filing cabinet drawers—its packages—are defined at the OMG's M2 level and contain classes and associations, which are also M2 level objects, that describe a particular area of interest in the data warehousing or business intelligence domains. For example, the CWM's Record package contains classes and associations allowing the description of data sources that use traditional record-oriented data layouts, such as a spreadsheet file or some older database management systems. The Record package in the CWM can be thought of as containing descriptions of many different record files, just as the Office Buildings drawer in the construction file cabinet contains plans for many different office buildings.

The descriptions of specific record files in the CWM's Record package are like the plans for specific buildings; they describe the structure of some real-world collection of things. At this M1 level in the OMG architecture, we find, for example, a description of the structure of the Customer file in the CWM and, in our construction example, a notation on the blueprints for the Acme Business Tower indicating that all bricks on the exterior façade are Red Fire bricks.

The lowest level in the OMG metamodel architecture, M0, contains details of specific customers and individual bricks. In the CWM, the M0 level contains the names of all customers who have records in the Customer file. At this level, the construction example might contain the location of every Red Fire brick used in constructing the exterior façade: "first brick, third row, west side," "second brick, third row, west side," as so on.

Finally, at the other most abstract end of the OMG architecture, the M3 level is implemented by the MOF. Because most CWM classes are defined at the M2 level, they are themselves instances of some MOF class. In fact, the objects within each level of the OMG architecture can be thought of as an instance of some class at the next higher level. In our construction example, the filing cabinet itself most closely represents the role played by the M3 level in the OMG architecture.

Table 4.1 summarizes how the CWM and our construction example map into the OMG metamodel architecture.

Table 4.1 Mapping CWM and Construction Example Elements to the OMG Metamodel Architecture

OMG METAMODEL LEVEL	OMG METAMODEL COMPONENT	CWM	CONSTRUCTION EXAMPLE
M3	MOF, XMI	MOF, XMI	Filing cabinet
M2	UML, XMI	CWM, XMI	Filing cabinet drawer
M1	XMI	Customer file	Building plans
M0	Storage device	John Doe	Bricks

Understanding the subtleties of layered abstractions is a challenging intellectual exercise that can be difficult even for experienced professionals. However, it is important to recognize that these concepts, although perhaps difficult to explain, are the foundation of a set of technologies—the OMG metamodel architecture—that are central to the CWM achieving its goal of vendor-neutral metamodel interchange.

How CWM Models the Data Warehousing and Business Intelligence Domains

Modern computers and the application systems they support can be very complex. In the data warehousing and business intelligence domains, this inherent complexity is multiplied because multiple computers are involved. Besides exchanging data, the computers involved also must resolve any incompatibilities that would otherwise impede interchange.

Today, such exchange problems frequently can be managed in computing environments in which the level of complexity is relatively low. For example, interchange of both data and meta data often can be achieved with relative ease if the participating systems reside on compatible hardware platforms and are running similar operating systems, and possibly, database management software. However, when the exchanging systems use different hardware, operating systems, databases, and application software, the number of incompatibilities that must be resolved can increase dramatically. It is precisely this heterogeneous environment that CWM must deal with to achieve a vendor-neutral interchange.

All this potential for high levels of heterogeneity in data warehousing and business intelligence environments means that the CWM must be able to describe the meta data of a broad diversity of data sources and warehouse targets. Even though CWM does not need to represent all of the complexity that heterogeneous systems may contain, it must represent sufficient complexity so that the desired interchange can be achieved. The result is that the CWM must represent data and meta data from a wide selection of systems using a number of data models. However, this breadth of coverage comes at a cost.

To capture this diversity of meta data, the CWM is a complex system in its own right. In its first release, the CWM package adopted by the OMG contains more than 200 classes, and future releases can be expected to grow even larger! The CWM design team knew that delivering such a large and complex metamodel in a single package would virtually ensure that it was never used. Indeed, early releases of UML had been the subject of similar complaints in OMG circles. UML, which is nearly the same size as the CWM, was organized into three packages (Foundation, Behavioral Elements, and Extension Mechanisms). The sheer size of the packages is one of the reasons that UML has been implemented incompletely in most of its product deployments.

For the CWM to be deployed in production-quality software, it had to be delivered in small, understandable packages that could be more easily implemented. Also, smaller packages made learning the CWM a much less daunting task that could be done in incremental, bite-sized chunks. To achieve this, the design team organized the CWM into 21 separate packages. Each package contains classes, associations, and constraints relevant to a specific area of interest in data warehousing and business intelligence. Twenty of the 21 CWM packages require the presence of one or more of the other packages in an implementation. The one package that does not require other packages is the most fundamental part of the CWM, upon which all other packages ultimately depend.

Comprehending the content and interrelationships of 21 packages can seem like a daunting task. To further promote understandability, the design team organized the packages into five stackable layers. The packages in each layer play similar roles in the overall architecture of the CWM. The 21 CWM packages are shown in their assigned layers in Figure 4.1 and are described in the next section, *A Survey of Core CWM Components*.

To understand a particular CWM package, one must understand only that package and the packages it depends upon; other packages can be ignored. To

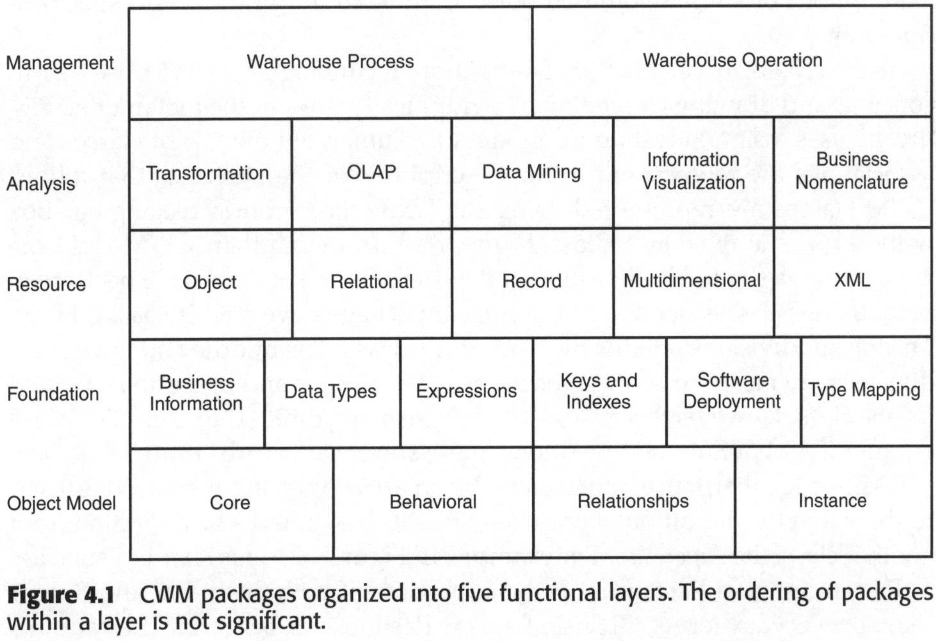

Management	Warehouse Process			Warehouse Operation		
Analysis	Transformation	OLAP	Data Mining	Information Visualization	Business Nomenclature	
Resource	Object	Relational	Record	Multidimensional	XML	
Foundation	Business Information	Data Types	Expressions	Keys and Indexes	Software Deployment	Type Mapping
Object Model	Core		Behavioral	Relationships	Instance	

Figure 4.1 CWM packages organized into five functional layers. The ordering of packages within a layer is not significant.

make this task as easy as possible, the CWM design team consciously kept the number of packages on which a particular package depends to a minimum. All other packages depend directly on the Core package. Nine of the packages depend on only the Core package; whereas the most dependent package, Relational, requires six additional packages. In Figure 4.1 are 22 packages, not 21 as noted in the preceding text; this is because the Object package in the Resource layer does not exist as a separate package.

A Survey of Core CWM Components

Because understanding the functional role of each package and its relationships to other packages is our primary concern, the descriptions that follow focus on the main ideas of each package. To reduce complexity, package descriptions have been simplified in ways that do not detract from their central ideas. Consequently, the class structure of each package is emphasized, and its associations receive reduced emphasis; their names, end names, and cardinalities have been omitted unless they are specifically discussed in the text. Because they are not critical to understanding package structure, attributes and constraints have been omitted completely from the package diagrams and are mentioned in the text only when they have direct bearing on the discussion. Also, some classes that provide support functions or are in other ways not central to the main ideas of the package have been omitted. Descriptions of all these omitted objects can be found in the CWM specification itself.

As described in Chapter 3, "Foundation Technologies," CWM uses UML concepts and drawing conventions to graphically present the metamodel. Figure 4.2 uses a simple restaurant model to summarize how CWM classes and associations are represented in the descriptions of the packages that follow. CWM classes are represented using the UML class icon, a rectangular box with three subdivisions. Classes imported from another CWM package appear with a shaded background and with the name of the source package in parentheses; classes defined in the current package have a white background. The top subdivision contains the name of the class. The middle and lower subdivisions are meant to contain the names of attributes and operations defined for the class. However, because attributes are being omitted for simplicity and because CWM defines no operations, these subdivisions are empty.

UML-style inheritance, represented by an arrow with an open head, is used to show that the definition of one class, the *subclass*, inherits its definition from another class, the *superclass*. For example, in Figure 4.2, Sushi Bar is a subclass of Restaurant, and Restaurant is the superclass of both Sushi Bar and Burger Joint. In everyday terms, all Sushi Bars are Restaurants, but not all Restaurants are Sushi Bars. Subclasses inherit all of properties of their superclasses and

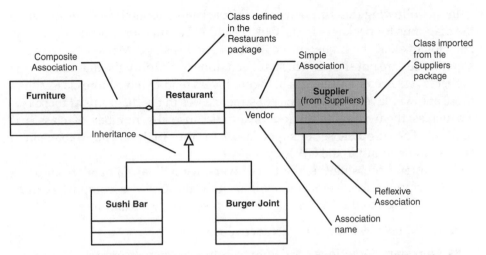

Figure 4.2 A simple restaurant model illustrating how CWM packages are described.

may redefine them as needed. Consequently, referring to the "furniture of a burger joint" is perfectly valid because Burger Joints inherit from their Restaurant superclasses an association to Furniture.

Associations define relationships between classes and are shown as lines connecting the classes. Three types of associations are used in the diagrams: *simple*, *composite*, and *reflexive*. Simple associations are shown as unadorned lines that connect related classes; restaurants have suppliers. Reflexive associations are special kinds of simple associations that link different members of the same class. For example, suppliers may resell supplies they have purchased from other suppliers. Composite associations represent ownership relationships between classes and are indicated by diamonds on the owning class. In Figure 4.2, the composite association between Restaurant and Furniture means that restaurants own the furniture they contain, and if a restaurant were to burn down, its furniture will burn as well. UML allows for both strong and weak ownership, representing strong ownership with a black diamond. Strong ownership means that the furniture will burn; weak ownership, that it will not. Although ownership diamonds are not black in these diagrams, all CWM composite associations are strong unless otherwise indicated. CWM associations are named, have named ends, and indicate how many objects may be present on each end (sometimes called its *multiplicity* or *cardinality*). Although these characteristics of associations may provide additional information about the nature of the associations, they are included here only when they are directly referenced to keep details to a manageable level. When present, association names appear adjacent to the lines representing the associations.

In the following descriptions of CWM packages, superclasses are shown in the diagrams for packages in the Object Model, Foundation, and Resource layers. However, at the higher, more abstract Analysis and Management layers, superclasses are not shown. This has been done to simplify the diagrams at the higher layers because packages in higher layers tend to have more classes than those at lower layers. The absence of superclasses in the diagrams at these layers makes them simpler to understand because the number of classes is reduced. The complete set of superclasses for the Analysis and Management layers can be found in the CWM specification.

Also, after discussing the first three layers, we will take a break from package descriptions for a while to explore how the CWM accomplishes three important tasks. In the *Methodology Interlude* section, we examine how

- CWM uses inheritance to achieve reuse
- Meta data definitions are tied to the physical data resources
- Resource packages support creation of instance data objects

By the time we get to this discussion, you will have seen enough of the CWM to understand why the issues are worthy of attention.

Object Model Layer

The Object Model layer contains packages that define fundamental metamodel concepts, relationships, and constraints required by the rest of the CWM packages. These concepts create an environment in which the remainder of the CWM packages can be defined in a crisp and clear fashion, enabling them to concentrate on their individual purposes and minimizing the extent to which they must deal with infrastructure and other housekeeping details. The Object Model packages constitute the complete set of fundamental metamodel services needed by the other CWM packages; no other services are necessary for the definition of the CWM.

The Object Model has strong ties to, and is a subset of, UML. Many Object Model classes and associations directly correspond to UML classes and associations. This correspondence is intentional. UML provides a strong, widely used modeling foundation, and CWM should leverage the substantial strengths of its UML heritage. Early working versions of CWM, in fact, incorporated the complete UML model in the role now occupied by the Object Model. However, initial implementation efforts by some of the CWM submitting companies identified a couple of important drawbacks to this approach. First, the sheer number of classes in UML (nearly 120 in the initial version; the Object Model draws directly from UML Versions 1.3 and 1.4 and anticipates certain changes expected in Version 2.0 as well) meant that generated CWM interfaces had many classes defined—because they are part of UML—that were unused by

CWM. This situation presented a large documentation challenge for every CWM deployment as well as complicated our understanding of the CWM with explanations that justifed the presence of all those unused classes. Second, the object-oriented superstructure of UML, which every CWM class inherited, created a need to explain why some commonly used concepts, such as Table and Record, had interfaces supporting object-oriented concepts like inheritance and associations that have no direct bearing on the concepts themselves The Object Model was designed as a response to these problems. It includes portions of UML that CWM heavily depends upon without requiring support for the unused parts. Furthermore, the Object Model package structure minimizes the number of object-oriented capabilities inherited by widely used, nonobject-oriented concepts.

Core Package

The Core package contains basic classes and associations used by all other CWM packages. As such, it depends upon no other packages. The Core includes the basic UML infrastructure required to define nonobject-oriented data stores, such as relational databases and record files, without introducing exclusively object-oriented concepts. The Core also contains support classes and data types widely used by other packages. The principle classes of the Core package are shown in Figure 4.3.

In CWM, every class in every package is, by definition, a subclass of the Element class. Element has no attributes and provides no services beyond being a single point from which all objects in a CWM description can be found. If you think of CWM as a tree-structured arrangement of classes, then Element is the root of the tree.

With the exception of a few support classes, such as TaggedValue in Figure 4.3, all CWM classes are also subclasses of the ModelElement class. ModelElement provides basic attributes—most importantly, a name—to all of its subclasses and serves as a common connection point for all classes. For example, the Constraint class, which defines rules restricting how CWM objects behave, has an association to ModelElement indicating the model elements to which the constraint applies. Structuring the Core package in this way allows constraints to be defined for any CWM model element regardless of its precise subclass; objects as different as relational database tables and business terms can all be constrained with a single construct. Although perhaps subtle in appearance, this technique of relating general-purpose classes to ModelElement is used throughout CWM to provide metamodel services to every model element. The notion of model elements is pervasive in the CWM and is used frequently to refer to any named CWM object (that is, any instance of the ModelElement class).

In addition to Constraint, other general-purpose service classes in the Core package are as follows:

Dependency.   A definition of how two model elements depend on each other. One model element is the *supplier*, and the other is the *client*.

TaggedValue.   A simple extension mechanism allowing usage-dependent attributes to be added to any model element. TaggedValues are recorded as name-value pairs. For example, a person's nickname might be recorded as "Nickname = Pookie"; Nickname is the name, and Pookie is the value. TaggedValues are a useful, easy-to-use extension mechanism, but their use can inhibit interchange. (See the *CWM Extension Mechanisms* discussion later in this chapter for details.)

Stereotype.   A form of extension mechanism that permits an existing CWM class to be labeled with a name that more accurately reflects the

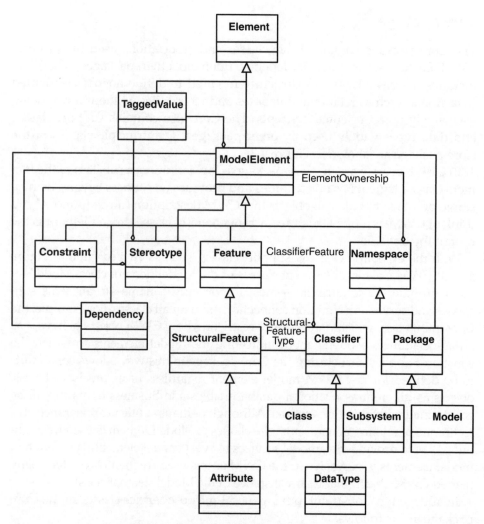

Figure 4.3   Principal classes in the Core package.

role it currently plays. As with TaggedValues, stereotypes can limit interchange if they are used injudiciously.

At its heart, the Core package provides for the description of things that have structure. Structured things include familiar computer system objects like relational database tables, records in a file, and members of OLAP cube dimensions. In UML terms, the individual items of a thing's structure are called *features* and are represented by the StructuralFeature class. For example, the features of a relational table are the columns in the table; for a record, they are an ordered list of the record's fields. CWM allows for nonstructural features as well; they are described by the Behavioral package. The Attribute class represents structural features that can have an initial value.

Features (including all StructuralFeatures) are owned by classifiers, via a composite association called the ClassifierFeature association. A classifier is a thing that has structure; both records and relational tables are types of classifiers. The notion of *classifier* is very similar to the idea of *type* used in modern programming languages. *Integer* and *character* are simple, frequently encountered programming language types; they are classifiers in CWM, but they have no features. *Address*, in contrast, is a compound type (classifier) whose features are *street*, *city*, *state*, and *postal code*. In the same way, a relational table is a classifier whose features are its columns, and a record is a classifier whose features are its fields. Note that StructuralFeatures are owned by one classifier (via the ClassifierFeature association inherited from Feature) and are related to another classifier. The former is the StructuralFeature's owner, and the latter, reached via the StructuralFeatuerType association, is its type. A StructuralFeature cannot have the same classifier as both its owner and its type.

The class named Class (Don't let the strangeness of a "class named Class" confuse you. These are the correct names, and such phrases are not uncommon in the world of meta data. The weakness is in our language, not in the concepts. Rely on the capital C to help keep things straight!) represents classifiers that can have multiple instances. So, tables are really instances of Class because they can contain multiple data rows. In contrast, the DataType class represents classifiers that have only one instance; *integer* and *character* are instances of DataType.

Although Namespaces have no attributes themselves, they are critically important because they ensure that individual objects can be uniquely identified by their names. Consequently, nearly every model element in a CWM description will be owned by some Namespace. Normally, the only model elements that are not owned by Namespaces are those representing top-level namespaces—that is, Namespaces that are not owned by other Namespaces. The composite association between Namespace and ModelElement, called the ElementOwnership association, allows Namespaces to own ModelElements, and hence, other Namespaces. This association is one of the primary structuring mechanisms within the CWM. This association enables model elements to be organized in hierarchical, or tree-like, arrangements in which the parent Namespace is said to contain, or own, its child ModelElements regardless of their ultimate type. The ElementOwnership association is reused throughout the CWM to indicate ownership relationships between classes at every level.

Because of the package structure of the CWM, model elements must be able to reference objects in other packages. This is achieved by the Package subclass, Namespace. Packages, because they are Namespaces, allow model elements of arbitrary type to be collected in hierarchies. However, because a ModelElement can be owned by at most one Namespace, we cannot use this mechanism to pull in ModelElements owned by different Namespaces. Instead, the Package class provides the notion of *importing* ModelElements from other packages. This technique, based on rules established by the underlying MOF specification, is used to associate objects across package boundaries and is the foundation for linking descriptions of database schemas and file layouts to the their physical deployments within an enterprise. Refer to the *Software Deployment Package* section later in this chapter for more information on this technique.

The ModelElement, Class, Attribute, DataType, and Package classes are the workhorses of CWM. They are the foundation on which the powerful structuring capabilities of the CWM are built.

Behavioral Package

The Behavioral package collects classes that provide CWM classes in other packages with behavioral characteristics frequently found in object-oriented systems. Software systems that include the Behavioral package can create classifiers capable of having the object-oriented concepts of *operation, method, interface,* and *event* specified as part of their definition in a CWM model. The organization of the Behavioral package is shown in Figure 4.4.

The package's object-oriented features are centered around the BehavioralFeature class. The BehavioralFeature class is similar to the StructuralFeature class described in the Core package in that both are classes of Feature and can be owned by classifiers. In everyday terms, BehavioralFeatures can be thought of as representing executable units of program logic that an object can perform. As such, they have a name, a set of parameter definitions describing their input and output values, and optionally, a returned value. The parameters of a behavioral feature are described by the Parameter class.

BehavioralFeatures are either operations or methods. An operation is a specification of a callable unit of programmatic logic shared by all of the methods that implement the operation. In contrast, a method represents the implementation of a particular programmatic unit in some programming language. The methods implementing a particular operation all perform the same task but may do so in different ways or may be written in different programming lan-

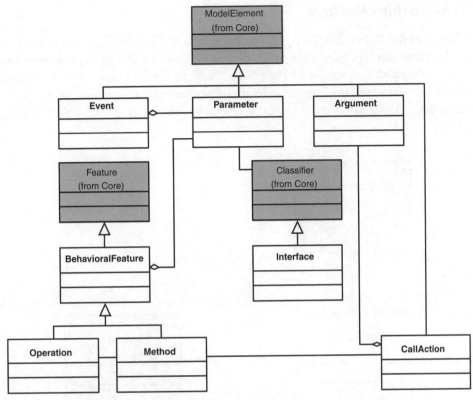

Figure 4.4 Behavioral package classes provide object-oriented characteristics.

guages. Actual invocations of methods can be recorded using the CallAction class. The ownership association between the CallAction and the Argument class enables the recording of the actual values of parameters used in the call.

An interface is a collection of operations defining a service that classifiers can provide to their clients. Individual classifiers may provide multiple interfaces. For example, an accounting system might provide an interface called GeneralLedger; this fact would be recorded in the CWM by a classifier with the name AccoutingSystem owning an interface named GeneralLedger via the ElementOwnership association defined in the Core package. Recall that even though this association is defined between the Namespace and ModelElement classes in the Core package, the AccountingSystem and GeneralLedger classifiers inherit the capability to participate in ownership relationships from the ElementOwnership association between their superclasses Namespace and ModelElement, respectively.

The Event class represents an observable occurrence and may have parameters. The CWM, however, does not record the action to be taken when a particular event occurs; this decision is left to individual application programs.

Relationships Package

Classes in the Relationships package describe how CWM objects are related to each other. Two types of relationships are defined by CWM—generalization and association—as shown in Figure 4.5. Because CWM classes are defined at the M2 level in the OMG metamodel architecture, the Generalization, Association, and AssociationEnd classes allow specific instances of other CWM

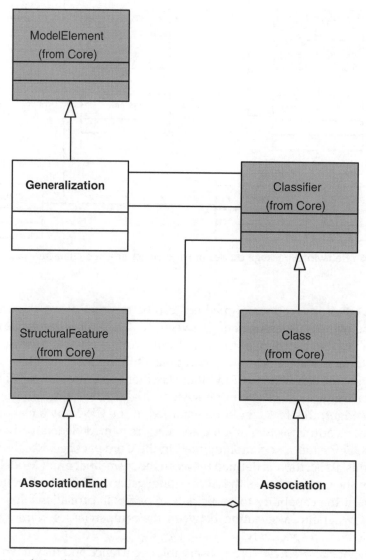

Figure 4.5 Relationships package classes.

classes to be related and arranged in hierarchies at the M1 level. MOF classes defined at level M3 also provide the framework that allows the M2 CWM classes shown in this chapter to be related and arranged in hierarchies.

Generalization is a relationship between more general objects and more specific objects that enables them to be organized into a *hierarchy*. In generalization hierarchies, the more general objects occupy the owning, or parental, position, and the more specific objects, occupy the owned, or child, position. Although generalization hierarchies, in appearance, are very similar to organizational structure diagrams, the semantic relationships between the parent and child objects more closely match that of taxonomic relationships in biology in which the child is considered to be a type of the parent. The Generalization class identifies two classifiers, one representing a parent and the other representing its child. Because a child can have children of its own, arbitrarily deep hierarchies can be created. The CWM allows children to have more than one parent classifier. Although multiple parent situations are not encountered frequently in CWM, they do exist. For example, the Subsystem class defined in the Core package (refer to Figure 4.3) has the classes Classifier and Package as parents. This means that Subsystems have the characteristics of both Classifiers (the ability to have features) and Packages (the ability to own and import model elements).

Associations define specific relationships between two (or more!) classifiers. Associations that relate two classifiers are *binary*, and those that relate more than two classifiers are *n-ary*. N-ary relationships are quite rare, and most applications of CWM will have no need to create them. (The CWM itself has no n-ary associations.) The ends of an association are represented by the AssociationEnd class. Associations own their ends using the ClassifierFeature association defined in the Core package. Association ends identify the classifiers to which they are connected via the Core package's type association between StructuralFeature and Classifier.

Instance Package

In addition to interchanging meta data with CWM, it is often useful to send along some of the data as well. The capability can be especially useful for data that represents the allowed values for some attribute, such as a column in a relational table. Such columns are sometimes categorical because they define the allowed types of rows that can be stored in the table. For example, a library database might have a table containing books with a column describing the type of each book; the type column would contain values like "fiction," "nonfiction," "reference," and so on. In another common usage, the Instance package could be used to exchange instances of the Core's DataType class, which represent the primitive data types of a programming language such as Java. In

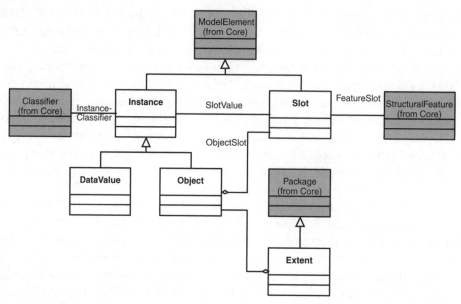

Figure 4.6   The Instance package.

this case, the values passed would be "boolean," "char," "byte," "short," "int," "long," "double," and "float." The CWM Instance package provides the infra-structure required to include data values along with meta data in a CWM interchange. The Instance package is shown in Figure 4.6.

All data instances are either DataValues or objects. An object is an instance of some classifier that defines the structure of the object. Objects own a collection of slots. Each slot represents the value of one of the StructuralFeatures (usually Attributes) of the classifier that describes the structure of the object. If a slot represents a StructuralFeature that is itself a classifier, the slot contains another object that owns still other slots. Otherwise, the slot contains a DataValue that specifies the data value.

An example of these relationships is shown in Figure 4.7. The figure shows both the meta data and one data record from a U.S. Presidential information database. In this database, the President class holds the first and last names of presidents, their hometowns, and the number of terms they served. Presidential hometowns are modeled by the CityState classifier that is embedded in the President class. The Instance package objects for the data for George Washington show how the Core package meta data objects (Classifier, Attribute, and DataType) are linked to Instance package objects (Object, DataValue, and Slot). The names of the associations used to record the linkages between the object are indicated in the upper part of the figure.

The Extent class is a subclass of the Package class from the Core package. This class is used to collect multiple objects of the same kind using the Ele-

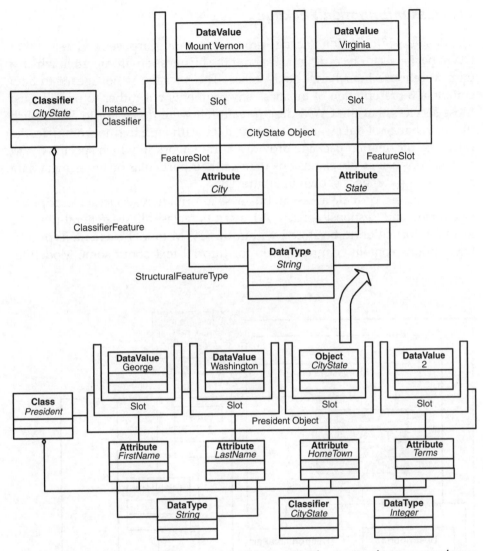

Figure 4.7 Linkage of meta data and data objects using the Core and Instance packages.

mentOwnership association. Extents might be used, for example, to own all of the objects

Foundation Layer

At the Foundation layer, the CWM contains packages that provide CWM-specific services to other packages residing at higher layers. In this respect, Foundation packages differ from Object Model packages whose services are of a general-purpose nature and not specifically designed for CWM.

Business Information Package

The Business Information package provides general-purpose services to other CWM packages for recording facts about the business environment in which a data warehouse interchange takes place. The package is not meant to be a complete representation of business environments but rather to provide just those services that the CWM design team felt were necessary to accomplish the interchange of data warehouse meta data. Although it is not complete, the Business Information package provides a framework in which specific CWM applications can create extensions to meet their particular business meta data needs. This package is shown in Figure 4.8.

Three classes provide access to business information services: Description, Document, and ResponsibleParty. A Description class allows general-purpose textual information to be stored within the CWM model element. Typically, Descriptions contain comment, help, or tutorial text about some ModelEle-

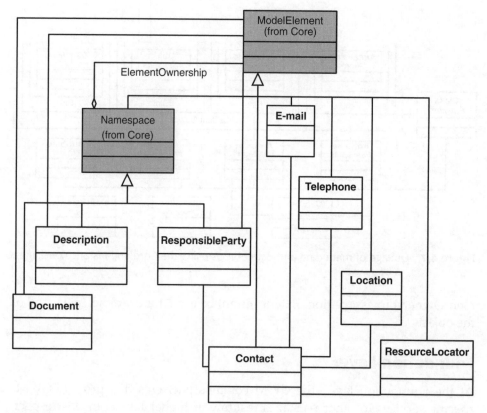

Figure 4.8   The Business Information package.

ment. However, descriptive text can service any required purpose. Descriptions can be tied to a single model element or shared by many. Descriptions can even contain text describing other Descriptions, because the model elements that the text is linked to are themselves Description objects.

Document classess are very similar to Description classess, except that they are assumed to be stored at some location outside of the CWM meta data. For example, you would find the text of a Description embedded in a CWM XMI interchange file, but a Document might be found in a filing cabinet in the corporate records department. In the XMI interchange file, you would find that the Document class has the notation "look in the filing cabinet in corporate records," but you would not find the Document's text. This distinction between descriptions and documents was created so that CWM interchange files would not be unnecessarily burdened with large or structurally complex text blocks. Because Documents are a subclass of Namespace, they can be arranged in hierarchies as well, permitting the complete structure of a complicated document—that is, all of its chapters, sections, subheadings, and so on—to be represented, if necessary. In this way, any ModelElement could be linked to its formal definition in a particular section of a complicated design document.

The ResponsibleParty class enables people or organizational units, such as the IT department, to be identified as responsible for, or at least, as interested in hearing about, every ModelElement. As with Descriptions and Documents, ResponsibleParties can be arranged in numerous ways including hierarchical ownership trees. Because of the close structural correspondence between trees and organizational structures, ResponsibleParty objects can be used to represent complete organization charts, allowing responsibility for particular model elements in an information system to be closely tied to the organizational units directly responsible for them.

ResponsibleParties also can be associated with multiple sets of contact information. Each set of contact information can have multiple telephone numbers, e-mail addresses, locations, or resource locators (typically, these would be in the form of Internet Uniform Resource Locators [URLs] but this is not a requirement). The associations between Contact objects and Telephone, E-mail, Location, and ResourceLocator objects are ordered so that contact priorities can be retained as well. For example, you might want to call the IT director at his office first, his mobile phone second, and his home third.

Because Descriptions, Documents, and ResponsibleParties can be arranged in tree structures with the ElementOwnership association and linked to *ad hoc* ModelElements with their individual associations to ModelElement, complex relationships can be constructed. These powerful structuring techniques were included in the CWM so that the semantics of potentially complicated business scenarios could be accurately expressed. However, as with all complex things, use them carefully.

DataTypes Package

The notion of *type*—a name that describes what kind of a thing something is— is central to most modern programming languages and data management systems. Types provide the foundation from which programming systems begin to capture the meaning and behavior, or *semantics*, of the real-world activities that they mimic by restricting the kinds of values and operations that are relevant for particular computer memory locations. Types have evolved from the loosely defined and easily circumvented memory overlays of assemblers and COBOL through primitive data types, such as *integer* and *boolean*, and structured types, such as C's *struct* and Pascal's *record*, to become perhaps *the* central idea in modern type-safe programming languages, such as Java and C++. In object-oriented programming languages and modeling languages like UML and CWM, the *class* construct is fully equivalent to the type concept. A class is merely a user-definable type. In CWM, type most closely corresponds to the semantic of the Core's Classifier class.

The collection of primitive types and type structuring capabilities of a programming language or database system is its *type system*. Most modern type systems share many important types in common. The notions of integer number, Boolean, float-point number, and fixed-precision number are widely supported. Within the boundaries imposed by various value representation techniques on their underlying hardware platforms, data characterized by such types can be exchanged between systems. However, no two type systems share collections of types that completely overlap. The success of an exchange can even be influenced by low-level hardware details of the particular systems involved. The result is that the exchange of data values between systems is fraught with difficulties and challenges. No guarantee exists that exchanging data between matching releases of the same software system running under identical operating systems on architecturally equivalent hardware platforms will always be trouble-free.

In the realm of data warehouse meta data interchange, a CWM-based tool must be able to recognize type system incompatibilities and respond accordingly. To do this, the CWM designer must be able to describe the type system of data resources that participate in CWM-mediated interchanges. After a data resource's type system is described in CWM, it can be exchanged with other CWM-compliant tools. The DataTypes package (see Figure 4.9) provides the infrastructure required to support the definition of both primitive and structured data types. Defining type systems and mapping data types between them is dealt with by the TypeMapping package, which is described later in this chapter.

Primitive numeric data types like *byte*, *short*, *integer*, *long*, *float*, *real*, and (single) *character* are defined by creating an instance of the Core's DataType class to represent them. The DataType instance appropriate for a particular attribute is referenced via the StructuralFeatureType association defined in the Core package. Primitive numeric data types that require additional information to com-

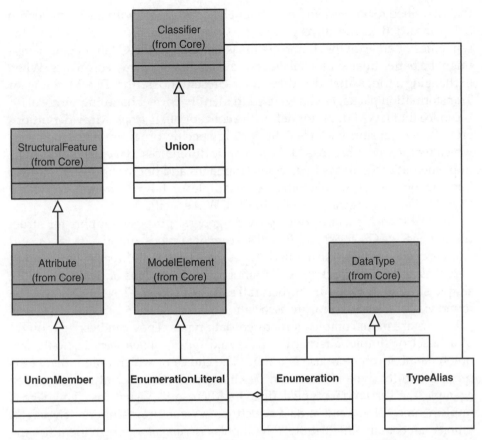

Figure 4.9 The DataTypes package provides the infrastructure for defining primitive and structured data types.

plete their definitions, such as *decimal* and *fixed* whose definitions require precision and scale values, are also created as instances of DataType. The values required to complete their definitions are, however, stored in the Attribute instance rather than with the DataType itself. Modeling parameterized data types in this way keeps the number of DataType instance to a manageable level. To enforce this style, a constraint defined on the DataType class prevents it from having attributes that could be used to store parameter attributes, such as precision and scale. (Examples of the correct handling of parameterized data types can be found in the Relational and Record packages in the CWM specification.)

The representation of string data types can be done in several ways; the appropriate choice usually is dictated by the semantics of the programming language whose types are being described. In languages whose strings do not have defined lengths, an instance of DataType can be used. If the language, even optionally, defines string lengths, creating a parameterized data type like that described for *decimal* and *fixed* might be appropriate with the string length being recorded in the corresponding Attribute instance. If strings have the semantics of an array of characters (as is the case in the C language), strings might be better treated as a subclass of the language's array constructs. When exchanging strings that use different representations, the TypeMapping or Transformation packages can be used to identify correct handling protocols.

Notice that CWM does not define the concept of an *array*. Array definitions are left to extension packages supporting specific programming languages, which require them because of the semantic differences that exist between the implementation of arrays by various languages and operating systems; direct interchange can be problematic. An example of how to define arrays for CORBA IDL language is provided in the CWM specification.

The DataTypes package does provide general-purpose support for structured types like C's *struct* and Pascal's *record* data types, union data types, and enumerations. Simple structured types are handled directly by creating instances of the Core package's Classifier class. The values or fields owned by simple structured types are StructuralFeatures of their Classifier and can be found via the ClassifierFeature association.

Unions are more complex structured data types. They can best be thought of as a set of simple, alternative structured types—*union members*; only one union member can be in use at a time. The choice of which union member is present is fully dynamic and can be changed by the user at any time. For example, the *Variant* data type defined by Microsoft's Visual Basic language is implemented using a union data structure. In some programming languages, unions can contain an attribute, the union's *discriminator*, which identifies the union member currently present. Discriminator attributes can reside either outside or inside the union members. (When placing discriminators inside union members, be sure to include the discriminator attribute in every union member!) Although some implementations of union data types allow the union members to be a sort of type overlay, accessing the same area of memory, CWM does not support this distinction.

Enumerations are named sets of constant values that can serve as the type of an attribute. The individual values in an enumeration are *enumeration literals* and are referenced by their names. For example, an attribute specifying a day of the week might have a data type called Weekday whose enumerated values are Sunday, Monday, Tuesday, Wednesday, Thursday, Friday, and Saturday. CWM allows optional numeric values to be associated with enumeration literals.

The TypeAlias class allows aliases, or other names, to be defined for data types but does not change the definition of an aliased data type in any other way. Although type aliases can be useful in any language, they were added to CWM specifically to support the needs of the CORBA IDL languages.

Expressions Package

In programming systems, an expression is an ordered combination of values and operations that can be evaluated to produce a value, set of values, or effect. As such, expressions can be used to describe logical relationships between their component values and to describe algorithmic sequences of steps. Indeed, some programming languages are considered to be elaborate expressions. Because one of CWM's chief goals is to promote meta data interchange in environments, the capability to exchange expressions is paramount. Unfortunately, this capability often does not exist in data warehousing systems. Rather, senders and receivers generally share little or no common language syntax or semantics.

Normally, expressions are encoded in the syntax of a specific language. However, in this form, their interchange can be achieved only if both the sender and receiver share the same language syntax and semantics. Such expressions are called *black box* expressions because their content cannot be discerned by an entity that does not share knowledge of the common expression format. For example, a C language expression is meaningless to a Fortran compiler. CWM provides direct support for the exchange of black box expressions with the Expression class and its subclasses in the Core package. (Expression classes were not explicitly discussed in the previous discussion of the Core package.) The Expression classes allow an expression's text and the name of the language in which it is written to be recorded and exchanged. Understanding of the content of a black box expression is left, however, to the sender and receiver; CWM has no knowledge of the meaning of the content of the expression text.

So that expressions can be exchanged between senders and receivers that do not share a common language, CWM also provides for *white box* expressions. In a white box expression, the individual components within an expression—its values and operations—are exposed to the CWM, permitting reference to operations and attributes already defined in CWM. In addition, white box expressions permit the tracking of the participation of individual attributes in expressions to facilitate analysis of the moment of data within a data warehouse process. White box expressions are defined using the metamodel shown in Figure 4.10.

To record an expression in the Expression package, it first must be converted to a form that is compatible with the structure of the classes in the package and at the same time be language-neutral. In principle, virtually any expression, irrespective of the language in which it is written, can be converted to a (possibly nested) sequence of function calls. Converting expressions to a function representation matches the object-oriented nature of the CWM and is a technique that can be executed by the vast majority of experienced programmers. For example, the famous equation $E = mc^2$ can be represented in a functional notation as follows:

```
Assign(E, Multiply(m, Power(c, 2)))
```

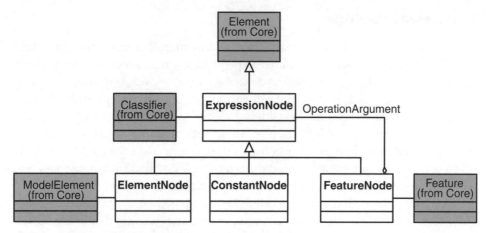

Figure 4.10   The CWM's white box expression metamodel.

Reading from the inside out, an equivalent English form of this functional expression might be, "Raise *c* to the second power, multiply the square by *m*, and assign the result to *E*."

To place a functional expression in the CWM, first define each of the functions as an operation of some classifier (perhaps, even one that was defined specifically for this purpose). In our example, operations named *Assign*, *Multiply*, and *Power* would be required. Second, create attributes to define the variables *E*, *m*, and *c* and create DataValue instances to hold each of their values. Finally, create instances of FeatureNode for each of the functions and values and a ConstantNode instance to hold the value 2. (A more complete description of this example is available in the CWM specification.)

Functional expressions can be stored directly in a hierarchical data structure. The tree-structure of the CWM Expression package is provided by the nested relationships between functions in which the result of one function (for example, *Power*) acts as an actual parameter to its containing function (*Multiply*). These tree relationships are recorded by the OperationArgument composite association between FeatureNode and ExpressionNode. FeatureNodes representing functions are linked to operations that define them via the association between FeatureNode and Feature (a superclass of Operation). Similarly, FeatureNodes representing variables are linked Attributes (a subclass of Feature) that define them via the same association. ConstantNodes directly hold the values of constants in a locally declared attribute and do not need to be linked to some Feature. The ElementNode class permits CWM expression elements access to any object in the CWM store that is not a Feature.

Every node in a CWM expression is an ExpressionNode. The association between ExpressionNode and Classifier allows the type of any node in an expression tree to be specified. However, specifying ExpressionNode types is optional and need be done only for the root ExpressionNode (the *Assign* FeatureNode in our example) when a return value is required. Type classifiers can be recorded for intermediate nodes whenever there is reason to do so. Each ExpressionNode also contains an attribute of type Expression; this attribute can be used at any node to record useful information about the node. For example, in an ExpressionNode tree describing a SQL query, the Expression attribute of the root ExpressionNode instance might be used to record the text of the complete query.

Here is a design tip for use when creating expression attributes in the CWM. It may not always be clear whether a black box or white box expression will be needed. In such situations, declare the type of the attribute as an ExpressionNode (a white box) rather than as an Expression (a black box). In this way, you can store either type of expression in the attribute. If a black box expression is needed, place the language name and expression text in the expression attribute of the ExpressionNode and create no expression nodes for it.

Keys and Indexes Package

Much like the one at the back of this book, an *index* is a list of elements arranged in an order other than the physical sequence of the elements themselves. In a database management system, an index is used as a performance optimization technique to specify alternate orderings of data objects. When an index exists that matches the structure of a query, database management software can use it to return data objects more quickly than it could if the index were not present.

A *key* is a set of one or more values that identifies, often uniquely, some record within a database. Also, keys may be used in indexes to identify the record at this index location and, in relational databases, as the basis upon which relationships between data rows are constructed.

Because keys and indexes are used by several CWM packages and by some extension packages (see Volume 2 of the CWM specification for examples), classes supporting them have been included at the CWM Foundation layer. The Keys and Indexes package is shown in Figure 4.11.

The Index class represents index data structures and is said to *span* a class. The association between these classes records this relationship and is required because an index that doesn't span a class is meaningless. Instances of the IndexedFeature provide links to the attributes of the spanned class; these links describe the index's key and are owned and ordered via the composite association to Index. Mapping index key features in this way allows them to remain attributes of their owning class and still participate in the definition of spanning indexes.

The UniqueKey class defines the notion of a key that uniquely identifies a member of a class. Although not shown in the figure, classes own their UniqueKey instances using the ElementOwnership association. Much like index keys, Unique-Keys are linked to, and ordered by, the association to

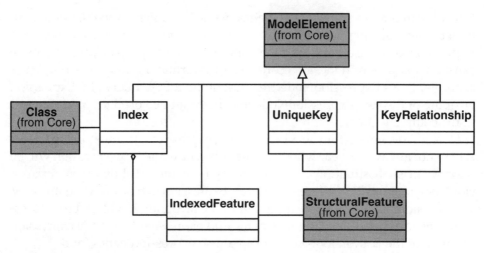

Figure 4.11   The Keys and Indexes package.

StructuralFeature (usually, its Attribute subclass). UniqueKey is a superclass of the relational database notion of a *primary key*.

KeyRelationship instances represent relationships that are based on shared key values, similar to the *foreign key* of relational databases. Like UniqueKeys, KeyRelationships are owned by the class that contains them. In relational database terms, the KeyRelationship is owned by the class that contains the foreign key, not the class containing the primary key. KeyRelationships are key fields linked by an ordering association to StructuralFeature.

To better understand how CWM models keys, note that they are *not* modeled as classifiers. Rather, they are ModelElements that represent the roles played by collections of fields. This distinction is important because the definition of the Core package does not permit Features to be owned by more than one classifier. Consequently, if keys were modeled as classifiers, fields could not be owned by both their class and, the possibly multiple, keys in which they might participate.

Software Deployment Package

The Software Deployment package records how software and hardware in a data warehouse are used. CWM-enabled warehouse management tools can use the information found here to locate hardware and software components of the warehouse. The package attempts to capture only as much of the operational configurations as is needed to service other CWM packages; it does not try to be a complete or general-purpose model of any data processing configuration. Figure 4.12 shows the package classes and associations.

Software packages are modeled as SoftwareSystem instances. A SoftwareSystem can be thought of as representing an installable unit of software

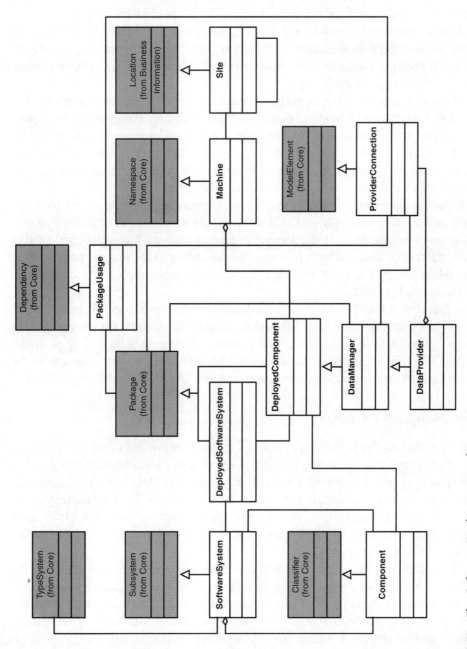

Figure 4.12 The Software Deployment package.

that you might purchase from a software vendor. Each SoftwareSystem can record identifying information such as *name*, *type*, *subtype*, *vendor*, and *version*. A TypeSystem instance can be associated with a SoftwareSystem providing a link to the data types that it defines. Individual parts of an installable software system are modeled by the Component class. Components are owned by SoftwareSystems. So that they can be shared without violating the single ownership nature of the ElementOwnership association, components can be imported by other SoftwareSystems.

The actual installation of a software package on a computer is modeled by the DeployedSoftwareSystem class, and an installed component is represented by the DeployedComponent class. DeployedComponents are linked to the Machines on which they are deployed, and Machines are owned by Sites, which may be arranged hierarchically to reflect organizational structure or similar relationships.

DataManagers represent software components that provide access to data, such as database management systems and file systems. As discussed in the following section, each of the Resource layer packages has a subclass of the Core's Package class, which inherits the relationship between Package and DataManager that is used to link the meta data resource's meta data to its physical deployment.

A DataProvider is a kind of DataManager that provides access to data stored in other DataManagers. This class is used to model data interfaces like ODBC and JDBC that do not actually own the data to which they provide access. The PackageUsage class allows DataProviders to provide access to other DataManager's data under names not used by the DataManager itself.

TypeMapping Package

As discussed in the DataTypes package, a key component of successful data warehouse interchange is the capability to correctly transfer data defined by the type systems of different software products. The DataTypes package provides the capability to define data types. In contrast, the Type-Mapping package defines the notion of type systems as a collection of data types and supports the mapping of data types between type systems. The package metamodel is shown in Figure 4.13.

The TypeSystem class represents a collection of data types defined by some software package or programming language. Type systems can be recognized by the names or the content of the version information attributes they contain. Best practice guidelines suggest that a convention about how type system names are constructed within an organization will simplify the process of finding a specific TypeSystem instance.

TypeSystem instances own two separate sets of objects. One set describes the data types that the TypeSystem defines; the other set identifies the TypeMapping instances, which describe how the TypeSystem's data types are mapped into the

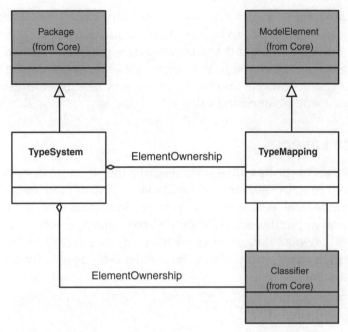

Figure 4.13   The TypeMapping metamodel.

type systems of other products. Because both sets of objects are owned via the ElementOwnership association, you will need to examine the type of each object to determine what it might be. Any object that is a TypeMapping instance represents how type mapping occurs; any other object type is a data type.

TypeMapping instances are unidirectional; they define movement of data from a source type in the current TypeSystem to a target type in another Type-System. Consequently, a reciprocal pair of TypeMapping instances is required to model a two-way transfer, one in each of the type systems involved. It is, however, perfectly acceptable for a type mapping to be defined in only one direction.

If a TypeMapping instance exists, the mapping that it describes is considered *permissible*. If no TypeMapping instance exists for a pair of data types, any desired mappings between them must be handled by the Transformation package in the Analysis layer. TypeMapping instances have two flags that provide additional information about how data interchange can occur. Because a type may be mapped successfully to more than one target type, the *isBest-Match* flag usually will be true for the available mappings that are the *preferred* mapping. If more than one TypeMapping instance between a source and a target is marked as a best match, it is up to the application to decide which one to use. Some type mappings are acceptable within some value ranges and not acceptable elsewhere; the *isLossy* attribute should be set to true in the latter case and false in the former. For example, a long data type can be mapped to another compatible long data type regardless of the value being interchanged. However, a long data type can be interchanged successfully to an integer data type only when the value of the data being transferred is less than the maximum value that can be stored in an integer data type. *isLossy* can be set to true in the latter case to indicate that the mapping may be subject to value truncation errors, depending upon the value interchanged.

Resource Layer

CWM packages in the Resource layer describe the structure of data resources that act as either sources or targets of a CWM-mediated interchange. The layer contains metamodel packages that permit descriptions of object-oriented databases and applications, relational database management systems, traditional record-oriented data sources such as files and record model database management systems, multidimensional databases created by OLAP tools, and XML streams.

Object Package

The CWM already contains a perfectly good object model (in the Object Model layer). Consequently, the CWM design team saw no reason to create another one. Instead, the Object Model layer Core, Behavioral, Relationship, and Instance packages can be used directly to create descriptions of object-oriented data resources. These packages can be used to describe the structure of object-oriented databases and of object-oriented application components that act as data sources, such as COM and EJB objects.

If you encounter an object-oriented data source with features or capabilities that cannot be handled by the Object Model packages, an extension package can be defined to add support for the additional capabilities. If you need to create an extension package, it will need to define only those classes and associations required to support the additional features. The modeling capabilities of the existing Object Model packages can continue to be used as they are; you should not need to duplicate any metamodel features already provided. See the *CWM Extension Packages* section later in this chapter for specific details.

Relational Package

Relational database schemata can be described by the Relational package. The metamodel for the Relational package (a portion of which is shown in Figure 4.14) supports the description of SQL99 compliant relational databases, including its object-oriented extensions. This standard was selected because of its widespread acceptance in the data processing community and because it is vendor-neutral. Although the CWM design team knew of no vendor's rela-

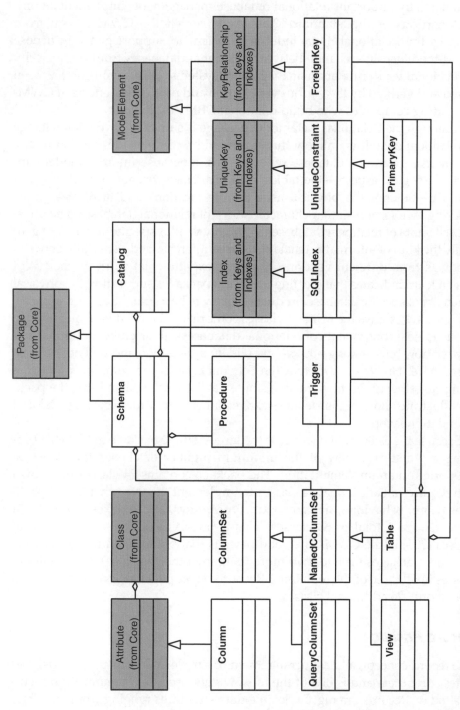

Figure 4.14 The Relational package supports SQL99 standard compliant relational database schemata.

tional database that had fully implemented the SQL99 standard, virtually all commercially important relational database managements implement significant portions of this standard. The result is that the CWM design team believes the Relational metamodel is sufficient to support general-purpose CWM-mediated interchange between relational databases from the majority of relational vendor database management systems. This conclusion has been tested and verified by the various verification and production efforts of CWM-submitting companies who build relational DBMS products.

Although the Relational metamodel package is sufficient for the interchange of relational data, it is unlikely that it can hold a complete description of any commercial relational database schema. This is because the metamodel supports the logical aspects—the tables, columns, views, trigger, procedures, and so forth—but not the physical aspects—file locations and attributes, index blocking factors, and similar characteristics—of relational databases. The physical schemata of relational databases are highly vendor specific and are not generally the kind of information that needs to be interchanged, especially between products from different vendors. However, experimental work by the CWM design team indicates that creating extension packages supporting the physical schemata of specific database products is likely to be a straightforward exercise.

Figure 4.14 shows the primary classes comprising the Relational metamodel.

The logical components of relational databases—their tables, columns, and key relationships, among others—are widely understood and will not be belabored here. However, note that the Schema class is the common point that brings together all of the parts of a single database schema and that the package illustrates how higher level packages inherit from the Object Model and Foundation layers.

Because the Relational package is the largest single package in CWM, it provides a worst-case view of the minimum number of classes that must be supported in an implementation. The package contains 24 classes of its own and requires an additional 44 classes to implement the five other CWM packages (Core, Behavioral, Instance, DataTypes, Keys, and Indexes) on which it depends, for a total of 68 classes. This is one-third of the total number of classes (204) in the CWM. The good news is that because it already depends on other packages (at five, two more than any other package) the remaining classes in all three of the remaining Resource layer packages can be added at a cost of only 24 additional classes.

Record Package

The record concept, a linear arrangement of simple and structured fields, predates computers and is one of the most widely used data organization methods today. Records are highly flexible data structures ranging from character stream files (in which each character is a record) to complex structures of interlinked records. Because of their flexibility and longevity, record-based files are pervasive in today's computing environments. Because they were compatible with disk and memory structures, records could be transferred directly between the two storage media without translation. Records became the foundation upon which first-generation database management systems were built, and they still underlie the physical storage of many of today's more advanced databases. The CWM Record package (see Figure 4.15) provides the infrastructure needed to describe a wide variety of record-oriented data structures.

The RecordDef class describes the field layout of a record. Each RecordDef owns an ordered list of Field instances via the ClassifierFeature association. Each Field instance defines a semantically meaningful area of the RecordDef. Because they are attributes, Fields inherit a data type via the StructuralFeatureType association. This classifier may be a DataType instance for simple field types like integer, or it may be a structured classifier, a Group, which describes the internal structure of the field itself. Note that Groups are not actually embedded directly into RecordDefs, but instead, serve as the types of Field instances. Although Groups can be thought of as an inline data type that has meaning only where they are directly declared, CWM permits Group definitions to be shared as needed by fields in multiple RecordDefs.

The FixedOffsetField class allows fields to be mapped to particular byte offsets with a RecordDef and can be used to record memory boundary alignments when required.

A RecordFile is an ordered collection of RecordDefs that can be instantiated physically as a file in some file system. The ordering on the association between

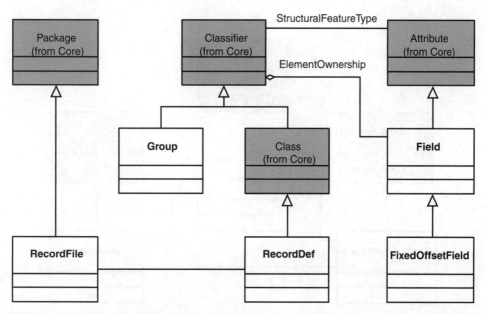

Figure 4.15 The CWM Record package.

RecordFiles and RecordDefs can be used to record required sequences of records in a file.

Multidimensional Package

Multidimensional databases are physical support structures created and used by OLAP tools. The objects in a multidimensional database directly represent OLAP concepts, such as dimensions and hierarchies, in a form that tends to maximize performance and flexibility in ways that will benefit the OLAP tools. The magnitude of improvements achieved can be sufficient to justify unloading warehouse data from more traditional data stores, such as relational databases and spreadsheets, and placing it in specialized multidimensional constructs. The CWM metamodel for multidimensional databases is shown in Figure 4.16.

The CWM Multidimensional metamodel does not attempt to provide a complete representation of all aspects of commercially available, multidimensional databases. Unlike relational database management systems, multidimensional databases tend to be proprietary in structure, and no published, widely agreed upon, standard representations of the logical schema of a multidimensional database exist. Instead, the CWM Multidimensional Database metamodel is oriented toward complete specification generality and is meant to serve as a foundation on which tool-specific extensions to the metamodel can be built. In situations like this, providing a stub metamodel like the Multidimensional package is valuable, because it allows tool-specific extensions that inherit directly from the stub to receive the breadth of other services that

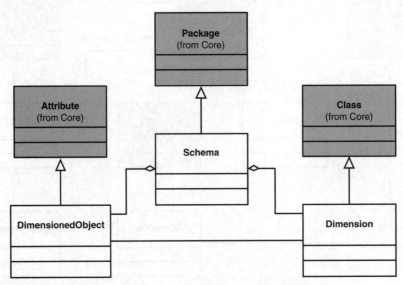

Figure 4.16 The CWM Multidimensional data resource package.

CWM packages can offer. For example, tying a tool-specific extension to the Multidimensional package allows the extension package to participate in transformations. In this way, the original sources of data in a warehouse and the transformations that move it into an OLAP cube can be recorded and shared with other tools. Fortunately, tool-specific extension packages are relatively easy to formulate, and examples for several popular OLAP tools are provided in Volume 2 of the CWM specification.

XML Package

The XML developed by W³C (www.w3c.org) is a vendor-neutral data interchange language that has rapidly become an integral part of many data processing environments, especially those with significant Internet activity. Because XML documents can be stored as standalone files and because they can be adapted easily to the structure of any particular data structures to be exchanged, they are becoming a popular storage format for data. The CWM XML package (see Figure 4.17) defines metamodel classes needed to support the description of XML documents as data resources in a data warehouse and it is compatible with the XML 1.0 specification.

The CWM XML metamodel does not contain an XML document with data to be interchanged. Rather, it contains the XML Document Type Definition that describes the structure of XML documents that can be interchanged. If you think of an XML stream as a database containing information to be exchanged, the DTD is the schema of that database and is represented by the Schema class. An XML Schema owns a set of ElementTypes. Each ElementType owns a set of attributes that describe the element type and, optionally, one Content instance that specifies the kind of data that the ElementType can contain. The Content can be either an ElementContent, which limits the content to XML tags, or MixedContent, which permits both XML tags and character data. Content instances can also own other ElementTypes. In this case, the ownership is of the weak kind, as is the ownership relationship between ElementType and Content and the recursive ownership on ElementContent.

XML DTDs have been criticized because they are not strongly typed. To response to this and other problems with DTDs, W³C continues to evolve the way in which XML documents can be described. The next step in this process will occur with the acceptance of the XML Schema specification, which will provide improved type support and other features and will replace DTDs as the preferred method for describing the structure of XML documents. Unfortunately, when the CWM was adopted by OMG, the XML Schema specification was not yet ready. Although the present XML package correctly describes DTDs and is fully usable for that purpose, you should expect that the XML package will be extended to include XML schemas soon after the specifications are adopted by W³C.

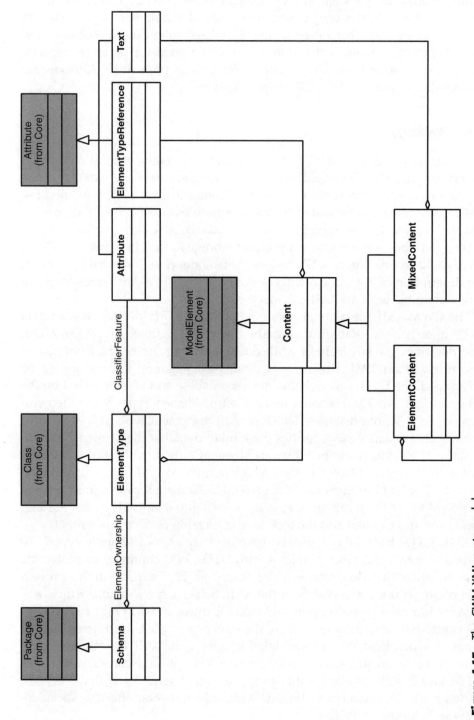

Figure 4.17 The CWM XML metamodel.

Methodology Interlude

At this point, we have seen enough of the CWM to take a moment to understand how it accomplishes three important tasks. This information will help you to understand the structure of the CWM and how to use its modular package design to best advantage.

How CWM Uses Inheritance to Achieve Reuse

The notion of inheritance—in which subclasses acquire the attributes, operations, and associations of all of their superclasses—is one of the most useful features of object-oriented technology. Inheritance is a powerful organizing principle that allows complexity to be managed in an orderly fashion. However, inheritance is well known only to those familiar with object technologies; no direct counterparts exist in the relational model, and only the dimmest reflections of inheritance can be found in the Record model. Because classes receive inherited features through their immediate superclasses only, inheritance hides much of the complexities of more ancestral superclasses (that is, those above the immediate superclass).

To keep the complexity and size of the foregoing package diagrams manageable, a few artist's license shortcuts have been taken in create them. If we take the time to understand what is really going on in one of the diagrams, we will see how inheritance achieves reuse and acquire a feeling for the true structural nature of the CWM. For example, Figure 4.18 contains a fragment of the XML package excised from Figure 4.17. Notice that composite associations between Schema and ElementType and between ElementType and Attribute are labeled with the names of associations defined in the Object Model's Core package. By redrawing these Core associations as if they were part of the XML package, we

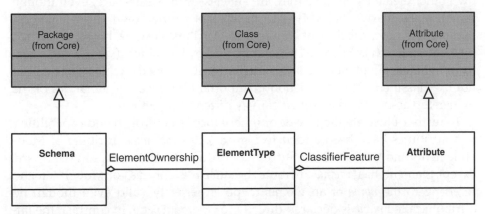

Figure 4.18 A fragment of the XML metamodel showing reused Core associations.

have shown which associations are reused to achieve the desired owner relationships without having to reproduce all of the superclass structure of the Core package to do so. This technique has been used repeatedly in the chapter and dramatically simplifies the metamodel diagrams. Diagrams redrawn in this way are completely correct representations of the desired relationships.

How can classes be kept from owning other classes that they are not allowed to own? For example, what prevents an XML Schema from owning a Relational Trigger? Apparently nothing is in the Core package that would prevent the creation of such nonsensical relationships. The CWM specification contains rules, *integrity constraints*, which are encoded in a special purpose language, OCL, which is a part of UML. OCL was described previously in the section on UML in Chapter 3. These constraints ensure that XML schemas can own only XML ElementTypes.

To understand exactly what is really going on, let's expand this fragment of the XML package to see how the relationships and inheritance really work. The CWM design team frequently resorted to expanded diagrams of this sort to clearly understand relationships and design issues during the development of the metamodel. The complete inheritance tree for the XML classes Schema, ElementType, and Attribute is shown in Figure 4.19 from the perspective of the XML package. Although diagrams of this sort greatly aid understanding, they are generally impractical in published works. However, you might find that constructing similar diagrams on your white board will help you understand the CWM as much as it helped the design team when building it.

The expanded figure makes the semantics of the Core associations and classes easier to see. Because inheritance provides classes with the attributes and associations of all of their superclasses and prevents the inheritance of attributes and associations of classes that are not superclasses, the XML classes acquire from the Core only those capabilities that are relevant to their location in the inheritance tree. For example, the Schema and ElementType classes can own other elements because they are subclasses of Namespace, even though remotely. Similarly, the XML Attribute class cannot own other elements because it is not a subclass of Namespace. Attributes can be, however, owned by Namespaces (via ElementOwnership) and by Classifiers (via ClassifierFeature), whereas ElementType and Schema can be owned by Namespaces but not by Classifiers. This distinction is important because the semantics of the ownership associations involved convey different capabilities.

To further illustrate the power of inheritance to control shared capabilities, two attributes have been added to Figure 4.19—the *name* attribute of ModelElements and the *initialValue* attribute of Attribute. Every class in the figure, except Element, has a *name* attribute, because it is subclass of ModelElement; referring to the *name* of an ElementType is perfectly valid even though no attribute called *name* is declared directly for ElementType. In contrast, the *initialValue* attribute is defined only for the Core's Attribute class and for XML's

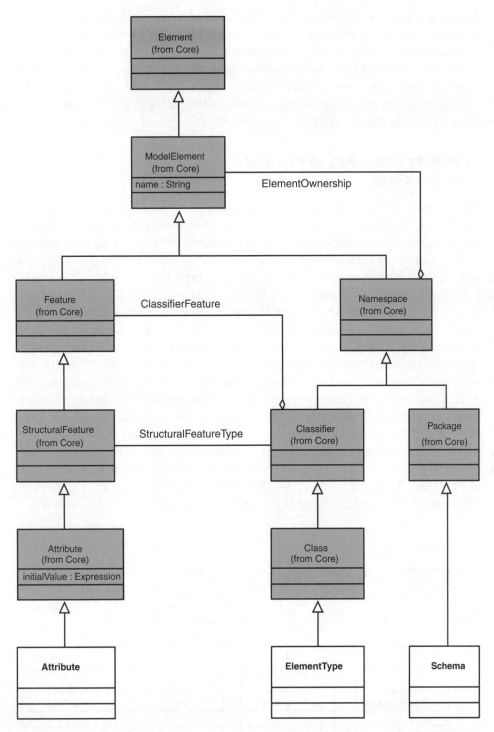

Figure 4.19 How the XML fragment really reuses Core associations and inherits attributes.

Attribute class. The concept of an initial value is not meaningful for the other classes in the figure, and they do not inherit it because they are not attributes.

Finally, note that the reuse of class names is not prohibited. There is no confusion between the Core's Attribute class and XML's Attribute class in a CWM implementation because rules defined by the MOF at level M3 in the OMG meta data architecture require that all names be qualified by the name of the packing in which they occur.

How Meta Data Links to Physical Data Resources

The primary purpose of the SoftwareDeployment package is to record the location of, and the software responsible for, data resources in the warehouse. The missing piece of information in this scenario so far is a link between the data resources and the meta data that describes its structure and characteristics. Figure 4.20 shows how this link is accomplished.

Each Resource layer package contains a class that is a subclass of the Core's Package class. These subclasses of Package collect the meta data information in their respective packages. Recall that for object-oriented data resources, the Core's Package class fills this role directly, and no subclass is needed. The link to the corresponding physical data resources (that is, the corresponding relational databases, files, multidimensional databases, or XML documents) is created by the DataManagerDataPackage association between SoftwareDeployment's DataManager class and the Core's Package class. In yet another example of the value of inheritance, a single association is reused for all data resources defined today, as well as any extension packages and data resource metamodels added in future CWM releases. All that is necessary is to make the top-level meta data container in a new data resource package a subclass of the Core's Package class.

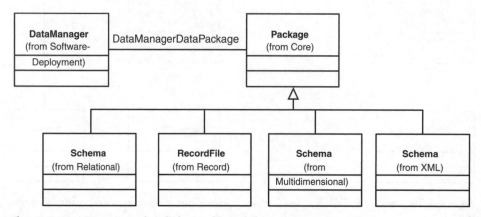

Figure 4.20 How meta data links to physical data resources.

Normally, this link technique might not be worthy of this much attention. However, because the DataManagerDataPackage association crosses the package boundary between SoftwareDeployment and Core, the MOF makes the situation more interesting. The MOF requires cross-package associations to be implemented in a way that may reduce their performance in some implementations. The reason for this is not really important here. Cross-package associations in MOF are guaranteed to be semantically correct; the only effect is on the performance of accesses across such associations in some implementations. By using a single cross-package association to capture the deployment relationship between data resources and their descriptive meta data, implementation of the DataManagerDataPackage association can be done once and leveraged for all data resources, present or future.

How Resource Packages Support Instance Objects

Each data resource metamodel in the Resource layer provides classes that directly subclass the Object Model's Instance package classes. These classes allow data instances, such as the DataType instances defined by a programming language's type system or the predefined values of categorical data fields, to be included in a CWM-mediated meta data interchange. The instance classes for each data resource type are shown in Figure 4.21. Data resource classes in each column are subclasses of the Object Model's Instance package class at the top of the column. For example, a relational RowSet is a subclass of the Extent class in the Instance package, and Row is a subclass of Object. The XML package has no subclass of DataValue, because it simply reuses the Instance package's DataValue class directly.

Now we will return to our overview of the CWM package at the Analysis layer. From here on, we will reduce our focus on the lower levels of the metamodel and concentrate more on the content of the upper layers. Because higher layer packages tend to have more classes in them than lower layer packages, we will reduce the diagram complexity and size by including Object Model and Foundation classes only when they are the endpoints of associations and not when they are used as superclasses. The precise superclasses of the Analysis and Management layer classes can be found in the CWM specification.

Analysis Layer

Packages in the Analysis layer support warehouse activities not directly related to the description of data sources and targets. Rather, Analysis layer packages describe services that operate on the data sources and targets described by Resource layer packages. The layer includes a Transformation package supporting extraction, transformation, and loading (ETL) and data

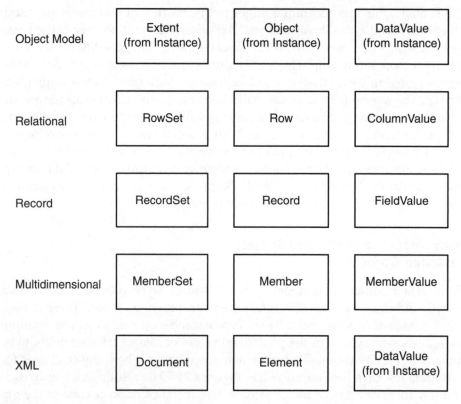

Figure 4.21   Data resource package Instance classes.

lineage services, an OLAP model for viewing warehouse data as cubes and dimensions, a data mining support metamodel, a foundation for storing visually displayed objects, and a terminology package supporting the definition of logical business concepts that cannot be directly defined by Resource layer packages.

Transformation Package

Two technical concerns are chiefly responsible for the separation of data warehousing and operational databases in today's enterprises. First, fundamental resource tradeoffs and consistency requirements in database management systems make it exceptionally difficult (most would say impossible) to tune a single data storage engine so that it simultaneously serves both update-intensive transactional application and retrieval-intensive warehousing applications with optimal efficiency. A database that tries to do both simultaneously does neither well. Second, high throughput retrieval can best be provided when data is organized in a fashion distinctly different from that used by operational databases. Many data warehouse retrievals can be optimized by using data summarization techniques whose maintenance could easily destroy the performance of operational data sources.

The cost of having separate operational and warehouse databases is that data must be moved, and transformed, from operational databases to warehouse databases on a regular basis without losing integrity in either the source or the target systems. Conversely, business analysts must be able to examine the source operational data supporting conclusions drawn from summarized data in the warehouse regardless of the complexities induced by any transformations that may have occurred. These requirements are addressed by the Transformation package (see Figure 4.22).

The Transformation class records the data sources and targets in a single transformation. Source and target data items are members of the transformation's DataObjectSet and can reference any ModelElement. Related transformations can be grouped into larger sets, TransformationTasks, which in turn, can be collected into TranformationSteps that can be sequenced using the StepPrecedence and PrecedenceConstraint classes. TransformationTasks own Transformations weakly so that Transformations can participate in multiple TransformationTasks. A TransformationActivity owns an unordered set of TransformationSteps and is the top-level class in the Transformation package. Execution of TransformationActivities and TransformationSteps can be scheduled using the Warehouse Process package described in the *Warehouse Process Package* section later in this chapter.

In conjunction with the Warehouse Process package, transformations can be scheduled for execution. The Warehouse Operation package records the execution activities of transformations and is the basis for determining the data lineage of information in the warehouse. Transformations may operate sequentially, passing intermediate result sets of subsequent transformations, or in parallel and can be associated with any operation or method recorded by the Behavioral package to indicate the exact code module that is responsible for effecting the desired transformation.

Transformations may be *white box* or *black box*. Black box transformations record information movement at large granularities, between entire systems or components, whereas white box transformations record information movement at a fine level of granularity, between individual classes and attributes. Transformations may even record information movement between objects of different granularities, such as moving an entire XML document into a column of a table, if the semantics of the situation so requires.

Some detailed white box transformations that are commonly reused can be recorded as TransformationMaps or as TransformationTrees. TransformationMaps can be used to preserve a detailed record of multiple movements of data between specific classifiers and attributes using the ClassifierMap, FeatureMap, and ClassifierFeatureMap classes, which might be performed by

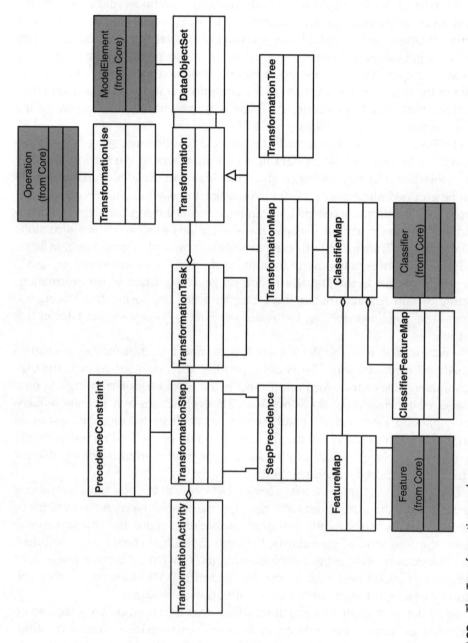

Figure 4.22 The Transformation package.

external agents (such as a method described in the CWM). In this way, detailed records can be kept to track the lineage of individual data items as they move from operation data sources to the warehouse. The TransformationTree class allows a transformation to be represented as an expression tree using the Expressions package metamodel.

As an example how the Transformation package can be used, you can coordinate the evolution of systems that have multiple levels of abstraction. For example, as shown in Figure 4.23, conceptual business objects, such as customers, might be modeled as concepts in the Business Nomenclature package. The customer concept can be mapped to a less abstract description in a logical data model, such as the Entity class in the CWM's ER extension package. At an even lower abstraction level, a table in a relational database might be used to implement customer Entities. Transformations can be used to evolve each of the abstraction levels forward, and TransformationMaps can be used to record how transitions between abstraction levels are accomplished. In this way, full data lineage can be recorded and traversed for multiple versions of multilayered systems. (For more examples of interesting things that can be done with TransformationMaps, refer to the OLAP chapter of the CWM specification.

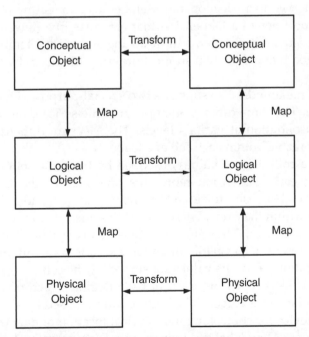

Figure 4.23 Transformations are used within abstraction layers, and mapping is used between layers.

OLAP Package

OnLine Analytical Processing (OLAP) is an analysis technique in which business data originating from multiple, diverse operational sources is consolidated and exposed in a multidimensional format that allows business analysts to explore it a retrieval-friendly environment. The ultimate goal of OLAP tools is to transform operational business data into strategic business insights.

OLAP tools can be used in many ways. However, many commercially important tools directly support the storage of multidimensional data in relational databases (ROLAP), multidimensional databases (MOLAP), or a hybrid of the two, making data resources described by the CWM's Relational and Multidimensional packages ideal candidates for OLAP analysis techniques. Mapping these data resources into OLAP systems and tracing the lineage of OLAP data back to its sources can be accomplished with CWM's Transformation package. The OLAP package metamodel is shown in Figure 4.24.

The Schema class owns all elements of an OLAP model and contains Dimensions and Cubes.

Each Dimension is a collection of Members representing ordinal positions along the Dimension. Dimensions (because they inherit from Classifier) describe attributes of their Members, which can be used to identify individual Members. The MemberSelection and MemberSelectionGroup classes support limiting the portions of a Dimension that are currently viewed. Dimensions can also contain multiple hierarchical arrangements of Members including two specialized hierarchies that support ordering Members by hierarchy levels and value.

The OLAP metamodel also supports two special-purpose dimensions: Time and Measure. The Time dimension supports time-series data in a form that supports consolidation at various levels. The Measure dimension describes the values available within each cell of a Cube.

A Cube is a collection of values described by the same set of Dimensions. Conceptually, each Dimension represents one edge of the Cube. A set of Dimension members, one for each dimension, uniquely identifies one, and only one, cell within the Cube. This cell contains one value for each member of the Measure dimension. The value of a Measure in a cell is often an aggregate value that represents a consolidation (often a simple sum, but other aggregate functions are allowed) of the values subsumed by the cell.

Cubes are constructed from a set of CubeRegions, each of which defines some subset of a larger Cube. CubeRegions are also used by some implementations as a device for controlling the physical location of data corresponding to CubeRegions. The CubeDeployment and DimensionDeployment classes are used to map portions of a cube to particular implementation strategies.

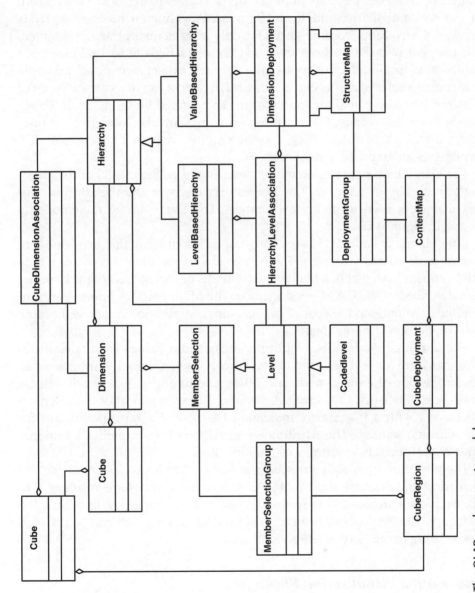

Figure 4.24 The OLAP package metamodel.

Data Mining Package

Data mining applies mathematical and statistical techniques to large data sets to detect patterns or trends that are not immediately obvious through visual inspection. For example, data mining tools can detect patterns that are present in the data but that would likely be missed by human business analysts because the patterns become apparent only after statistical analysis. Often, this happens because patterns are based on interactions of several measured values. Statistical and learning techniques such as factor analysis, principle component analysis, clustering, and neural networks can detect these types of patterns, but with visual inspection of the sort offered by OLAP tools, detection is much less certain. Data mining techniques are also attractive because, being discovery oriented, they do not require analysts to form and test hypotheses about possible relationships.

The Data Mining package contains descriptions of the results of data mining activities by representing the models they discover and the attribute values that were used to in the exploration. The Data Mining metamodel is shown in Figure 4.25.

Data Mining metamodel classes are grouped into three main areas—the core model, settings, and attributes. The core model represents the result of a data mining operation—that is, a mathematical model of some aspect of the information described in the CWM—and includes the MiningModel, SupervisedMiningModel, MiningModelResult, MiningSetting, ApplicationInputSpecification, and ApplicationAttribute classes.

The settings area describes input parameters and values for model attributes that were (or will be) used to construct a mining model. MiningSettings are a collection of mining model attributes, and five specific types of settings are defined: Statistics, Clustering, AssociationRule, Classification, and Regression along with a CostMatrix indicating the cost of a misclassification for classification settings. The AttributeUsageRelation class provides additional information about how settings use mining attributes.

The attributes area elaborates on the MiningAttribute class allowing for numerical and categorical attributes. Categorical attributes are arranged into taxonomic hierarchies and may have a collection of properties describing the Category. The OrdinalAttribute class is used to describe categories in which the ordering of category levels is significant.

Information Visualization Package

Because of the volume and complexity of data that can reside in a data warehouse, graphical presentation and summarization capabilities are essential for the effective analysis and understanding of business information gleaned from warehouses. Information recorded in the warehouse must be able to be

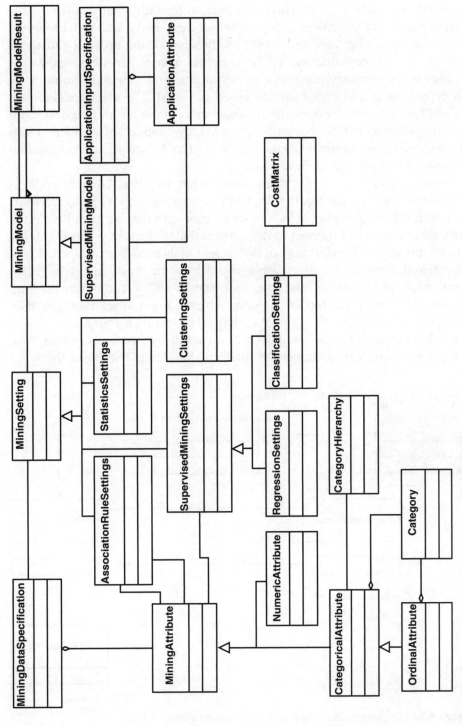

Figure 4.25 The Data Mining package metamodel.

presented in any of an ever-growing number of presentation styles (*renderings*) and on a dynamically evolving collection of traditional display media, such as paper and screens as well as more modern media like Web browsers, XML/XSL rendering, and audio players. Because of the breadth and rapid pace of this problem domain, CWM provides a very generic visualization package whose primary purpose is to permit the rendering of information of any type to be interchanged for any object in CWM. The metamodel classes defined here provide a framework in which more elaborate and capable models can be defined to interchange complex M1 level models of relevant to specific rendering environments and tool sets. The Information Visualization metamodel is presented in Figure 4.26.

The RenderedObject class acts as a stand-in for any ModelElement in CWM and contains specific information about the rendering of the object, such as its relationship to neighboring objects or its location on a display grid. Rendered-Objects can reference a number of Renderings that indicate how the objects are actually presented. Renderings can be thought of as transformations that turn a RenderedObject into a displayable object in some rendering style (table, chart, graph, and so on) or rendering tool. RenderedObjects describe the logical rendering aspects of ModelElements, whereas Renderings alter how they are represented without changing their logical rendering information.

RenderedObjects can be composed of an arbitrary number of other RenderedObjects and can reference neighboring RenderedObjects. In this way,

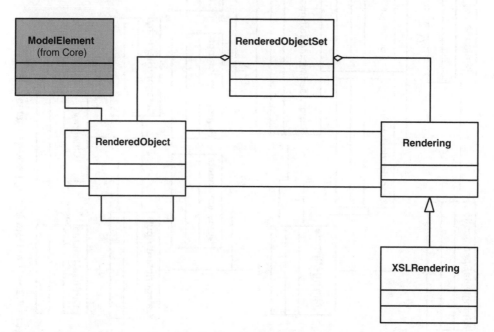

Figure 4.26   The Information Visualization package metamodel.

complex RenderedObjects can be constructed from simpler ones. Indeed, RenderedObjects may themselves be the targets of complex transformations described using the Transformation package.

XSLRendering is a useful subclass of Renderings that uses XSL to create HTML documents for display by Web browsers.

Business Nomenclature Package

Most of the CWM packages are focused on information that is already organized and structured in ways that can be easily represented in computer systems. However, computer systems, at their core, model real-world systems and processes that are not necessarily so tidily defined. In fact, many of the business concepts and ideas that computer systems represent are structured, artificially limited expressions of ideas and concepts that are best defined in natural languages. For example, the business notion of a customer is a clearly understood concept in most situations (even though we might disagree about how to describe them). Taking an understandable intellectual shortcut, computer professionals can come to equate the business notion of a customer with a specific set of tables in some database that contains customer information. Although nothing particularly is wrong with this transition, the businessman understands that the customer tables in the database are merely one of possibly many representations of a useful idea. The idea of customers and their importance to a business remain very real no matter how many times or in what formats they are presented in computer systems. In fact, customers are just as real as ever to businesses, even if they have never been computerized.

Representing generic ideas, like customer, in a form that is purely conceptual and not tied to any particular implementation technique is useful because it conveys an independent existence to ideas and is the foundation for permitting the lineage of ideas to be traced across the multiple implementations that are likely in a data warehouse environment. The CWM Business Nomenclature package captures generic business concepts in the form of a structured vocabulary—an *ontology*—which is independent of any computer implementation format or data model and appears in Figure 4.27. An important side-effect of having a generic description of business concepts close at hand is that they can foster communication between business and technically oriented employees and can help clarify a business' understanding of its own processes.

The Business Nomenclature package expresses concepts as collections of terms that can be organized into hierarchies of taxonomies and glossaries. Concepts capture semantic relationships, can be related to similar concepts, and identify terms that describe them. A taxonomy is collection of concepts, and a BusinessDomain is a definable business area that owns a set of taxonomies that are relevant to its activities.

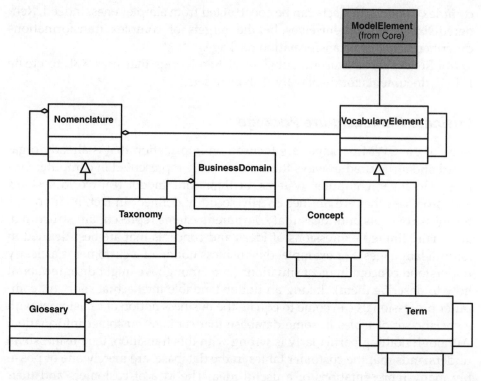

Figure 4.27 The Business Nomenclature package metamodel captures generic business concepts.

Terms are collected into glossaries and may be related to each other. Terms may be *preferred*—the best term representing a concept—or may be *synonyms* that reference preferred terms and allow for shades of meaning. Hierarchical arrangements of terms into more general and more specific elements allow the substitution of narrower terms for more specific terms where appropriate.

A VocabularyElement, the superclass of Concept and Term, is a stand-in for any ModelElement in the CWM, captures conceptual descriptive information about the ModelElement that documents its business meaning, and allows it to be related to other VocabularyElements. VocabularyElements are the words and phrases of the Business Nomenclature package.

Management Layer

Packages in the Management layer provide service functions that can support the day-to-day operation and management of a data warehouse. These packages can make the CWM an active, well-integrated part of your data warehouse environment. Besides acting in the roles described here, these packages can serve as a foundation upon which more elaborate warehouse management activities can be built using CWM extension packages.

Warehouse Process Package

The Warehouse Process package (see Figure 4.28) describes the flow of information in a data warehouse. Information flows are expressed as transformations described by the Transformation package and may be documented at the level of a complete TransformationActivity or one of its TransformationSteps. Warehouse events are the triggers that begin the flow of information between data warehouse components; they can be scheduled or provoked by either internal or external events.

A Warehouse Process is either a WarehouseActivity or a WarehouseStep depending upon whether it represents a TransformationActivity or a TransformationStep, respectively. Related Warehouse Processes can be collected into Process packages as needed.

WarehouseEvents trigger the initiation of Warehouse processes. A scheduled WarehouseEvent occurs at a predetermined point in time, or it can recur after a specific period of time has elapsed. An external WarehouseEvent is a response to some happening or stimulus that has occurred outside the data warehouse. Finally, CascadeEvents and RetryEvents can fire internal WarehouseEvents at the completion of a preceding WarehouseEvent; these events can be used for many activities including starting the next WarehouseProcess, scheduling a retry or the next occurrence of the current WarehouseProcess, and posting activity records to the ActivityExecution and StepExecution classes in the Warehouse Operations package.

Warehouse Operation Package

The Warehouse Operation package (see Figure 4.29) records events of interest in the warehouse. Three types of events are recorded—transformation executions, measurements, and change requests.

After transformations have been completed, the results of their activity can be recorded by the ActivityExecution and StepExecution subclasses of TransformationExecution. This recording can be done in response to the occurrence of an InternalEvent in the Warehouse Process package or by any other equivalent means. Start time, end time, various progress and result indications can be recorded for each TransformationExecution; for StepExecutions, the actual arguments used in executing the transformations can be recorded using the CallAction class from the Object Model's Behavioral package.

The Measurement class allows metrics to be recorded for any ModelElement. Measurements can hold actual, planned, or estimated values for any item of interest in a particular tooling, analytic, or administrative function.

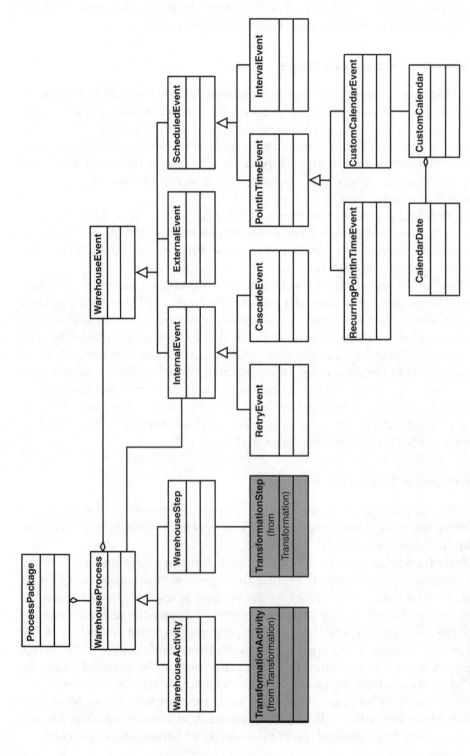

Figure 4.28 The Warehouse Process package.

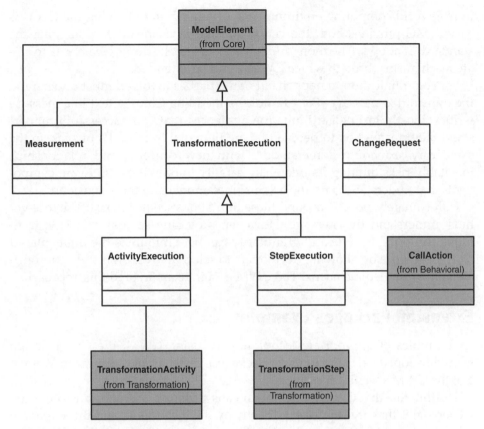

Figure 4.29   The Warehouse Operation package records events of interest.

ChangeRequests permit the recording of proposed alterations affecting any ModelElement. A number of attributes describing the change are provided, and historical as well as planned changes can be kept as needed.

CWM Extension Packages

Computer software standards developers walk a thin line between doing too much and doing too little. Do too much, and the standard is stiff and unused. Do too little, and the standard is inoffensive but also unused. The history of software standards is replete with examples of both outcomes. If it's going to be a useful standard, CWM must do what it can to walk the thin line of usability.

To remain usable in an industry as dynamic as computer software, a standard must be flexible. Flexibility means being *changeable,* to evolve with the industry as it changes, and being *extensible,* to adapt as needed for deployment in real-world computing environments. Changing and evolving the CWM is easy; OMG provides both the venue and the mechanisms for changing the standards it adopts. The more difficult task facing the design team was to create mechanisms through which CWM could be extended.

For communication to happen, all of the parties involved must understand the transmitted message. For example, embedding Chinese text in a message written mostly in English limits the audiences that can successfully understand the transmission to people that are bilingual in those languages. In the same way, extending a metamodel with new concepts and relationships inevitably risks limiting its interchangeability to only those software components that understand both the original metamodel and the extensions.

Unfortunately, no way around these limitations seems to exist: The receiver must understand the message. However, providing several extension techniques differing in style and granularity can help minimize the limits placed on the audience by allowing developers to select an extension style appropriate to their immediate needs. The CWM design team favored this approach.

Extension Packages Examples

As examples of appropriate techniques for using CWM, the CWM design team developed several extension packages. The examples appear in Volume 2 of the CWM specification.

The thin line that CWM must walk means striking a useful balance between technologies that are supported directly by the metamodel and those that are relegated to extension packages. A technology was included in the CWM if, in the judgment of the design team, it was in sufficiently widespread use and if general agreement exists as to the major metamodel concepts. (Usually, but not always, this meant that a well-known standard could be identified.) Technologies that failed either of these tests became candidates for extension packages. As an example of the latter case, the entity-relationship (ER) model met the widespread usage test but failed the general agreement test; Many ER implementations exist in design tools and in standardized practices, but many of them differ in incompatible ways. However, because of its importance to the industry, the ER model was provided as an example extension package in Volume 2 of the CWM specification (and is presented in the *Subclass Extensions* section later in this chapter). In another interesting case, the COBOL Data Division model (also in Volume 2) meets both criteria for inclusion, but because CWM (and even UML) does not model program logic, the COBOL Data Division became an extension package because it is an incomplete representation of the language.

After a technology was selected for inclusion, it was modeled sufficiently so that meaningful interchange could occur. Features that fell outside this definition were also candidates for extension packages. For example, the relational data model was modeled to the point that logical database descriptions could be interchanged between vendors. However, no attempt was made to model vendor-specific extensions to the logical model, nor were the physical attributes of relational databases modeled. Both were relegated to vendor-specific extension packages. Except for the ER and COBOL Data Division packages, the remainder of the example extension packages presented in Volume 2 fall into this category.

Sometimes the criteria for including a technology in the CWM meant that the resulting package became little more than an attachment point for extension packages. As noted, this was the case for the Multidimensional package, and to some extent, for the Record package as well. However, this is not a problem because the attachment point package allows its extension packages to directly leverage important CWM capabilities, such as transformations, lineage tracking, conceptual business models, and the services of the Foundation layer. Example extension packages are available for both the Record (DMS II and IMS) and the Multidimensional (Essbase and Express) packages in Volume 2.

To emphasize the point that the CWM can be used for modeling both traditional and nontraditional components of data warehouses, the design team also included the Information Set and Information Reporting extension packages in Volume 2. The Information Set extension treats the domain of survey data, such as might be collected by a questionnaire, and extends the OLAP package, and Information Reporting covers reporting tools and extends the Information Visualization package.

CWM Extension Mechanisms

Three mechanisms for creating extensions to the CWM are described in this section. When creating an extension package of your own, you should select the mechanism that best meets your needs. These mechanisms can also be combined to produce a CWM extension package tailored to your needs.

Subclass Extensions

CWM is built using subclassing (inheritance) techniques, so using the same technique to extend it seems highly sensible. In fact, the design team preferred this extension mechanism, and all of the CWM extension packages in Volume 2 use it exclusively. The Entity-Relationship package from Volume 2 is provided as an example in Figure 4.30.

Except for the RelationshipEnd and Domain classes, the ER extension classes are all subclasses of corresponding CWM classes. Because these extension classes do not add attributes, the only function they serve is to rename the CWM class so that they match the names expected by users

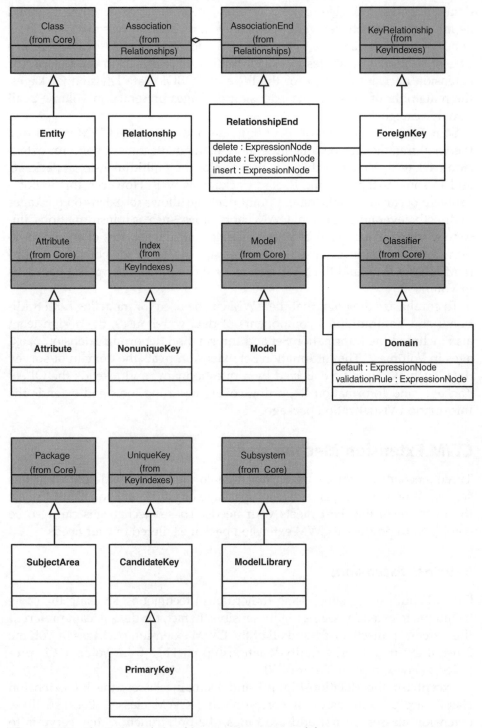

Figure 4.30 The Entity-Relationship extension metamodel.

familiar with the ER model. That so many of the ER classes rename existing CWM classes speaks to the model power of CWM. Nearly all of the concepts required by ER were already present in CWM, except that their names were spelled wrong!

The Relationship and Domain classes are true extension classes because they add attributes that are unique to the ER model. In addition, the ER package adds two associations that are unique to this model—between RelationshipEnd and ForeignKey and from Domain to Classifier. Notice that the Attribute and Model classes were added, even though they have the same name as their subclasses from the Core package. Subclassing these two classes was not strictly necessary; the corresponding Core classes could have been reused as they are. They were subclassed so that it was clear that they were included in the ER model.

TaggedValue and Stereotype Extensions

A sometimes-heard complaint about subclassing as an extension technique is that it is too heavyweight for most simple situations, especially when the only extension that may be needed is to add an attribute or two. Although such concerns are generally based in worry that subclassing techniques will have detrimental performance impacts, in some legitimate situations subclassing techniques may be pretty heavy-handed. The CWM Core Stereotype and TaggedValue classes were created to address these situations. As an example of the use of these simpler extension techniques, the ER extension package has been recrafted in Figure 4.31 using Stereotypes and TaggedValues instead of subclassing.

In the figure, the labels on classes enclosed in double brackets indicate stereotypes; for example, <<Entity>> is a stereotype on the Class class from the Core package. Stereotypes are special-purpose labels that convey extra semantic information about the intended use of the class they adorn. The meaning of a stereotype is usually significant only to humans; they do not directly carry significance for software systems. Note that the Attribute and Model classes from the Core package are reused and do not require stereotypes because their current name completely conveys their semantic intent.

TaggedValues are arbitrary name-value pairs that can be added to any ModelElement. In the figure, they are used to hold the values of needed attributes unique to the ER model and are shown as instances of the TaggedValue class owned by the relevant classes. The tag attribute of the TaggedValue instances holds the name of the extended attribute. However, the modeling of extended attributes does not work completely in this case because the data type of the new attribute *must* be *string*. This means that nonstring values, such as *integers* or *ExpressionNodes*, must be converted to strings prior to saving them in TaggedValues and must be reconverted to their native data types when they are retrieved.

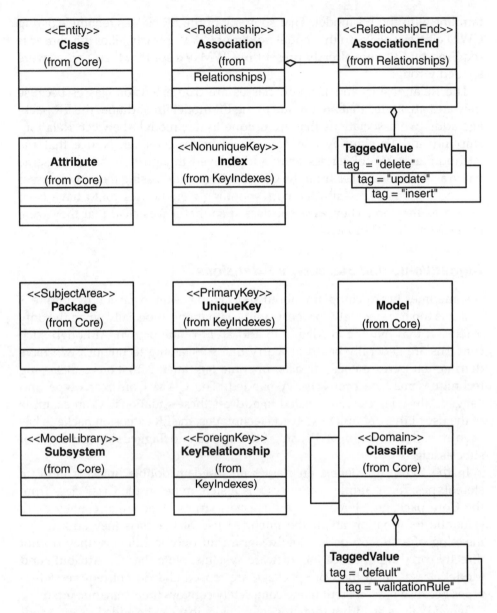

Figure 4.31 ER package modeled using Stereotypes and TaggedValues.

Stereotype and TaggedValue extensions are created as instances of their respective classes in the Core package. These classes provide the necessary links that allow the extensions to be owned by ModelElements and allow Stereotypes to own a set of TaggedValues. This latter mechanism allows a set of TaggedValues to be associated with any class that has been assigned the Stereotype that owns the set.

These extension techniques are simpler to use than subclassing, but they fall short of subclassing in another way as well; they provide no mechanism for adding associations to the ER model. Consequently, the association between the RelationshipEnd and ForeignKey classes in Figure 4.30 could not be modeled in Figure 4.31.

As with subclassing, opinions differ as to the value of Stereotypes and TaggedValues as extension mechanisms. Their chief advantage is their simplicity and ease of use; they require no additional metamodel changes and are lightweight. Complaints about Stereotypes and TaggedValues as extension mechanisms often revolve around their incomplete modeling of the desired extensions. In our example, the *string* problem and the inability to add associations are indicative of these complaints. Most of the problems that these simple extension mechanisms experience stem for the fact that they are sort of a degenerate subclassing mechanisms: They do only part of the job. You can see that any usage-definable character string, which both Stereotypes and TaggedValues are, whose base purpose is to add some extra information about the role or function of particular instances of some classes are little more than a shorthand for a subclass hierarchy. The unfortunate aspect of taking such shortcuts is that the sending and receiving applications must be aware of the meaning of specific strings, which limits the interchange to tools aware of the extensions. Ultimately, the question of which to use comes down to whether the simpler Stereotypes and TaggedValues will provide you with the modeling power that you need in your application. If they do, use them, but if you are unsure, subclassing is a safer, more robust, and semantically cleaner choice.

XMI-Based Extensions

An additional extension technique is available to the CWM developer—XMI extensions. Because CWM meta data interchanges are accomplished using XML files that conform to the OMG's XMI specification, XMI's native extension techniques can be used with any CWM interchange.

XMI extensions support the full modeling power of XMI and so do not suffer from the incompleteness problems, which can plague Stereotypes and TaggedValues. Also, because multiple sets of extensions can be added to an XMI file, it is a useful way to pass around sets of tool-specific parameters. Each tool's XMI parser need only ignore extensions that were meant for some other tool. For example, XMI extensions might be used to transfer display-oriented information, such as the layout of graphical objects, from one copy of a tool to another copy. Also, they might be used to pass vendor-specific physical attributes of a relational database schema that is exchanged with the CWM Relational package.

The chief drawback of XMI extensions for interchanging CWM meta data is extensions that are not directly part of the CWM meta data being interchanged. Although XMI extensions successfully will deliver extensions to the receiving tool, they, in a sense, *tunnel* under the CWM and may not be directly visible via CWM-aware software that isn't preconditioned to understand the semantics of the specific extensions transmitted.

Although XMI extensions are technically complete and general-purpose, the details of their delivery are quite technical and are summarized here. That said, using XMI extensions might best be left as a technique intended for professional programmers interested in building tool-specific CWM interchange definitions.

The bottom line on selecting extension techniques for the CWM is to choose one or more techniques that accomplish your goals for your extended CWM environment and, at the same time, match the skill sets of the personnel available to do the work.

Summary

In this chapter, we investigated the architecture of CWM in considerable detail. In particular, we demonstrated how CWM's architecture leverages and extends the OMG's standard metamodeling architecture (initially described in Chapter 3). We showed how CWM is structured as a collection of interrelated packages, where each package addresses the modeling requirements of some particular subdomain of data warehousing and business analysis. This is a key characteristic of CWM that facilitates the management of complexity in the modeling of large data warehouses and information supply chain architectures by breaking up the descriptions of both the problem domain and its solutions into easily managed and reusable chunks.

We provided a comprehensive survey of the architectural layers of CWM, and each of the metamodel packages residing at each layer. In particular:

- ObjectModel, which effectively represents a subset of the UML and is used as the base metamodel for all other CWM packages
- Foundation Layer, which defines a number of packages that facilitate the modeling of common services and constructs found in most data warehouses and ISCs, such as the modeling of data types and key and index structures
- Resource Layer, which supports the modeling of the various, physical information resources found in a typical ISC, such as relational and multidimensional databases

- Analysis Layer, in which typical business analysis meta data is defined on top of the various resource models. This includes the modeling of data transformations, logical OLAP schemas, data mining and information visualization, and business nomenclature

- Management Layer, which allows for the modeling of common data warehouse management tasks and processes, and supports the tracking of these activities and other significant events within the data warehouse

The Methodology Interlude section discussed several key aspects of CWM that fundamentally relate the architecture to its use in modeling. This included

- CWM's use of inheritance (in the typical object-oriented sense) to achieve reuse of key meta data constructs (recall from Chapter 2 that meta data reuse has been established as one of the key determiners in enhancing ROI).

- How meta data models can be linked back to their physical resources: This an important aspect of CWM model building that is investigated in considerable detail in Chapter 5.

- How each of the various Resource packages of CWM support the inclusion of data instances: This means that a CWM model is fundamentally capable of representing meta data together with the data described by the meta data.

Finally, we surveyed the CWM Extension package, which consists of technology-specific metamodels that extend the core CWM to represent vendor-specific meta data. This further demonstrates the support that CWM provides for meta data re-use, and enables users of CWM to develop their own meta-models. What is perhaps most relevant about this is the fact that very same architectural nuances characterizing the structure of CWM itself (for example, the use of inheritance and package structuring) automatically provide the means by which CWM may be extended and customized.

In Chapter 5, we will see how the concepts presented throughout Chapters 3 and 4 are actually employed in the formulation of data warehousing and business analysis meta data. Chapter 5 provides a number of concrete examples of combining CWM with *use case methodology* to realize the model driven approach to meta data integration.

CHAPTER

5

Using CWM

This chapter describes how CWM models are constructed from use cases. A *use case* is a description of how a typical function within a system or application is performed, most often from the perspective of an end user of the system. In the case of CWM, we are primarily concerned with use cases describing the construction or specification of system models that translate directly to meta data. This chapter presents a simple use case that is used as the basis for constructing relational meta data using the CWM Relational package. Then, the relational model is expanded into a dimensional model using the CWM OLAP and Transformation packages. This model refinement process illustrates both the logical and physical modeling of the same use case scenario, using CWM as the modeling language. The reader is provided with a better understanding of how CWM is used in practice to construct models of typical data warehousing and business intelligence use cases, and how these models are subsequently used as meta data.

A Use Case Based Approach to Understanding CWM

CWM covers a broad spectrum of meta data information about the data warehouse. Our discussion of CWM use is based on a single, and comprehensive, use-case scenario. To cover as much of the model as possible, this use case takes the reader through a complete data warehouse scenario, from concepts to design, implementation, and end-user analysis. Although this use case is rather large, it represents only a fraction of the total CWM metamodel. This particular use case was chosen because it covers many of the basic concepts and constructs used throughout the CWM metamodel and describes the complete data warehouse life cycle, from concept to end-user analysis. The CWM metamodel supports the wide variety of definitions required to go from one end of the life cycle to the other. To set the stage, let's consider Figure 5.1.

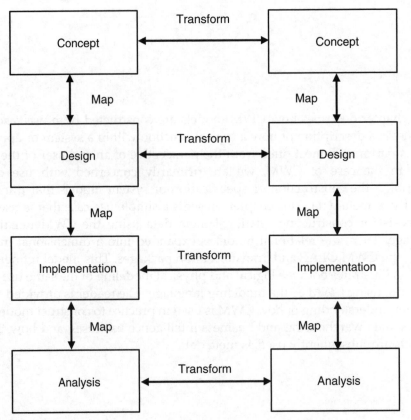

Figure 5.1 Data warehouse life-cycle conceptual levels and activities.

In Figure 5.1, we see that the process of traversing from one level to the next level is *mapping*, and traversing between levels is *transforming*. CWM uses this paradigm extensively in the construction of models, and it is one of the most important aspects of the overall CWM design. With this basic understanding of how the CWM modeling process moves between conceptual levels, we can begin the discussion of the use case.

First, we need to define what a use case is: A use case, in terms of CWM, is some standard way of using meta data, from the viewpoint of an end-user of that meta data. Use cases can be very simple, describing a specific low-level meta data definition, such as how a relational table is defined and used. Use cases also can be very complex, describing the entire interaction of meta data from concept to analysis. In this chapter, we use a series of use cases to describe how to use the CWM metamodel. At the end of this chapter, the series of individual use cases is put together to form a single use case that will describe the complete interaction of meta data, from its use in a conceptual design tool to its use in an end-user analysis tool. Note that the descriptions in this chapter attempt to give the reader a feel for how to use CWM to solve problems.

Secondly, readers should not feel intimidated by the notation used to describe how CWM satisfies the use cases. We will use instance diagrams to depict the CWM objects necessary to satisfy the use cases. These diagrams are a convenient and compact way to describe CWM meta data. The reader doesn't require a highly technical background or any knowledge of object-oriented programming to understand the instance diagrams.

To illustrate how an instance diagram works, let's consider the simple metamodel found in Figure 5.2, as well as an instance of that metamodel.

Figure 5.2 shows a simple UML metamodel containing two class definitions, ClassA and ClassB. An association between the two classes indicates that ClassA *owns* all instances of ClassB. Each class has a pair of attributes, one naming each instance of the class, and the other defining a link between the two classes.

Figure 5.3 shows four object instances of the classed defined by the metamodel in Figure 5.2. The metamodel governs how the objects are constructed and associated. The metamodel indicates that a ClassA object can *own* a collection of ClassB objects. The instance diagram in Figure 5.3 depicts a particular

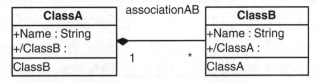

Figure 5.2 Simple metamodel.

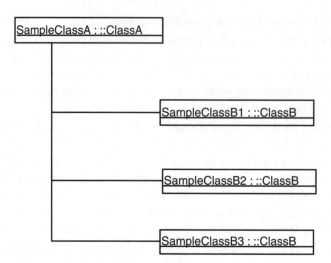

Figure 5.3 An instance of the simple metamodel.

instance of the metamodel (a *model*). The object named SampleClassA is an instance of ClassA. This object owns three instances of ClassB: SampleClassB1, SampleClassB2, and SampleClassB3.

Now that we have a basic understanding of instance diagrams, let's begin the use-case studies by describing a few simple CWM objects. We start in the Design layer of Figure 5.1, with the definition of two physical structures: a relational table and a record file.

The first use case demonstrates how to physically represent a set of data. The data we want to model is shown in Table 5.1. The data is presented in tabular form, but we will use this data in the two different physical representations.

To model the data in Table 5.1 as a physical relational table, we will use CWM's Relational metamodel. The use case will define a relational table called *Product* with five columns, with one column for each of the data columns in Table 5.1. The use case also will define a key on the relational table that will be used to uniquely identify the different rows of data. To produce

Table 5.1 Sample Data for the Use-Case Study

UPC	NAME	SIZE	BRAND	CATEGORY
111222	Dave's Candy Bar	4 oz	CompanyA	Candy
111223	Michele's Cookie	24 oz	CompanyA	Food
112223	Good Cola	8 oz	CompanyA	Beverage
112222	Better Cola	8 oz	CompanyB	Beverage

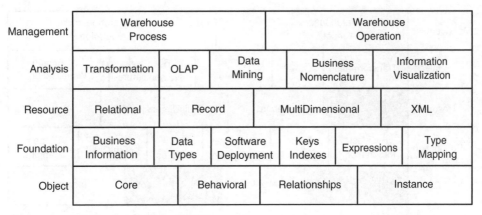

Management	Warehouse Process			Warehouse Operation		
Analysis	Transformation	OLAP	Data Mining	Business Nomenclature		Information Visualization
Resource	Relational	Record		MultiDimensional		XML
Foundation	Business Information	Data Types	Software Deployment	Keys Indexes	Expressions	Type Mapping
Object	Core		Behavioral	Relationships		Instance

Figure 5.4   Layered CWM metamodel.

the use case instances, we first must determine which CWM packages we actually need.

Figure 5.4 shows the layered CWM metamodel structure originally presented in Figure 2.10. One of the basic design principles of CWM is that metamodels residing at one particular layer are dependent only on metamodels residing at a lower layer. This structure allows individual implementations to use only those portions of the CWM metamodel that are germane to their problem space. A result of this dependency structure is that little or no *package coupling* exists between metamodels on the same level, or from a lower level to a higher level. This means that a given CWM metamodel is dependent only on packages below itself in the block diagram (but not necessarily all packages below). In addition, no dependencies exist along any horizontal plane of the packages. An implementation of a given metamodel package requires the accompanying implementation of all other metamodel packages that it depends on, but no others.

The relational use case, therefore, requires the selection of only a subset of the entire metamodel. The packages required are illustrated in Figure 5.5. Notice that not all the packages from any one horizontal level were selected. In this example, the Relational package was selected because the relational table and relational column modeling elements reside in that package. In addition, we need to define a unique key on the table, so we also need a relational constraint. These objects are dependent on the Keys and Indexes metamodel from the Foundation layer and are dependent on the Core metamodel from the Object layer.

The actual use case instance described previously is shown in Figure 5.6. In this figure is an instance of Relational Table called Product. The Product table has five columns: UPC, Name, Size, Brand, and Category. The Product table

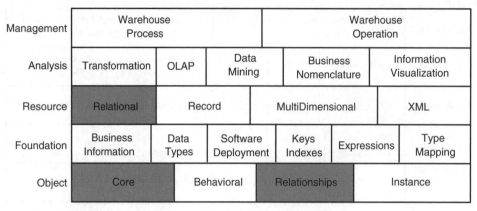

Management	Warehouse Process			Warehouse Operation	
Analysis	Transformation	OLAP	Data Mining	Business Nomenclature	Information Visualization
Resource	Relational	Record		MultiDimensional	XML
Foundation	Business Information	Data Types	Software Deployment	Keys Indexes	Expressions	Type Mapping
Object	Core	Behavioral		Relationships	Instance

Figure 5.5 CWM packages required for the relational use case.

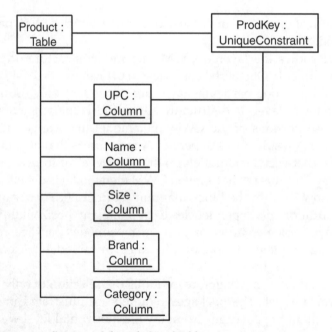

Figure 5.6 Instance diagram of the relational table.

also has a unique constraint, ProdKey. This example shows how the CWM metamodel can represent Relational Table as a design element. In the next use case, we take the same data and use the Record package to represent the design of a Record File.

Another tool used by the CWM working group to validate the metamodel is a sequence diagram, and these diagrams show the message interaction between objects in the system. We introduce these diagrams to give the reader a flavor of how an API of the CWM metamodel might work. Another reason to introduce sequence diagrams is to give the reader more insight into how to use the *classifier equality* feature of the CWM metamodel. We will completely define this feature a little later in this chapter and will show you how it solves certain problems.

The easiest way to describe a sequence diagram is to look at the diagram and walk through the syntax. The sequence diagram shown in Figure 5.7 is for the instances of the Relational Table shown in Figure 5.6.

The sequence diagram in Figure 5.7 shows a sample set of API calls to create and associate the Relational objects. The CWM specification does not contain this API. Rather, this API is a projection based on best practices of API design used by the authors. A slight embellishment exists in the preceding diagram: No RelationalObjectFactory object exists in the CWM metamodel. This object is used to show that the objects must be created in some fashion, and the sequence diagram provides a convenient vehicle to use such an object. In the preceding sequence diagram, messages are sent to the factory object. These method calls are used to create the Relational objects. These messages are also directed to the Product table object. Notice that the method is addFeature. The addFeature method is used because in the CWM metamodel, a Relational Table is a type of classifier and, as such, inherits an association to a Feature

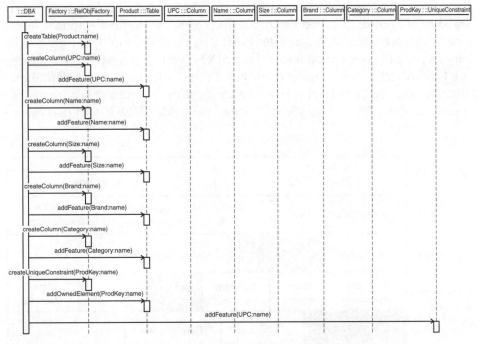

Figure 5.7 Sequence diagram for creating a relational table.

from Classifier. In the Relational metamodel, a column is a type of feature and as a result, no special association is necessary to link Relational Tables to Columns. This same type of association reuse is found in the UniqueConstraint class in the Relational package. The UniqueConstraint is a type of UniqueKey found in the Keys and Indexes package. The UniqueKey object provides a relationship to some Structural Feature. Therefore, a UniqueConstraint in the Relational package can be related to a Relational Column via this inherited relationship. This feature of the CWM metamodel turns out to be very powerful to users of CWM. We will show how this feature works later in this chapter in the context of a dimensional modeling scenario. This is because we need an example of another resource to fully understand the significance of the UniqueConstraint.

In the next use-case scenario, we will take the same data definition shown in Figure 5.4 and use the Record package of CWM to produce the design of a Record File. The structure of the file will be the same as the structure of the Relational Table, but we will replace the Relational Table with a Record File. The Relational Columns will be replaced with fields, and the UniqueConstraint will be replaced with a UniqueKey. To start this use-case scenario, we again use the block diagram depicting the CWM packages and identify the packages necessary to solve this use case.

Figure 5.8 shows the packages required for this use-case scenario. The diagram differs from the Relational scenario only at the Resource level. The instances of the Record Package are shown in Figure 5.9. This figure shows an instance of RecordFile called Product, which correlates to the Relational Table. The CWM definition of RecordFile is that it can support multiple record definitions per file, so we must add a RecordDef object. The next set of instances are Field objects. These objects correspond directly to the Column definitions from before. The last object is that of a UniqueKey. This object represents the intention of the designer to identify one of the fields of the record that can be

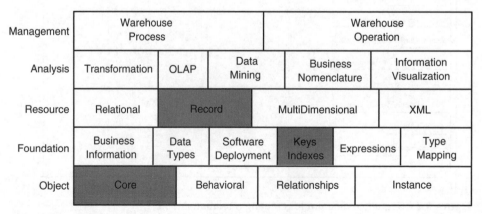

Figure 5.8   Packages required for producing a record file.

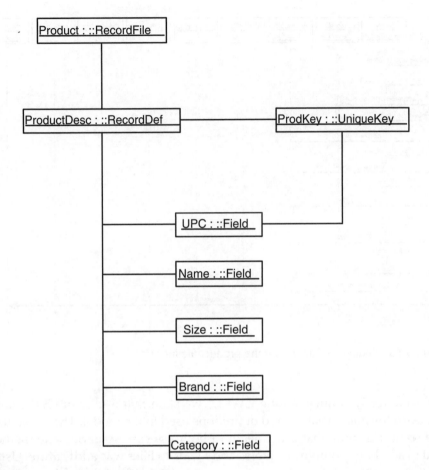

Figure 5.9 Instance of a record file.

used for record identity. This idea is a parallel concept to the Relational UniqueConstraint.

Figure 5.10 shows the sequence diagram that describes the API calls, which might be made to create the Object instances shown in Figure 5.9. This set of API calls is again only a projection based on the definition of the Record Package in CWM. The sequence diagram uses an Object factory for the creation of the objects.

The most important aspect of illustrating these two use-case scenarios is the resulting instance and sequence diagram. An important result is that if the reader takes a close look at both examples, she will realize that the only differences are in the object creation and the base types of objects. The structure of both the Relational Table and the Record File are identical. In fact even the projected API calls are the same. This is no accident. Further investigation will result in the discovery of what we previously called classifier equality.

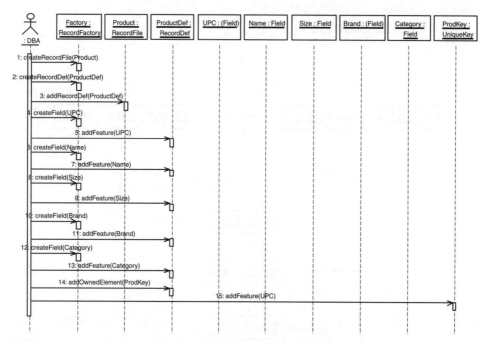

Figure 5.10   Sequence diagram for the product file instance.

In Chapter 7, "Implementing CWM," we state that a user of CWM must first learn the nomenclature and definitions used in the model. These two use-case scenarios show that exact need. In both use-case scenarios, the method used to add both Columns to Tables and Fields to Files was addFeature. Using the same method, addFeature may seem strange at first, but this is a good example of why the user of CWM must become familiar with the overall methodology used to design the CWM metamodel. In this case, if the user was looking for an addColumn method on Table and didn't find it, he may have come to the conclusion that the CWM metamodel didn't have the correct semantics for his use. This could not be farther from the truth. The CWM metamodel has the complete definitions necessary to model Relational Database objects. The key is that CWM has abstracted many common features that belong to warehouse definitions and placed them in one place. These features are inherited down the metamodel and used by a great number of object definitions. The CWM working group used this design technique throughout the construction of the CWM metamodel.

The benefits were two fold: First, this technique allows users of CWM to slice and dice the implementation of the model down to exactly the portions of the metamodel needed for their specific tool. The design eliminates package coupling by placing the commonly used associations between class definitions in the lowest level packages. As more specific packages and specific class definitions were added to those packages, most of the common structural associations were already there in the lower levels of the metamodel.

Second, this design created the classifier equality that we have been talking about. Classifier equality means all classifiers are created equal, and all features are also created equal. In data warehouse meta data, this turns out to be a very important definition. The CWM metamodel can model constructs from concepts to analysis, with design and implementation in between. The underlying concept behind this methodology is that at their core, all these types of objects inherit from the same common root, the classifier. This classifier equality made trivial the construction of a common way to navigate from any type of resource to any other type of resource. In fact, this construct is the basis for the design of a very, very small transformation package that effectively can describe the movement of data from any resource to any resource. This package also can describe the logical mapping from any level of classifier to any other level of classifier. Figure 5.11 shows the classifier equality in the model. The diagram depicts that Schemas, Packages and Record files are equal. The diagram also depicts that Classifier, Table, RecordDef, Dimension, and ElementType are equal. Finally, the diagram shows that Feature, Column, Field, DimensionedObject, and Attribute are equal. This equality also provides the CWM user the benefit of learning how one package works; they get a greater

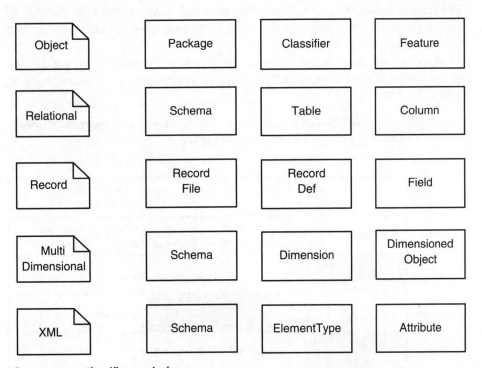

Figure 5.11 Classifier equivalence.

understanding as to how other like packages will work. This can reduce the ramp-up time in adding new packages to a given implementation.

To cover more of the CWM metamodel, the use-case scenario can be extended to include a physical implementation of the preceding example. The Relational use case will be extended to place the Relational Table into a Schema. The Schema, in turn, will be placed into a Relational catalog. By adding these two objects, the object graph now can be associated with a particular installed database instance. This use-case scenario will use the fictitious database company TablesAreUs. This company makes a relational database that will house the Table definition from the preceding use-case scenario. CompanyA has purchased the TablesAreUs relational database and will install it on one of their servers, Ethel. This new use-case scenario now describes the meta data necessary to locate a particular database table in a particular instance of a relational database running on a machine. Again, we use the block diagram in Figure 5.5 to identify the packages necessary to complete this use case. Figure 5.12 shows the packages necessary for this use case. Notice that it was only necessary to augment the packages by one. The SoftwareDeployment package contains both the definition of the software package and the machine object. The meta data associated with the additional objects is shown in Figure 5.13. The physical link, from the table definition to where it is located, is through a Deployed Software System. In terms of the CWM metamodel, implementing the physical location was as simple as adding one package implementation and providing the associated objects and object associations.

This use-case scenario demonstrates another important aspect of the design of the CWM metamodel—its use of Namespaces. A Namespace as defined by CWM is

> . . . a part of a model that contains a set of ModelElements each of whose names designates a unique element within the namespace.

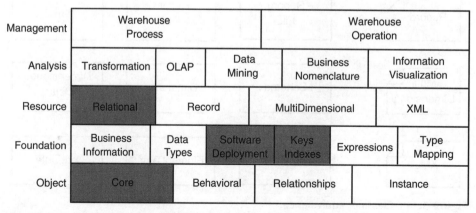

Figure 5.12 Packages needed to physically locate the relational table.

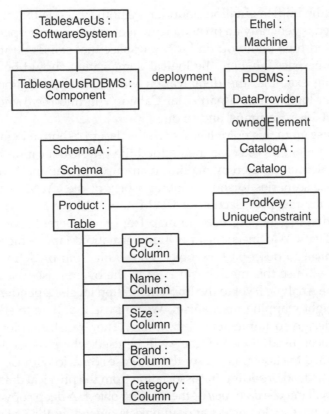

Figure 5.13 Physical deployment of the product table.

In the metamodel, a Namespace is a ModelElement that can own other Model Elements, such as Classifiers. The name of each owned ModelElement must be unique within the Namespace. Moreover, each contained ModelElement is owned by at most one Namespace. The concrete subclasses of Namespace may have additional constraints on which kind of elements may be contained. *(CWM, 2001)*

This definition allows users of CWM to use Namespace as a logical demarcation between local and enterprise-wide definitions. In the preceding use-case scenario, let's assume that there was only one machine and only a single instance of the installed database. In that case, carrying the additional enterprise meta data is unnecessary. The CWM metamodel is constructed to allow the meta data definition to stop at the catalog object. This use makes an implicit assumption that the meta data is used to describe a Local instance. In addition, when a user of such a system makes a connection to the meta data, a location is implied, and all meta data definitions are part of the connection. This type of CWM use is completely supported by the metamodel, but care must be used when determining where an implementation can set up meta data boundaries. A good rule of thumb is to always use a Namespace (or some subtype) as the implementation boundary. Another rule is that if the Namespace selected is generally an owned element of another Namespace, walk the owner relationships until you find a Namespace that stands on its own. The topmost Namespace is where the logical demarcation should be applied. In the preceding example, the demarcation would be the Relational Catalog object. A user logging into a particular Catalog will find the owned Schemas and in turn Tables, Columns, and so on.

The use case up to this point has shown the design of both a Relational table and a Record file. The use case then added the physical location to the Relational Table definition, thereby making it an implementation. We can use the same use-case scenarios to show another aspect of the CWM metamodel by introducing the mapping section of CWM. In CWM are two types of mappings. The first is generally used to map from the different levels shown in Figure 5.2. That CWM mechanism is TransformationMaps, which are a general mechanism to describe how objects are built from or defined by other objects. We will use this mechanism later in the overall use-case scenario to map from the Analytic level to the Implementation level. Dependency is a second lightweight mapping mechanism. We will use that here to show how to map from design to implementation. (Note: The TransformationMaps also could have been used; however, they will be used where dependency could not. We decided to show this part of the use-case scenario with Dependency.)

This time, instead of adding the association from the physical database to the catalog, we will make a *deep copy* of the Catalog object. A deep copy means that we will copy the Catalog object and all objects owned by the Catalog. In this specific case, it means a copy of the Catalog, the Schema, the Product Table, the Columns, and the Unique Constraint. We will use the Dependency mechanism to link the first Catalog object to the copied Catalog object. The second Catalog then will be associated to the physical database. We will repeat the process a second time with a second instance of the database on a different machine. This new set of instances will show that the CWM metamodel can be used to design a relational table and implement that table on two different database instances.

The instances shown in Figure 5.14 could represent the meta data test and production instances of the TablesAreUs database. The set of instances representing the design of the table are shared via a dependency between the two database instances. This mechanism can be used to provide both dependency tracking and design to implementation specification. In Figure 5.14 , we have shown the dependency object used to link the design specification of the table to the implementation of the table. In fact, additional Dependency objects probably would be between the columns to complete the use case. These objects were omitted for brevity and because they look identical to the Dependency objects between the Table objects.

The use-case scenario has now covered the middle two portions of Figure 5.2. Two levels remain in the diagram: Concept and Analysis. The decision as

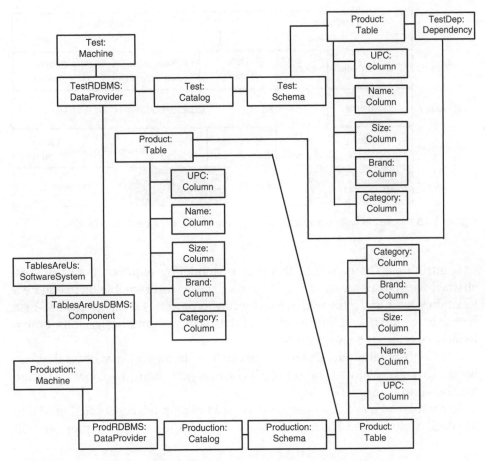

Figure 5.14 Test and production implementation of the product table.

to which to cover first is arbitrary, but to make a cleaner flow of the overall concepts, we will discuss the conceptual level first.

To add the conceptual portion of the CWM metamodel, no further packages have to be implemented. No other packages were needed because in the CWM metamodel, the Design and Implementation structures are dependent on the conceptual level. This fact is highlighted in Figure 5.15, which shows the packages necessary to implement the conceptual area of the metamodel.

If we apply the concepts of the Object layer to the Relational use-case scenario, we can add a conceptual design to the overall use case. To make the use-case scenario concrete, assume that we have some visual modeling tool to construct our conceptual model. This particular tool has the capability to model data entities as classes and data attributes as features of those classes. In addition, we will model the connection between the two associations that connect the classes via an association end object. This long-winded explanation is another way of saying that some data structure will have some set of

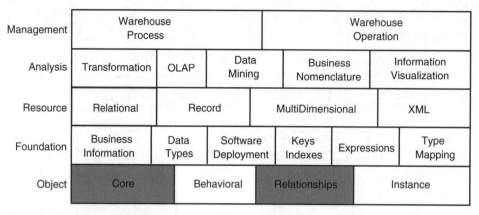

Management	Warehouse Process			Warehouse Operation	
Analysis	Transformation	OLAP	Data Mining	Business Nomenclature	Information Visualization
Resource	Relational	Record		MultiDimensional	XML
Foundation	Business Information	Data Types	Software Deployment	Keys Indexes	Expressions	Type Mapping
Object	Core		Behavioral	Relationships	Instance

Figure 5.15   Core package is the only package needed for conceptual modeling.

data attributes. The nature of this type of modeling requires us to use very abstract words, but the meaning is simple. These words enable us to equate a Relational table and a file with a fixed record type at this level. In this use-case scenario, we can now define an abstract data structure and design it for both a Relational table and a Record file.

The Conceptual model shown in Figure 5.16 defines a DataGroup that can have many DataValues. The set of CWM instances from the Object package are shown in Figure 5.17.

To complete the use-case scenario, we need to map the conceptual model to the design model (see Figure 5.18). As we did earlier in this chapter, we will

Figure 5.16   Conceptual model of a data group.

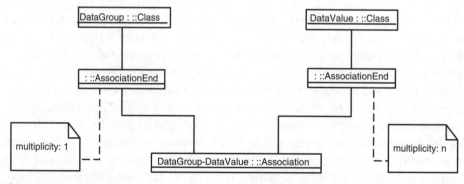

Figure 5.17   Object instances from the Object package representing a conceptual model.

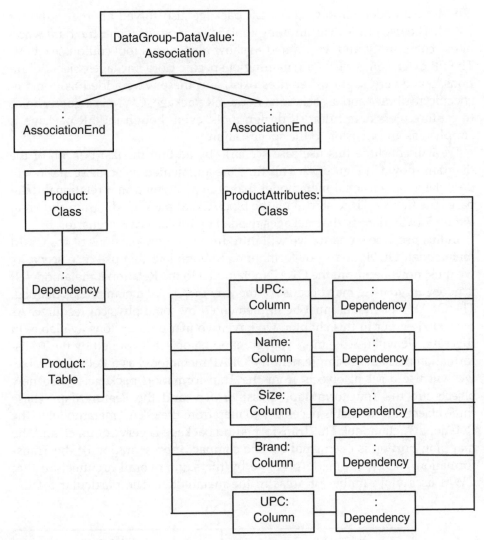

Figure 5.18 Instance diagram mapping the conceptual and design levels.

use the Dependency object to map the DataGroup to a Relational table and a DataValue to a Column.

The modeling tool used in this portion of the use-case scenario used classes and other objects from the Core package. The example could have been done just as easily with an ER modeling tool. The objects in the Core package were used as the basis for one of the CWM extension packages, the ER extension. We mention this here because many of the conceptual or design tools used provide ER diagramming tools. The ER extension package is not part of the normative part of the CWM specification. The CWM team did, however, supply a sample ER package with the specification to show how to extend the

CWM metamodel. Supplying the ER package also solved another issue for CWM. The use of ER diagramming tools is very pervasive in the data warehouse community, and we wanted to show how such a tool could use CWM. The ER extension is really a renaming of specific Core package object definitions. Some very slight differences exist, and these were added as domain-specific attributes and associations in the ER package. CWM is a good choice to capture meta data from ER design tools, even though the ER package is supplied as an extension to the specification.

We will conclude this use-case scenario by adding the last portion of the diagram shown in Figure 5.2. This time the augmented use-case scenario will describe a Dimensional metamodel that is implemented in a relational database. The first step is to start with the block CWM package diagram shown in Figure 5.19 to identify the packages needed by this use-case scenario.

In this use-case scenario, we will introduce two new portions of the CWM metamodel: OLAP and Transformation. To complete this use-case scenario, we must now map from the OLAP metamodel to the Relational metamodel. It is necessary to use a map because of the way the OLAP metamodel is defined. The OLAP metamodel must be implemented by some physical resource. As we stated earlier in this chapter, we have two mapping options available. In this case, we will use the more robust mapping objects supplied by the Transformation package. To implement the OLAP metamodel as a Relational table, we will use a set of objects from the Transformation package. These new objects are the TransformMap, ClassifierMap, and the FeatureMap. These three objects are all that is necessary to map from the OLAP metamodel to the Relational metamodel. The Transformation package is very compact, and the mapping portion is even smaller. The compact representation of the Transformation package is made possible by the same overall architecture that CWM uses in a number of areas in the metamodel. The particular feature

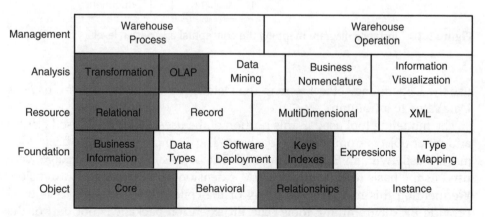

Figure 5.19 Packages required for dimensional use-case scenario.

exploited here is that all physical warehouse structures are a subtype of classifier. This feature means that a metamodel that can link classifiers can link any two objects that are of type Classifier. This design methodology was also extended to the OLAP package. By creating the CWM metamodel in this way, a CWM user can map any OLAP metamodel to any type of classifier. In turn, Attributes of the OLAP metamodel can be mapped to any type of Feature. The mapping metamodel does support one additional type of mapping—from Feature to Classifier. This additional object was defined because certain types of features, more specifically collections of features, will result in a Classifier. A good example of this is a set of Relational columns that are often equated with a single Dimension of a Multidimensional database. This Dimension object is the physical Dimension object found in the Multidimensional package and should not be confused with the Dimension object from the OLAP package.

The following use-case scenario may seem long and intimidating to the reader; however, a large portion is a rehash of the use cases we have already examined. The complete set of object instances has been provided for completeness and to give the reader an end-to-end example. In this use-case scenario, we also will add some object instances from the BusinessInformation package to introduce that portion of the CWM metamodel. In this use-case scenario, we will omit the deployment information about the Relational tables. The reader could infer this information by adding the deployment information from the preceding use case. The new use-case scenario will be to define an OLAP metamodel that consists of a single Dimension and a Cube dimensioned by that Dimension with one measure. Cubes will have more Dimensions in the real world in general, but adding more dimensions would only lengthen the description and instance diagrams and add little more information. The OLAP metamodel in this example is implemented as a standard *star schema* in a relational database (Kimball, 1996). The specifics of the use-case scenario are as shown in Figure 5.20.

The following set of figures describes the object instances to fulfill this use-case scenario. We start with the instances of the Relational metamodel that represent the star schema shown in Figure 5.20.

Figure 5.21 contains the object instances for both the Product table as well as the Fact table. In this example, we have introduced a new Relational object type: ForeignKey. This object is the standard Relational foreign key definition and is used to connect tables with many-to-one relationships.

Now, we start to define the Dimensional OLAP metamodel. The initial set of diagrams presents the Dimension and the Dimension's related structures. We then map the Dimension to the Product table of the star schema.

Figure 5.22 shows a set of instances that describe the Product dimension. Notice that the Dimension has a UniqueKey object attached to it. The use of *keys* is another concept that has been abstracted for use in almost all parts of

■ Dimension: Product

Attributes: ID, Name

Levels: UPC, BRAND, and CATEGORY

Hierarchy: Standard

Levels in Hierarchy

CATEGORY

BRAND

UPC

Cube: SalesCube

Cube Dimensions: Product

Cube Measures: Sales

Tables: Product, and SalesFact

Figure 5.20 Physical layout of the star schema.

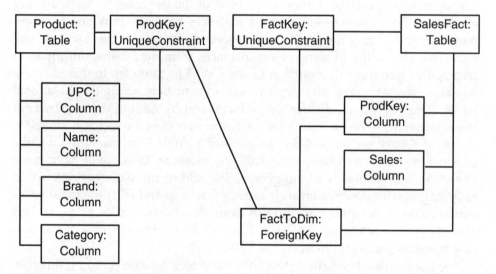

Figure 5.21 Star schema instances.

the metamodel. The intended use is to describe some set of Dimension attributes that will return a unique list of Dimension values. Figure 5.22 also depicts the standard hierarchy of the Product dimension. The diagram has numbered the associations from the hierarchy to the HierarchyLevelAssociation objects. The numbers have been placed in the diagram to show the ordered association. The diagram should be read as Category is the top of the hierarchy followed by Brand and finally UPC.

In the CWM metamodel, Dimensions, Levels, Hierarchies, and Hierarchy LevelAssociations are all types of classifiers. All these objects are types of

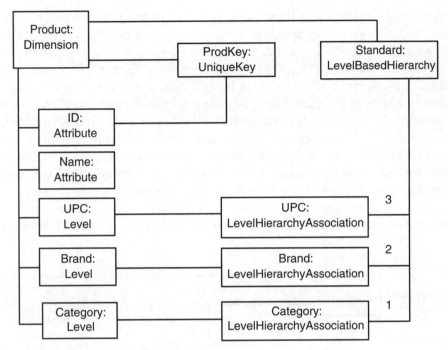

Figure 5.22   Instance of the Product dimension.

classifiers because in a Dimensional metamodel, each one of these types of objects can expose a set of attributes. In addition to exposing attributes, the Dimensional metamodel could be mapped at any and all of these objects. In general, the physical mapping is done on Levels and Level attributes and HierarchyLevelAssociations and their attributes. In this example, we will map only the HierarchyLevelAssociation attributes to the star schema. The other object mappings have been omitted for brevity of the example, and showing the additional mappings would add no new information. However, we will supply the mapping from the Dimension to its associated Levels. This mapping could have been done between the Dimension and the HierarchyLevel Associations, but again we are trying to describe the various features of the metamodel, and the two types of mappings are identical.

Figure 5.23 looks very complicated, but it really isn't. The key feature that this diagram depicts is that the Product dimension is made up of a logical union of its components. The logical union is shown by the ClassifierMap with a single target (the Product dimension) and three sources (the three Levels). The next important CWM concept is shown by this diagram: It illustrates a particular Attribute of a Dimension, which is also composed as a logical union of its components. In Figure 5.23 notice that the names of the Level attributes are different from the Dimension attributes. This was done to show that the mapping between these items is based on the FeatureMaps and not some naming convention. It is also worth pointing out that the various Levels expose a differing number of attributes. This was one of the requirements of the OLAP metamodel. The last thing to notice about Figure 5.23 is that in the Category level, one of the attributes is used as a source for both the ID and Name attribute of the Dimension. An important feature of the OLAP metamodel not shown is that the Attributes of the Levels are independent of the Attributes of the Dimension. This means that Attributes defined for the Levels may or may not be exposed by the Dimension. The reason for this is that many Level attributes make sense only for a particular Level. Forcing the Dimension to expose these Attributes is arbitrary and may not match a users view of the system. This design provides a CWM user with the most flexibility to solve the demands of their users. In general, the Attributes exposed by the Dimension

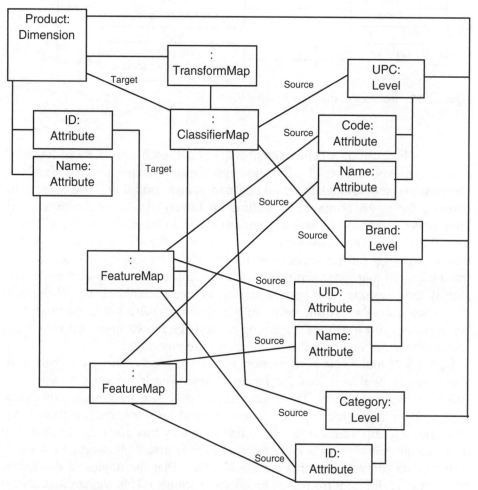

Figure 5.23 Mapping from a dimension to its levels.

will be a subset of the union of all Attributes exposed by the Levels. This is a general use of the metamodel but is not mandated.

Next, we turn our attention to mapping the OLAP metamodel onto an implementation. Before we can do that, we need to add some structure to the LevelBasedHierarchy and its owned objects. HierarchyLevelAssociations are a type of classifier. We also indicated that the maps support mapping only between classifiers and attributes. To link the OLAP metamodel to the Relational metamodel we must now define a set of attributes on the HierarchyLevelAssociations. In this example, we will define a special attribute for each named ID. This will be used when retrieving the set of values for the Hierarchy. In addition, we will add another special attribute, PARENT, to the HierarchyLevelAssociations representing the Brand and UPC levels. This attribute will serve as the immediate parent in the hierarchy. Finally, we will add a Name attribute to each of the HierarchyLevelAssociations.

In Figure 5.24, we have introduced a new set of objects, DeploymentGroup and DimensionDeployment. These object definitions enable users of CWM to provide multiple deployments of a specific OLAP metamodel. A few key features of CWM are highlighted by the instances in Figure 5.24. First, the LOV StructureMap is connected to the DimensionDeployment via the listOfValues association. This set of objects should be navigated to provide the list of values for the Category level in the Standard hierarchy. This activity is critical to the

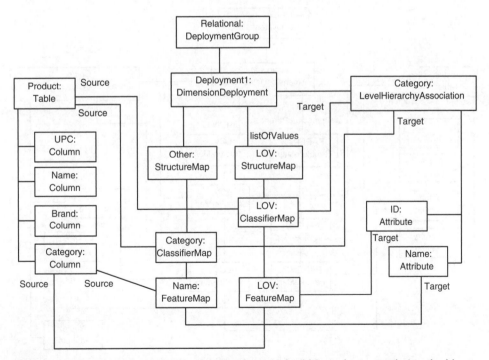

Figure 5.24 Mapping of Category level in the standard hierarchy to a Relational table.

construction of a hierarchy and was, therefore, given a special association to navigate in the OLAP metamodel. Second, users can reuse physical structures in mapping to the OLAP model. This is shown by the Category column, which represents both the list of values and the name of the Category elements in the hierarchy.

Figure 5.25, which depicts how to create an instance for a lower level in the hierarchy, is almost identical to the top-most level shown in Figure 5.24. The main difference is the introduction of the second special association, immediate Parent. The capability to navigate an association to the immediate parent in the hierarchy also was considered critical to the construction of the Hierarchy metamodel. Thus, a special association was added. The proper interpretation of the instances from Figure 5.24 and Figure 5.25, with regard to retrieving both the values of the Hierarchy and the immediate parent in the Hierarchy, is that of the logical union of the various pairs of listOfValues and immediateParent associations for the set of levels of the hierarchy.

(In Figure 5.25 the mapping of the Attribute name was omitted to keep the diagram less busy. The mapping is identical to that shown in Figure 5.24 except that the FeatureMap source would be the Brand column.)

To complete the mapping of the Standard hierarchy to the star schema, we would produce a third set of mapping structures similar to those shown in

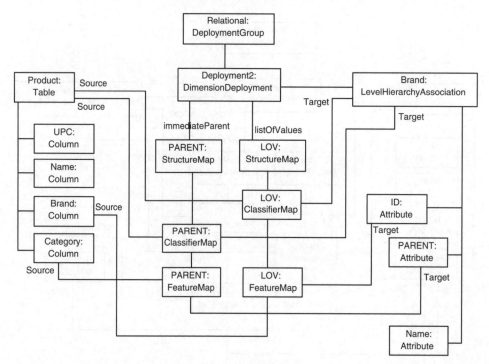

Figure 5.25 Mapping of category level in standard hierarchy to a relational table.

Figure 5.25. This set of objects would be for the UPC level in the Standard hierarchy. These mappings are not shown, but would essentially map the listOfValues to the UPC column, the immediateParent to the Brand column, and the Name attribute to the Name column. With the Dimension now mapped, we turn our attention to the other side of the OLAP metamodel: Cubes.

In this use-case scenario, we have a single Cube with one Dimension and one Measure. The process for Cubes is similar to that of Dimensions. First, we define the logical Cube model, and then we map that model onto a physical implementation. In this case, we will map the Cube onto the SalesFact fact table. Figure 5.26 shows the instance of the logical Sales cube. In the OLAP metamodel, the Cube is dimensioned by using a set of CubeDimensionAssociation objects to identify the Dimensions of the Cube. This structure is used to enable a CWM user to identify sparsity patterns in Cubes. A Dimension may be dense in one Cube and sparse in another. This functionality is made available by the intermediate CubeDimensionAssociation object. Figure 5.26 also shows that the Cube has a Measure called Sales. This association is not shown directly in the CWM specification, which rather shows another instance of the reuse of associations. The Cube is a subtype of Classifier, and the Measure is a subtype of Feature. The Cube reuses the Classifier-Feature association to imply that a Cube can contain a set of Measures.

Like Dimensions, Cubes must be implemented to represent actual values of the data warehouse. The process of implementing a Cube is slightly different than that of implementing a Dimension. The OLAP metamodel uses the CubeRegion construct to provide this functionality. A CubeRegion is necessary because of the varied ways in which data is stored in Data warehouses. The main difference between mapping a Cube and a Dimension is that the data represented by the Cube could be many orders of magnitude larger than the data represented by the Dimension. To illustrate how the volume of data represented by the Cube could explode, consider Table 5.2.

By definition, the Cube represents a set of data equal to the cross product of the number of values of its Dimensions. As Table 5.2 shows, a single structure representing the entire Cube might need to be enormous. A Cube structure

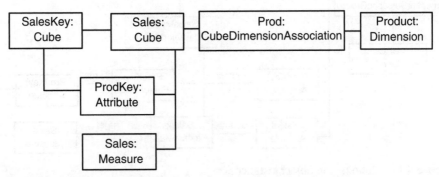

Figure 5.26 Logical cube definition.

Table 5.2   Data Volume Explosion

STRUCTURE	NUMBER OF DATA VALUES
Product dimension	100000
Geography dimension	1000
Time dimension	1000
Channel dimension	100
Sales: Product × Geography	100,000,000
Sales: Product × Geography × Time	100,000,000,000
Sales: Product × Geography × Time × Channel	10,000,000,000,000

this large could be either too large to be efficiently handled or may not be implementable in a given database technology. In general, Cubes are split into sections of the Cube that represent some manageable slice of Cube data because of the possibility of data explosion. The data slice usually represents some predefined section of each Dimension of the Cube. The various types of physical implementations lead CWM to construct the OLAP metamodel to parallel the storage flexibility needed by the implementers of Cubes. The definition of a CubeRegion is that the Dimensionality of the region is exactly the same as that of the Cube and represents some proper subset of the Measures of the Cube. In this use-case scenario, there is only one Measure. Thus, the CubeRegion defined in Figure 5.27 represents all the Measures of the Cube, but this is not mandated by the OLAP metamodel.

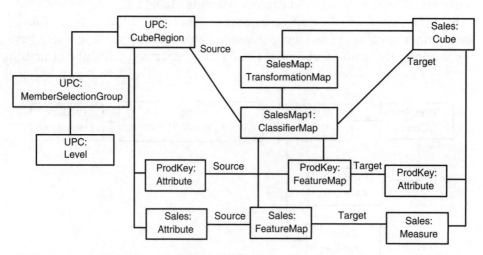

Figure 5.27   Cube region object instances.

Figure 5.27 depicts the object instances to create a CubeRegion for the Sales Cube. This CubeRegion represents a slice of data at the UPC level. This is defined in Figure 5.28 by the MemberSelectionGroup linked to the UPC level. The OLAP metamodel MemberSelectionGroup should contain one association for every Dimension of the Cube. This structure completely describes the slice of data represented by the CubeRegion. In the OLAP metamodel, the CubeRegion can contain any number of MemberSelection-Groups. This is because a particular physical slice of data may represent many logical slices of data. This metamodel can represent any portion of the Cube, with the smallest MemberSelectionGroup identifying a single value of the Cube. The next portion of this use-case scenario is to map the Cube Region to a physical implementation: the SalesFact Table. By combining the object instances in Figure 5.28 and Figure 5.29 a compete definition of the UPC CubeRegion is provided. The object instances show the specific mapping of the Cube to a physical implementation. In this case, the Sales Cube has a single physical implementation at the lowest level through the UPC Cube region.

The last portion of this use-case scenario is to link the Cube and Dimension objects. In CWM, a type of Namespace is typically used, which is provided by the CWM OLAP metamodel as an object called a schema. The Schema object is a Namespace and the entry point to the OLAP metamodel. The Schema object

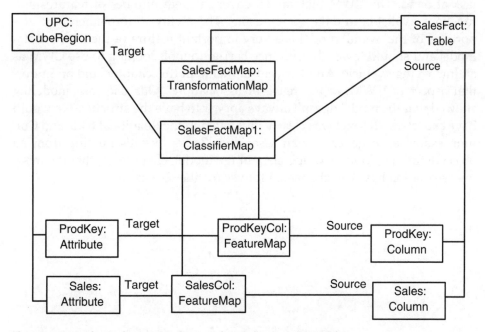

Figure 5.28 Physical mapping from Cube region to a fact table.

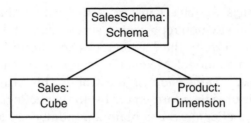

Figure 5.29 The OLAP schema and owned Cubes and Dimensions.

also serves to provide an overall namespace for Cubes and Dimensions. Figure 5.29 depicts the OLAP schema object instance along with the SalesCube and Product Dimension.

Summary

In this chapter, we saw how a CWM model is constructed from a simple use case. In the process, we illustrated several standard usage patterns for the CWM metamodel. We also demonstrated that a particular usage of the CWM metamodel (that is, to solve a specific modeling problem of interest to a particular CWM user) could be restricted to only those packages germane to the task at hand. The CWM metamodel covers a great number of features and functions available in data warehousing. The ability to implement and use portions of the overall model is a very important feature of the CWM metamodel and should lower the entrance barrier to tools looking to use CWM as an interchange vehicle. Another central theme in this chapter, and an important aspect of CWM, is the reuse of associations. Our use case modeling showed that the model doesn't always appear to have the structure we would have expected. This fact was clearly illustrated in the Relational table and Column example. In general, if an association looks like it's missing from an object definition, look to a superclass in the model; chances are that the missing association has been abstracted for use by like objects.

Developing Meta Data Solutions Using CWM

The preceding chapters have described CWM in considerable detail. In particular, we have seen that CWM is a standard specification for defining data warehousing and business analysis meta data in terms of descriptive models. These models are independent of any particular technology and live outside of the various software products that use them as the basis for integration. We also have seen how one goes about constructing CWM models to represent common problems in data warehousing and business analysis.

This chapter provides a much broader description of how CWM relates to the overall problem of building a comprehensive meta data integration solution. In particular, this chapter describes the implications that CWM has for both meta data management strategies and meta data integration architectures. We also describe the necessary architectural components required to deploy CWM integration solutions in the data warehousing and business analysis environments.

The Need for a Meta Data Management Strategy

In Chapter 2, "The Value Proposition for CWM," we learned that two of the major components necessary for a successful, model-based meta data integration solution, which were not specifically defined by CWM, are the following:

- A meta data management strategy
- A corresponding meta data integration architecture

In fact, both are required for any successful meta data integration effort, not just the model-based approach taken by CWM. However, the use of CWM for a model-based, meta data integration solution has certain implications for both strategy and architecture (perhaps more so for the architecture than the strategy, which is more high-level).

A *meta data management strategy* is the overall definition of what is to be accomplished by any meta data integration effort and the management policies, requirements, and constraints necessary to ensure the successful integration of the environment at the meta data level. Meta data integration architecture is the technical, system architecture that largely *realizes*, or implements, the meta data management strategy. This subsection discusses meta data management strategies in general, and the following subsections address their architectural realizations and the implications of using CWM as the basis for such architectures. Note that this chapter does not define, nor recommend, any particular strategy or architecture, but rather highlights the salient features and describes the CWM *touch points* that are relevant to these features. For a more thorough treatment of meta data management and meta data integration architectural techniques, see David Marco's *Building and Managing the Meta Data Repository* (Marco, 2000).

The Importance of a Meta Data Management Strategy

For any meta data integration effort to be successful, it must be grounded in a coherent and sound management strategy. This management strategy defines the objectives and requirements for meta data integration, sharing, and reuse in the target environment. Any given meta data management strategy is specifically tailored toward a particular data warehousing or business analysis or ISC deployment. However, any such meta data management strategy must adhere to general principles to be successful.

Often, the need for a meta data management strategy either goes unacknowledged or is naively assumed to be a problem largely addressed by software tools or technology standards. The need for sound meta data management, however, is not solved by technological capabilities. Meta data integration tools and enabled software products, no matter how powerful or robust, are no substitute for a sound and coherent meta data management strategy. In fact, strategy must precede the definition of meta data integration architecture and tool selection if the overall integration effort is to be successful. Regardless of how meta data management is ultimately carried out in the target environment (whether meta data is managed by a centralized repository or a distributed or federated network), some central, global policy must define the overall requirements and behaviors for meta data management.

The industry experts have been very clear on this matter for quite some time. For example, consider several reports on this issue by Gartner Group. In *Meta Data Management Alternatives for DWs and Data Marts* (Gartner, 1999), it is acknowledged that tool capabilities alone are no panacea for meta data management problems and that any decisions on tool selection should be based on an overall meta data management plan and architecture. The report, *Data Warehousing Business Meta Data Management Issues* (Gartner, 2000a), elaborates further, concluding that a sound meta data management strategy will maximize meta data reuse and enhance ROI, in part by helping to overcome the cultural and political issues impeding meta data integration. The companion report, *Data Warehousing Technical Meta Data Management Issues* (Gartner, 2000b), states that technology alone cannot solve the meta data integration problem if an organization is unable to secure agreement on fundamental meta data management issues.

Another recent Gartner report on CWM, *OMG's Common Warehouse Metamodel Specification* (Gartner, July 2000), acknowledges CWM as being a positive step toward ensuring meta data integration and reuse but also recognizes that CWM by itself will not be effective when an organization has no agreed-upon meta data management policy. Where such a policy does exist, however, the report states that CWM will indeed allow for a much greater semantic understanding between CWM-enabled technologies. The report goes on to state the importance of encouraging vendors to adhere to the CWM and XMI standards to maximize meta data reuse.

Finally, David Marco, in *Building and Managing the Meta Data Repository*, clearly delineates the need of ownership of meta data (the concept of *data stewardship*, pp. 61–62). He discusses prerequisites to the success of any meta data repository or integration effort as including clear management direction, backing, and policy (see p. 185 and pp. 115–121). Also provided throughout the book are numerous recommendations and checklists for verifying the efficacy of any meta data integration or repository effort.

Issues of organizational culture, politics, and budget rarely have technological solutions. Neither does the overall absence of a meta data management strategy. However, when a clear, well-understood, and widely agreed-upon management policy is in place, organizations can significantly benefit from the use of a model-based, meta data integration standard like CWM. The use of CWM will greatly enhance meta data integration, sharing, and reuse, and the presence of a sound and coherent meta data management strategy ensures that nontechnical issues (political, cultural, lack of ownership, agreements on meaning and semantics, and so on) will not subvert a meta data integration solution.

Elements of a Meta Data Management Strategy

What defines an effective meta data management strategy? The authors of this book do not attempt to define a meta data management strategy, because any particular strategy must be specific to a particular meta data integration problem or environment. However, we will attempt to delineate some of the essential elements of an effective meta data management strategy in the following list. This list could be used as the basis for evaluating any proposed meta data management strategy. Also, wherever CWM supports the realization of these policy elements is noted in the descriptions. (Recall that any meta data integration architecture is an implementation of some meta data management strategy and that CWM is a key component of any model-based meta data integration architecture.)

Any sound, coherent meta data management strategy will generally incorporate most of the following essential characteristics:

- An overall security policy for meta data
- Identification of all meta data sources and targets
- Identification of all meta data elements
- Agreement on the semantics of each meta data element
- Ownership of each meta data element
- Rules for sharing and modifying meta data elements
- Rules for republishing meta data elements
- Versioning of meta data elements
- Reuse targets for meta data elements
- Elimination of manual processes
- Elimination of meta data redundancy

These essential characteristics are further elaborated on in the subsequent subsections.

An Overall Security Policy for Meta Data

Security is a vitally important (and oft neglected) aspect of meta data management (Marco, 2000, pp. 62–63 and 196). Meta data is a highly sensitive and strategically valuable information asset because it describes almost all aspects of an information system or computing environment. Meta data is strategically valuable because it inherently contains a wealth of information regarding the characteristics of business data and forms the basis for strategic, business knowledge. Meta data cannot be comprised. A sound meta data management strategy must include a comprehensive security policy ensuring that meta data will be given adequate protection and safeguards.

CWM avoids defining a security model for meta data, and there is a good reason why. Although a more-or-less general consensus exists about the basic components of a good security model—single sign-on capability, authentication, authorizations based on user roles or locations, and so on—many security models are defined throughout the industry. Most software products provide some implementation of some security model. Security, however, is still very much a technology- and implementation-specific functionality. Because CWM strives primarily to be a technology-independent language for describing meta data, it avoids defining its own security model. CWM relies on each implementation of CWM to provide security functionality using mechanisms provided by the technology platform and in a manner that conforms to the specific security mandates of the meta data management strategy.

Identification of All Meta Data Sources and Targets

The meta data management strategy must identify all possible system components that may serve as either producers, consumers, or both of meta data. In particular, the strategy must define all situations in which a deployed product or tool might play either of these roles. For example, an ETL tool could be a consumer of meta data defining detailed mappings between source systems and the dimensional data warehouse. The ETL tool might be required to obtain the latest copy of this mapping from a central repository or modeling tool each time it runs. The ETL tool also may produce additional meta data that needs to be used to update certain models stored in the repository upon completion of its processing step. An analysis or reporting tool, however, may never be a producer of data warehouse meta data, only a consumer.

The notion of a meta data source or target is not a static property of a product or tool, but rather a specific role that can be assumed by a software component at different times and for different reasons. In fact, essentially five distinct meta data roles may be assumed by a software component:

- Author
- Publisher
- Owner
- Consumer
- Manager

The role of author applies to any component that initially generates some meta data element. For example, data modeling tools often serve as meta data authors. Publisher applies to any component that somehow makes a meta data element available to other components or to the environment at large (for example, a central meta data repository). Owner is the software component that ultimately has some ownership association to a meta data element. The owner may or may not be the original author of the meta data. A consumer is any software component that obtains a copy of a meta data element and uses it for some purpose. Finally, the role of manager applies to any component that assumes ongoing responsibility for long-term management and control of meta data. This term usually is associated with a repository or modeling tool.

For example, a relational data model (as a single, cohesive piece of meta data) might be authored by a modeling tool, published via a central meta data repository, and consumed by a relational database management system for the purpose of building its internal schema. The relational model continues to be managed by the repository. It may be owned either by the repository, the relational database, or the modeling tool. (We will have more to say about these *meta data life-cycle roles* in the subsequent section on meta data architecture.)

The meta data management strategy must clearly define what components serve any of these specific roles, at what times, and in collaboration with other components throughout the overall processing flow of the data warehouse or ISC. Because these roles are clearly implementation issues, CWM makes no attempt to define any supporting meta data.

Identification of All Meta Data Elements

The meta data management strategy must define how a given meta data element is to be uniquely identified. In general, meta data elements can be tagged with a unique identifier of some kind (for example, a *universally unique id* (UUID), which is a string of numeric characters that uniquely identifies objects across both time and space. For example, in an XML document, a given element can carry such a unique ID as an attribute of its defining tag. Similarly, meta data elements stored in a repository can be tagged in this manner. For example, the Meta Object Facility (MOF) requires that each MOF-compliant model element be assigned an immutable, unique ID when created. That ID must be unique within the repository or unique across all repositories in a federated environment.

The problem, however, is that in a largely collaborative computing environment, the assigning of a unique ID to a meta data element does not guarantee the unique identification of that element after the element has been published to the environment. For example, consider the case of a meta data element representing a relational table, as part of a relational model defined by a modeling tool. The relational model is published to the environment and subsequently consumed by a relational database management system, which uses the model to build its internal schema. Later, some other meta data consumer queries the relational database for its schema definition. The same table definition is supplied to the consumer in an XML document. You have no guarantee that the relational database manager will not supply *a new value for the unique ID* in the XML document! The various interchange and interoperability standards (CWM, MOF, and XMI) do not prescribe general rules for the use of such fields as UUIDs, only that they be generally supported. It is left up to the underlying implementation or technology platform to decide what is the best way to manage meta data element identity.

Thus, a meta data management strategy must define a coherent policy regarding how specific meta data elements are to be identified, as well as defining when unique identification is not required. The various tools comprising the meta data integration architecture must follow this policy faithfully.

Agreement on the Semantics of Each Meta Data Element

Complete agreement must exist on the semantics of each type of meta data element used by software components in the data warehousing and ISC environment. Otherwise, the tools and products implementing the ISC may not have a common understanding of what a given meta data element means (that is, how the meta data describes some specific piece of data). This property is sometimes referred to as *semantic equivalence* (Gartner, 2000b). A given element of meta data is said to be semantically equivalent to the data it is intended to describe if all consumers of that meta data element can use it to attain the same understanding of the described data element. Semantic equivalence can be *strong* or *weak*, and the stronger it tends to be (on average) within a given meta data integration solution, the more effective the solution is deemed. Clearly, the degree of semantic equivalence provided by any meta data integration solution directly affects meta data sharing and reuse (and ROI).

The CWM approach largely resolves these issues by providing a comprehensive, standard metamodel of the data warehousing and business analysis environment. The semantics of any type of meta data element (represented by a class in the CWM metamodel) is clearly defined by the CWM specification itself. Any software tool that has been enabled to understand the CWM metamodel will know how to interpret a CWM meta data instance. The same interpretation is guaranteed across all CWM-enabled tools, products, and applications.

Regardless of the amount of coverage of the data warehousing and business analysis domains that the CWM metamodel provides, in some cases unique features of the environment, which are not accounted for in the standard metamodel, will need to be represented in the meta data. As described in Chapter 2, "The Value Proposition for CWM," CWM accounts for this by providing standard extension mechanisms to the CWM metamodel (derived from the UML concepts of *Tagged Value*, *Stereotype*, and *Constraint*). In cases in which a weak semantic equivalence exists between modeled concept and model, this semantic gap can still be accounted for in a standard way. However, tools need to impose some uniform convention on how to interpret these nonstandard meta data elements.

Ownership of Each Meta Data Element

The meta data management strategy must identify what individuals or groups are the ultimate owners of a given meta data element. Note that this is not to be confused with the meta data life-cycle *owner* role that might be assumed by some software components with regard to an element of meta data. Rather, this is more akin to the concept of *data steward* (see Marco, 2000, pp. 61–62). A data steward is an individual, or perhaps a group of individuals, usually from the end-user community, who is responsible for some portion of the meta data as its owner. This role is critical, because it ensures that the ownership of the meta data ultimately falls within the realm of the key stakeholders in the meta data (that is, the data warehouse end-users or customers) rather than the data warehouse technical administrators or development staff. Meta data ownership is an important and necessary component of any sound meta data management strategy (Gartner, 2000c).

The CWM metamodel directly supports the encoding of this information in the meta data itself, by virtue of the *Business Information* package of CWM (see Chapter 4, "An Architectural Overview of CWM"). Any CWM-compliant meta data instance can be tagged with elements defining the responsible or affected parties of that meta data, along with detailed contact information. This may be done at any level of granularity desired. The CWM metamodel permits any meta data element to be tagged with such ownership information, although in practice, this tagging would be performed at a more coarse-grained level. For example, the root element of a complete model might be tagged with the name and contact information for the data steward responsible for that model.

Rules for Sharing and Modifying Meta Data Elements

The meta data management strategy must provide a general set of rules for sharing and updating meta data elements. Read-only sharing of meta data is allowed, within the boundaries of security access constraints. Consumers may be required to access meta data from certain designated repositories or meta data publishers. Modification of meta data elements must also be handled in a controlled and security-oriented fashion. Generally, the owner or manager of a model must provide some form of coordinated *check-in* and *check-out* functionality, in which only one client with sufficient access privileges can check-out, modify, and check-in a unique meta data element.

This problem is beyond the purview of CWM and needs to be addressed by the meta data management strategy and its subsequent realization in the form of some meta data integration architecture. This problem typically is addressed by a meta data repository product.

Rules for Republishing Meta Data Elements

Because meta data directly affects the structure of storage schemas and the behavior of software tools, care must be taken in reintroducing a modified or extended meta data element back to the environment. Often, certain tools will subscribe to the owner or manager of a piece of meta data for notification of any modifications made to that meta data. When notified, the tool may request a copy of the modified meta data element. It is then the responsibility of the tool to determine how to deal with the meta data change. In other environments, some central authority or process might shut down active tools affected by changes to meta data, then initiate a push of the modified meta data to the affected tool, and subsequently restart the tool, instructing it to incorporate the modified meta data into its internal implementation model. Regardless of the capabilities of available technology for performing these operations, a clearly defined policy must be in place for each dependent tool affected by changes to meta data.

This problem is beyond the scope of CWM and needs to be addressed by the meta data management strategy and its subsequent realization in the form of some meta data integration architecture. This problem typically is addressed by a meta data repository product, in particular, repositories that support *active* or *bidirectional* meta data flows between tools and repository (for example, see Marco, 2000, pp. 68, 202–203).

Versioning of Meta Data Elements

The meta data management strategy must set specific rules for the versioning of managed meta data elements. In particular, both metamodels and their related meta data instances must be capable of versioning. Associated with versioning is the issue of *granularity* of the versioned meta data. For example, the versioning of a metamodel usually applies to the metamodel as a whole (one would never implement portions of a metamodel that are of different versions). We term this coarse-grained versioning. Individual meta data elements might lend themselves to *fine-grained* versioning, particularly if they have been extended from their core definitions in some fashion. Also, complete packages (submodels) of meta data elements also might be subject to a *medium-grained* level of versioning.

The meta data integration architecture needs to track, control, and publish the various versions of metamodel and meta data available to the environment. It is ultimately a consuming tool's responsibility to determine what versions of metamodel or meta data it requires, but the meta data integration architecture must provide a means by which a tool can discover and request copies of the versions it requires. The rules governing this interaction must be prescribed by the meta data management strategy.

This problem is also beyond the scope of CWM, because versioning, along with the related issue of meta data *persistence*, is closely tied in with meta data repository implementation architectures.

Reuse Targets for Meta Data Elements

The meta data management strategy should set targets for the degree of semantic equivalence and the reuse of meta data elements attained by the overall meta data integration solution. (It must also define how such targets are to be *measured* over time.) Exactly what is a reasonable threshold for semantic equivalence is hard to judge. Gartner Group claims that even 80 percent semantic equivalence and reuse is an aggressive target for most environments to attain (Gartner, Jan. 2000b). This means that, in addition to setting such targets for reuse, the meta data management strategy must also prescribe what to do to minimize the effects of weak equivalence. Prescribing a convention for using the standard extension mechanisms of CWM is an example of where the management strategy can leverage a CWM infrastructure in this quest.

Eliminate Manual Processes

As described in Chapter 2, "The Value Proposition for CWM," any reliance the meta data integration solution has on manual processes or manual intervention, even if infrequent, has a dramatic, negative impact on the ROI of the overall data warehouse or ISC solution. The meta data management strategy should highlight any manual processes currently required and should provide a plan for eventually automating them. One of the single biggest advantages in a meta data integration solution is to have fully automated and repeatable processes (see Marco, 2000, p. 188).

Eliminate Meta Data Redundancy

Because one of the objectives of our meta data management strategy is to maximize sharing and reuse of meta data, our strategy should also strive to eliminate or at least minimize any unnecessary duplication of meta data in the environment. A single distinct copy of any particular meta data element should exist across the environment. Tools go to the owner or manager of this single copy to read it. Of course, no redundancy issue exists if a tool creates and maintains private copies of meta data for its own internal use and for efficiency reasons. In fact, a tool generally does this anyway, by virtue of the fact that it is using global meta data to populate its own internal implementation model. The point is that, as far as the globally available meta data is concerned, no published, duplicate copies should exist.

Developing a Meta Data Integration Architecture

In the preceding subsection, we described the importance of establishing a coherent and sound meta data management strategy prior to defining the meta data integration architecture. We described how the meta data management strategy must identify all of the meta data sources, their life-cycle roles, the owners of meta data, the agreed-upon semantics of the meta data, and the measurable goals for reuse and sharing. We also showed where CWM, as an anticipated component of the entailing meta data integration architecture, provides direct support for many of the essential characteristics of such a strategy.

This subsection delves further into the concept of the meta data integration architecture. As suggested previously, any meta data integration architecture is largely a realization or implementation of a meta data management strategy. We show the advantages that CWM, as the standard infrastructure for a model-driven approach to meta data integration, provides: CWM supports the overall integration architecture; it simplifies the integration and ensures its effectiveness (that is, results in the best-possible implementation of a coherent meta data management strategy).

Survey of Architectural Patterns

Like a meta data management strategy, any particular meta data integration architecture is specific to its target environment. Integration architectures must possess complete specificity to be effective but must also be founded on sound principles if they are to work. Whereas a sound meta data management strategy must adhere to certain, essential characteristics (as elaborated in the preceding subsection), sound meta data integration architecture must also be based on certain essential design patterns that have been proven to solve the problem. We define our architecture by selecting one of these proven patterns and then tailoring it to our specific implementation or environment. We also demonstrate how the model-based integration approach taken by CWM helps us to define superior concrete architectures from the more general architectural patterns.

The term *architecture* can be regarded as the use of abstract models or high-level specifications that describe something to be constructed. In Chapter 2, we described at great length how meta data is essentially an abstract model of data and how a metamodel like CWM is very much an abstract model of meta data in a particular domain. We likened models to architectural blueprints for the building of a house. We also noted that one particular model or blueprint does not necessarily provide all the viewpoints required by the various contractors involved in constructing a house. For example, we need an electrical blueprint for the electrical contractor, a plumbing blueprint for the plumber, a framing blueprint for the builder, and so on. Each of these blueprints is a separate model of the house, and collectively, they define the overall architecture of the house. Each blueprint defines a separate and necessary viewpoint on the overall architecture. No single description of the house's architecture is sufficient for all contractors.

Also, no single expression of a meta data integration architecture is sufficient for all purposes. We need to deal with several specific architectural viewpoints to provide a comprehensive description of our meta data integration solution. Two of the key viewpoints are as follows:

- Meta data interconnection architecture
- Meta data life-cycle architecture

Meta Data Interconnection Architecture

A *meta data interconnection architecture* (*topology*) describes, from a high level, the physical meta data interchange connections established between software products and tools within the deployment of an actual data warehouse or ISC.

Figure 6.1 illustrates a simple meta data interchange scenario between several data warehouse tools. A modeling tool is used to define a data warehouse model consisting of a relational database schema, transformation mappings

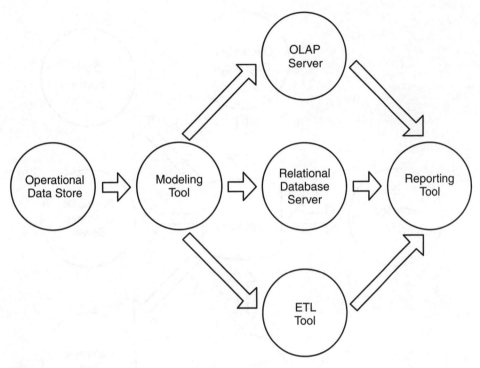

Figure 6.1 Simple meta data interchange scenario.

from a source operational system to a relational database, and an OLAP analysis application and its mapping to the relational schema. Portions of this model are exported to an ETL tool, a relational database engine, and an OLAP server. In each case, this meta data needs to be translated to three different formats that each of the three target tools can understand (each flow line in the diagram is implemented by a product-wise meta data bridge). Finally, a reporting tool imports the meta data that it needs to facilitate its analysis reporting and data drill-down capabilities. The sources of this meta data are the ETL tool, relational database, and OLAP server. Product-wise meta data bridges are used to translate the ETL, relational, and OLAP meta data into some format that is intelligible to the reporting tool.

Figure 6.2 shows the same scenario, except with a meta data repository included as the central clearing house for managing and publishing all meta data relevant to the software tools comprising the data warehouse. Note that this has the effect of simplifying the scenario somewhat. The modeling tool is still the primary source of meta data for the data warehouse, and the ETL is still both a consumer and a secondary source of meta data. Neither the relational database, the OLAP server, nor the ETL tool need serve as a direct meta data source to the analytic reporting tool. Instead, each tool obtains its meta

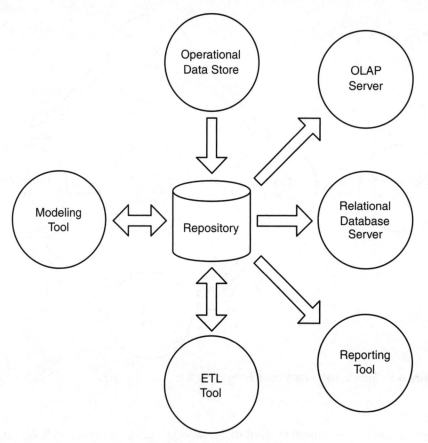

Figure 6.2   Repository-based meta data interchange scenario.

data from the repository. Note that fewer product-wise meta data bridges are required. Furthermore, these bridges translate between tool-specific formats and a single format defined by the repository product. So, their overall complexity is somewhat reduced.

Figure 6.1 is an example of a *point-to-point*, or *network*, meta data interconnection architecture, and Figure 6.2 illustrates a *hub-and-spoke*, or *centralized*, meta data interconnection architecture. We can abstract these two meta data interconnection architectures into two general patterns. Figure 6.3 shows a generalization of the point-to-point interconnection architecture involving four software tools. Because this diagram represents the most general case, we assume that any of the tools can equally be producers or consumers of meta data. Each link in the diagram represents a meta data bridge joining a pair of tools, and it is assumed that each bridge is bidirectional. (We also can assume that each link is composed of two unidirectional bridges.)

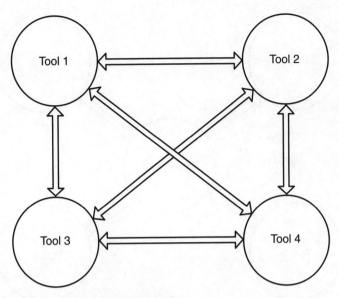

Figure 6.3 Generalized point-to-point model.

Similarly, Figure 6.4 illustrates a generalization of the hub-and-spoke meta data interconnection architecture consisting of four tools interconnected via a central meta data repository. Notice that the number of required meta data bridges has been reduced from six to four. In general, the point-to-point model requires a total of $n (n - 1) / 2$ bidirectional meta data bridges to interconnect n tools; whereas the generalized hub-and-spoke model requires n bidirectional bridges to interconnect n tools. This should give some indication of why point-to-point bridge building can be such an expensive and complex undertaking when the number of tools that need to be interconnected is large. For 100 tools, the generalized point-to-point solution requires 4950 bidirectional bridges; whereas the generalized hub-and-spoke solution requires only 100 bidirectional bridges to fully interconnect all tools.

This illustration is something of a *worst-case* scenario, in which we naively assume that each tool requires to be interconnected to every other tool. In any real-world situation, this is usually not going to be the case. This example, however, does serve to illustrate the fact that, *on average*, point-to-point interconnections using product-wise meta data bridges (for example, a bridge that performs a custom mapping between one proprietary metamodel and another) can be expected to be far more expensive than an equivalent hub-and-spoke solution. This is because a hub-and-spoke solution introduces a single, common metamodel (that is, implemented by the repository) with which tools need to interface. Each tool requires a single meta data bridge that

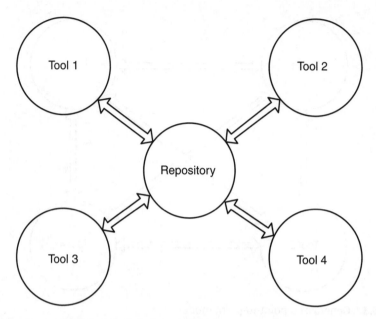

Figure 6.4   Generalized hub-and-spoke model.

translates between its own proprietary metamodel and a single metamodel defined by the central meta data repository product.

Note that, although we've reduced overall cost by standardizing on a particular, repository-based metamodel, we have still not provided the ideal, *minimal-cost* solution. This is because the common metamodel is still proprietary to the meta data repository. Each meta data bridge is required to translate between product-wise metamodels. We need fewer bridges, and the bridges are somewhat less complex, because the interface to the repository is the same for each bridge. If we wanted to substitute another vendor's repository product, however, we would need to acquire a whole new collection of bridges, unless the other vendor's repository implemented the same metamodel and interfaces as the previous vendor's. This is precisely what CWM enables us to have—a common and product-independent meta data and interface definition that we can use to construct meta data interchange architectures in a plug-and-play and minimal-cost fashion. Before considering how CWM enhances meta data integration architectures, let's consider several more variations on the basic meta data interconnection topologies.

Figure 6.5 illustrates an interconnection architecture in which two hub-and-spoke topologies are connected together via their repositories. We generally refer to this type of meta data integration architecture as being *distributed*, *decentralized*, or *federated*. (Note that a point-to-point topology is inherently decentralized, but here we use the term *decentralized* to refer to repository-oriented

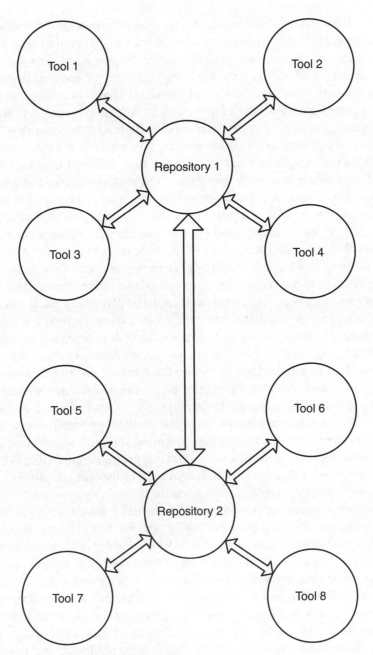

Figure 6.5 Decentralized meta data architecture.

topologies.) The two repositories in Figure 6.5 are interconnected via a meta data bridge. If the repositories implement different metamodels and interfaces, the bridge is another product-wise bridge that must be capable of translating meta data between the two metamodels. If each repository implements the same metamodel and interfaces, or some subset of the same metamodel, the bridge represents a simple, physical connection between repositories.

A number of reasons exist for building this form of meta data integration architecture. In the case of dissimilar metamodels, the architecture still provides a single, managed environment for meta data. A meta data client of repository R1 (in Figure 6.5) can have access to meta data defined in repository R2, assuming that the bridge properly maps this meta data between the two metamodels. This architecture might be used to combine two different business domains, with different descriptive metamodels, such as a sales domain and a manufacturing domain. In this case, either repository is primarily responsible for servicing meta data clients of its supported domain. Each repository maintains meta data specific to its particular metamodel and domain. Whenever necessary, meta data clients are still able to access and share meta data from the foreign domain (as long as adequate metamodel mapping and translation is provided). This approach facilitates cross-domain sharing and reuse of meta data.

In other situations, it may be advantageous to physically partition a single, common metamodel and distribute it across several repositories. For example, tools requiring only certain subsets of the overall data warehouse or ISC meta data might be designed as going to one particular repository hosting only that meta data. This might be done to ensure the efficient use of processing cycles and network bandwidth in a multitier environment. An analysis tier might host a repository containing meta data specific to analysis and visualization only, and the dimensional data warehouse itself might reside on a different tier with its own meta data repository defining the data warehouse and ETL processes. In any case, the entire meta data integration architecture is based on a single metamodel that gives it both semantic unity and simplified interconnections. We sometimes refer to this scenario as *model distribution*.

Yet another scenario supported by decentralized meta data integration architectures is that of *controlled meta data replication*. We stated in our requirements for a meta data integration strategy that redundant meta data definitions should be avoided or minimized. In certain situations, however, replication of meta data is necessary. For example, when the meta data repositories are geographically dispersed, it might be necessary to replicate some meta data between repositories to ensure adequate response times for the meta data clients at a remote location. This replication is acceptable, as long as a specific policy is in place that defines how and when meta data is to be replicated and how modifications are to be handled. Usually, modification to the meta data is restricted to one particular repository and that repository is designated as the master repository, with respect to any replicated meta data at other points in the topology.

Figure 6.6 illustrates a variation on the decentralized model that supports the model distribution paradigm in a specific way. This variation is referred to as a *hierarchical* or *star* topology. Note that this is essentially a hub-and-spoke

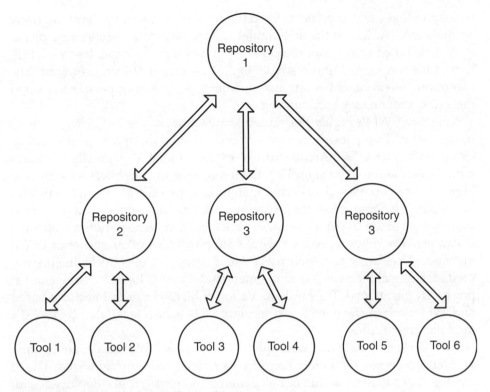

Figure 6.6   Hierarchical meta data architecture.

architecture in which the central repository hub has other repositories as its client tools. In this case, the *root* repository implements common portions of the metamodel (and corresponding meta data instances) that are common to the overall meta data environment. Each of the *leaf* repositories implements one or more specific subsets of the common metamodel and stores meta data instances corresponding to those subsets only. A given meta data client primarily accesses the leaf repository hosting the meta data in which it is primarily interested, but also has access to the global meta data stored in the root, as well as any subset meta data stored by other leaf-level repositories.

Note that this architecture gives us the ability to optimize the use of system resources (that is, processing cycles and network bandwidth) based on the principle of *locality of reference*. A given client usually accesses a single, specific leaf-level repository most of the time for its meta data needs. On occasion, the client may need to go to the global root or one or more of the other leaf-level repositories. Most of the time, the client's meta data requirements can be satisfied by one particular repository, and that repository can be collocated on the same physical computing tier as the client (or on a tier close by). So the majority of the client's meta data requests do not impact the rest of the interconnection architecture. However, a single, common and consistent metamodel (and corresponding collection of meta data) can be maintained and centrally administered. Although the metamodel and its meta data instances are physically distributed across the interconnection topology, a single, logical definition of the metamodel and a single, logical collection of instances exist. The computing environment is optimized (from a performance perspective), and meta data redundancy is eliminated.

Note that CWM's highly decoupled architecture, based on packaged metamodels with clean package separation and minimal interpackage dependencies (see Chapter 4, "An Architectural Overview of CWM"), greatly facilitates model distribution. For example, if the interconnection architecture shown in Figure 6.5 represents a distributed metamodel, two CWM-enabled repositories would be deployed in this environment. One repository would support some subset of the CWM metamodel packages (and corresponding meta data instances). The other repository would support some other subset of CWM metamodel packages and their meta data instances. Collectively, the distributed metamodel represents a single metamodel that is logically coherent, yet physically partitioned. The implementation of hierarchical architectures based on CWM, such as the one shown in Figure 6.6, is also facilitated by CWM's modular architecture.

We will demonstrate in a subsequent section how CWM relates to the integration topologies presented here. In particular, we will show that CWM enables these various architectural patterns to be physically deployed with minimal implementation complexity and cost, far less than what is currently possible with product-wise, or repository-product-wise meta data bridges. First, we need to consider the other key perspective on meta data integration architecture—*meta data life-cycle architecture*.

Meta Data Life-Cycle Architecture

In the preceding subsection on meta data management strategy, we alluded to the fact that a distinct meta data life cycle consists of the following activities:

- Authoring
- Publishing
- Owning
- Consuming
- Managing

Authoring generally implies the creation of new meta data. *Publishing* consists of somehow making the existence and location of meta data known to the environment at large or specific interested parties. *Owning* refers to some specific tool or process asserting certain privileges regarding how a piece of meta data is used. *Consuming* refers to a tool reading meta data and using it for some purpose, usually to effect its own internal operations or to build its internal information structures. Finally, *managing* refers to the overall management and control of meta data, including modifying, extending it, and controlling its access by other tools or processes.

Corresponding to the meta data life-cycle activities are a corresponding set of meta data life-cycle *roles:*

- Author
- Publisher
- Owner
- Consumer
- Manager

Each role describes how a particular software tool (or type of software tool) usually functions in some specified meta data integration architecture. For example, a modeling tool usually plays the role of meta data author. A repository often plays the role of publisher and usually the role of manager, as well. An analysis tool (for example, an OLAP server or reporting or visualization tool) is more often than not a consumer of meta data.

Note that these roles are not hard and fast. Specific software products and tools may assume different roles at different points in time. In many cases, roles may overlap. For example, the author of a particular model may also continue as the model's owner and manager. Or, the author may relinquish management of the model to a repository but still continue as the model's owner and have certain access privileges regarding the model.

These roles are clearly important to any meta data management strategy as well as its related meta data integration architecture. In fact, the roles define another viewpoint on the meta data integration architecture, one more behavioral in nature, and not necessarily readily apparent from the interconnection topology alone. We refer to this as the meta data life-cycle architecture. This architecture defines the overall meta data flow and behavioral characteristics of our meta data integration architecture; whereas the interconnection topology tends to define the static structure of the meta data integration architecture.

Consider again the meta data interchange scenario illustrated in Figure 6.1. A point-to-point interconnection topology capable of supporting this interchange is shown in Figure 6.7. Each of the links connecting the various tools is assumed to be a single, product-wise, bidirectional meta data bridge (for now, anyway). Figure 6.8 depicts the meta data life-cycle architecture supporting the interchange scenario. Now, a number of important points are revealed by the life-cycle architecture. The flow of meta data defining the life cycle is from

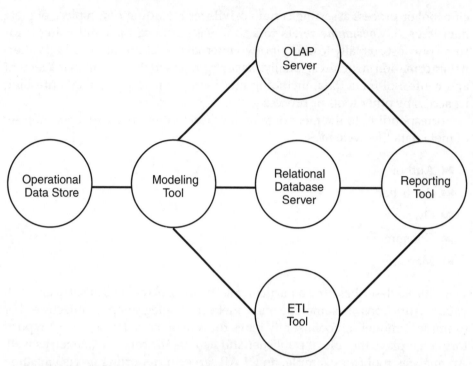

Figure 6.7   Point-to-point interconnection architecture.

left to right in the diagram. So it appears that the meta data bridges implementing the point-to-point network need only be unidirectional, although still product-wise. (Note, however, that some other life-cycle flow could easily impose other requirements on the same interconnection architecture, including the use of bidirectional bridges or mixtures of both bidirectional and unidirectional bridges.)

The various life-cycle roles of the participating tools are also shown in Figure 6.8. The operational data store is both an author and publisher, in the sense that its major role is to define and introduce *new* meta data to the environment. The modeling tool is the primary consumer of the ODS meta data. The modeling tool, via its meta data bridge to the ODS, captures enough essential meta data describing the ODS information structures to build a model mapping the ODS to the relational store. The modeling tool also creates new meta data in the form of a comprehensive warehouse model defining the relational database and OLAP schemas. So, the modeling tool plays the roles of consumer of published meta data, author of new meta data, and publisher of the combined model. The relational database and OLAP server are primarily consumers of meta data and republishers of existing meta data; that is, they use

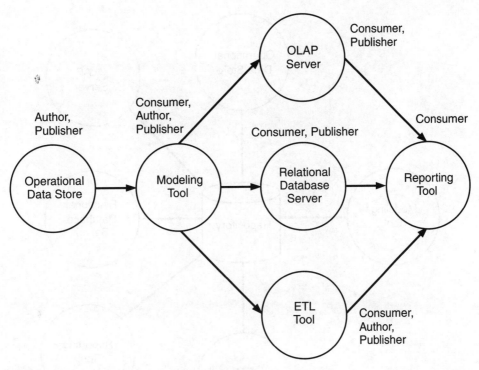

Figure 6.8 Point-to-point life-cycle architecture.

the meta data they import from the modeling tool to build their internal infor-mation structures and then forward that same meta data on to the reporting tool. The ETL tool is a consumer, author, and publisher and republisher, because it generates some new meta data as a by-product of its data transfor-mation, cleansing, and normalization process. Finally, the reporting tool con-sumes only meta data made available by the relational database, OLAP server, and ETL tool.

One of the roles obviously missing from Figure 6.8 is that of meta data man-ager. Quite a bit of authoring, publishing, and consumption of meta data goes on in this life cycle, but there does not appear to be any clear ownership or man-agement functionality roles assumed by any of these tools. Given the intercon-nection architecture and the necessary life-cycle flow, no one particular tool in this environment really seems suitable to assume this role. We will see how this situation changes when we introduce a centralized interconnection architecture.

Recall that Figure 6.2 showed the same meta data interchange scenario orig-inally illustrated in Figure 6.1, but introduced a central repository, converting the point-to-point interconnection architecture to a centralized one. Figure 6.9 shows the meta data interconnection architecture supporting this interchange

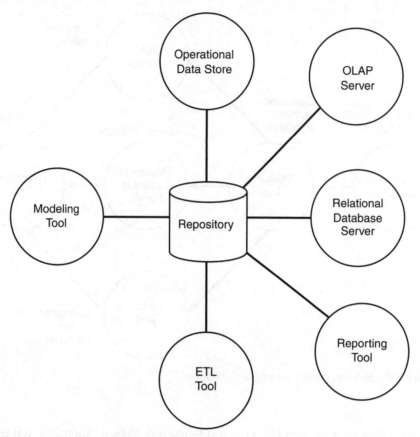

Figure 6.9 Centralized interconnection architecture.

scenario, and Figure 6.10 illustrates the equivalent, centralized life-cycle architecture (based on the same life-cycle flow implied by the interchange scenario of Figure 6.1).

Note that in this case, the roles are far more crisply defined than in the previous depiction of the life cycle. The ODS and modeling tools are clearly the primary authors of meta data in this environment. Although it is true that the modeling tool also consumes ODS meta data to perform its authoring function, its more dominant role is that of meta data author, even though we have labeled it as both a consumer and an author. The repository clearly plays the roles of publisher and manager and will consider it to be the owner of the meta data, as well. (One could also stipulate that the modeling tool and ODS share ownership of the meta data and that the repository manages the meta data on behalf of these two tools. For this example, declaring the repository the owner of all meta data is simpler.) The ETL tool is both a consumer and an author, and this is emphasized by the presence of a bidirectional bridge

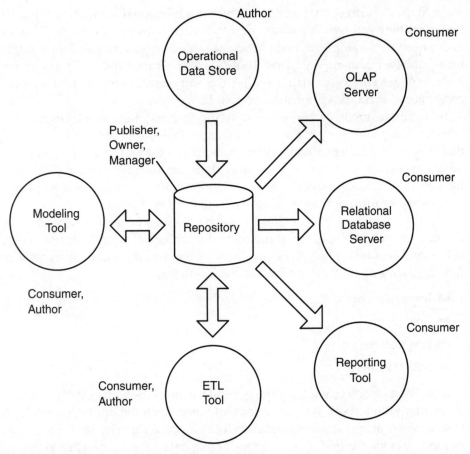

Figure 6.10 Centralized life-cycle architecture.

between the ETL tool and repository. The relational database, OLAP server, and reporting tools are now strictly consumers of meta data. The relational database and OLAP server are no longer both consumers and republishers of meta data (a rather bothersome and clearly extraneous term that the point-to-point topology forced us to use).

Before taking up the discussion of how CWM enhances these various interconnection and life-cycle architectures, let's briefly consider several of the important nuances often associated with these various approaches.

We described the use of meta data bridges as a means of implementing the links shown in the preceding diagrams. We also said that a given meta data bridge is either unidirectional or bidirectional. A unidirectional bridge is capable of transporting meta data in one direction only, from source tool to target tool. A bidirectional bridge is capable of transporting meta data in both directions and is generally equivalent to two unidirectional bridges between the same tools. A bidirectional bridge (or two unidirectional bridges) is typically deployed between two tools that need to switch between the roles of source and target. For example, in one particular interchange scenario, Tool A might be a publisher of meta data, and Tool B is a consumer, although in another interchange scenario occurring within the same environment, Tool A is the consumer of meta data published by Tool B.

To facilitate meta data transfers, a bridge must be capable translating between the proprietary metamodels of its source and target tools, assuming that they have different metamodels. Obviously, if they share a common metamodel and common interfaces for meta data, the transfer of meta data from the source tool to the target tool is straightforward and requires the use of a much simpler form of bridge, which we will term an *adapter*.

Certain behavioral nuances of meta data bridges or adapters need to be decided upon when specifying the meta data integration architecture. These behavioral features concern the initiation of the actual meta data transfer or flow and are generally categorized as the following:

- Import-export
- Push-pull
- Request-response
- Subscribe-notify

Import and *export* often refer to the general nature of the behavior of the bridge or adapter with respect to a particular tool with which the bridge interfaces. A tool currently acting as a meta data producer in some capacity is said to export its meta data via the bridge or adapter. A meta data consumer is said to import its meta data via the bridge or adapter. This generally means that the processing logic of the bridge generally reads meta data from the tool's proprietary meta data interfaces, in the case of a meta data export operation, or writes to the tool's proprietary meta data interfaces, in the case of a meta data import operation.

Push and *pull* are concepts almost synonymous with import and export, except that they more closely describe a meta data transfer from the viewpoint of the initiator of the transfer, rather than from the viewpoint of how the bridge interfaces with the source or target tool. If the source tool initiates the overall transfer process to a target tool, the transfer is usually referred to a *meta data push*. If the target tool initiates the transfer process, it is usually called a *meta data pull*. If neither source nor target initiates the transfer, the terms push and pull still apply but are relative to the process initiating the transfer. That is, the initiating process pulls the meta data from the source and pushes it to the target (relatively speaking). This is illustrated in Figure 6.11.

Request-response is essentially the opposite of the push-pull. In this case, a meta data target issues a request to a meta data source for some specific meta data instance. The source then transmits the requested meta data instance to the target, and the target imports the instance. Note that the request-response

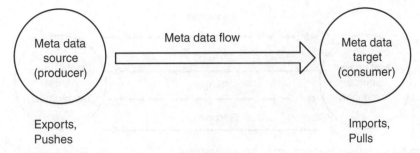

Figure 6.11   Push-pull interchange protocol.

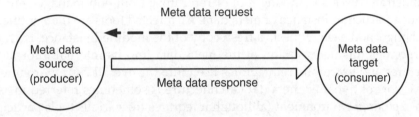

Figure 6.12   Request-response interchange protocol.

paradigm tends to be more message-oriented and synchronous than the push-pull or import-export paradigms, which are batch-oriented and asynchronous in nature. The request-response paradigm also offers more opportunity for finer-grained interchanges, because the meta data target has an opportunity to request precisely what meta data elements it needs from the source. Figure 6.12 depicts the request-response paradigm.

Finally, *subscribe-notify* refers to the capability of a meta data target to request (subscribe) that a meta data source notify it when some specific meta data instance is modified or otherwise made available in some published form. The source notifies the target that the requested instance is available, and the target issues a request for the instance using the fine-grained request-response paradigm (unless the notification message also includes a copy of the requested instance). This is shown in Figure 6.13.

Note that these various behavioral classifications apply primarily to the initiation of meta data movement between source and target tools and do not describe how metamodel mapping or meta data translation is to be performed. These behavioral classifications represent, however, an extremely important aspect of the meta data integration architecture, because they define the dynamic capabilities and overall robustness of the architecture. For example, consider a situation in which the various data warehousing or ISC tools are all served by a single, central repository. The repository has subscribe-notify capabilities built into it, and tools subscribe for notifications whenever any meta data instances they have a vested interest in are modified. An

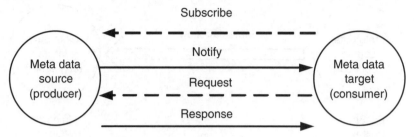

Figure 6.13   Subscribe-notify interchange protocol.

administrator uses a modeling tool or repository front-end management tool to alter a particular instance of meta data. All affected tools are then notified of the change, and each requests a fresh copy of the modified instance. Each tool incorporates this new version of the meta data into its internal information structures and gracefully reintegrates itself into the overall ISC environment.

This sort of dynamic meta data architecture is sometimes referred to as an *active repository* environment (although it requires the various tools participating in the environment to be just as active as the repository itself). Numerous advantages exist to such an architecture, including the central administration of changes to meta data, the automatic propagation of those changes to any affected tools, and the opportunity that each tool has to adjust its internal models accordingly and to reintegrate back into the environment. David Marco classifies this sort of meta data integration architecture as *bidirectional meta data*. He also discusses another variation of this behavior, referred to as *closed-loop meta data*, in which modified operational meta data is automatically applied to the affected operational system. Marco suggests that these types of meta data architecture will become quite prevalent in the near future (see Marco, 2000, pp. 311–314). Figure 6.14 illustrates a dynamic, centralized architecture, based on the active repository concept.

CWM-Based Meta Data Integration Architecture

In the preceding subsections, we investigated meta data integration architectural patterns in considerable detail. We noted that two key viewpoints exist for any meta data integration architecture:

■ Meta data interconnection architecture

■ Meta data life-cycle architecture

The meta data interconnection architecture defines the static connections between the various tools of a meta data-driven environment. The life-cycle architecture defines the general behavior and flow requirements of the meta

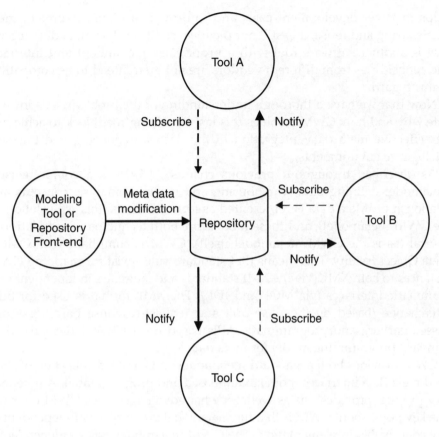

Figure 6.14   Dynamic centralized architecture.

data interchange process, embellishing the static interconnection topology with additional information on the dynamics of the overall meta data integration architecture.

Each static connection or link in the interconnection topology represents a meta data bridge, a software process that enables the flow of meta data between meta data source and target components. In addition to transferring meta data, the bridge is responsible for translating meta data between source and target components when the components have dissimilar, internal metamodels and proprietary meta data interfaces. We saw that the construction of a meta data bridge is a complex and expensive process, mainly because a large number of bridges must be implemented to integrate a wide variety of tools. We also saw that providing a meta data repository helps to mitigate this cost somewhat, because the repository, as a central hub for all meta data management and interactions, offers a single metamodel with which all tools integrate. Bridges are used to link tools with the common repository, rather than to link individual tools in a pair-wise fashion. Although this solution helps to lower development costs and to provide a higher degree of meta data sharing and reuse, it is still not the ideal solution. The meta data repository is another software tool with a proprietary metamodel and interface, and repositories from different vendors are not guaranteed to be compatible in this regard.

Now that we have a thorough understanding of the problem, let's investigate why and how CWM resolves this last remaining roadblock to achieving cost-effective meta data integration in the data warehousing and business intelligence environments.

As described throughout previous chapters, CWM is a comprehensive metamodel defining data warehousing and business analysis concepts and relationships. Meta data is represented as formal models (that is, instances of the CWM metamodel), and these models are both technology- and platform-neutral (as is the CWM metamodel itself). CWM is compliant with OMG's Meta Object Facility. This means that standard rules exist for mapping CWM instances to both XML (via the XMI standard) and language-independent programmatic interfaces (via MOF and IDL). The XML format is used for bulk interchange (based on the push-pull and request-response paradigms discussed earlier), and programmatic APIs based on the CWM IDL provide a standard programming model for meta data access.

CWM provides both a standard metamodel and a related collection of standard meta data interfaces (both stream-based and programmatic). Any repository product provides this as well. So what advantages does CWM offer us? The key point about CWM is that the metamodel is completely independent of any conceivable implementation. The CWM metamodel exists independently of, and outside of, all technology platforms and products. And, so do any instances of CWM. Therefore, using CWM, we can formulate highly expressive and semantically complete models of information structures (meta data) that can exist outside of any particular software product or tool. Meta data, therefore, is no longer confined to the proprietary metamodels and interfaces of specific products. Data warehousing meta data is liberated from products and tools and can exist on its own, as a valuable information resource in its own right.

CWM models can be constructed to any required degree of complexity. They can be sufficiently descriptive to be used as the basis for building the internal implementation models of a wide variety of data warehousing products and tools. Conversely, a given product or tool can easily export its internal meta data in the form of a standard CWM model, with little or no information loss, because the CWM metamodel is semantically rich. The meta data interfaces defined by CWM (both the XML and programmatic APIs) are also completely independent of any particular implementation or product, because they are based on standard mappings of the CWM metamodel.

All CWM-enabled software products, tools, applications, repositories, and so on, share a single, common metamodel that is totally independent of any particular implementation model. And, all CWM-enabled products implement the same common interfaces for meta data interchange. This means that any CWM-aware software component can readily understand the meta data instances exposed by another CWM-enabled component and can access that meta data through the standard set of CWM meta data interfaces.

This has profound implications for meta data bridges. In an environment consisting of CWM-enabled tools, the heavyweight, product-wise bridges we discussed earlier can be replaced with lightweight bridges termed *CWM adapters*. An adapter is a piece of software that understands the CWM metamodel, as well as the internal metamodel and proprietary meta data interfaces of the software product for which the adapter is written. One side of the adapter, the *public side*, implements the CWM standard interfaces. The other end of the adapter connects to the product-specific interfaces. Processing logic within the adapter translates between CWM-compliant meta data instances and product-specific meta data. A CWM adapter for a given software product or tool need be written only once. This represents considerable savings over the development of product-wise bridges, even when the bridge is targeted toward a repository product. A CWM-enabled product can readily integrate into any environment consisting of other CWM-enabled products and tools.

So let's investigate how CWM enhances the various meta data integration architectures described earlier. Consider the point-to-point meta data interchange scenario first defined in Figure 6.1. Figure 6.8 shows a life-cycle architecture describing the interchange. Each directed link in this diagram represents a unique, product-to-product bridge facilitating meta data interchange between pairs of products, along with the various life-cycle roles ascribed to each product instance. Figure 6.10 illustrates the equivalent centralized version of the life cycle, in which a meta data repository is introduced as the central meta data hub. The architecture is simplified to the extent that the bridges now interconnects product-specific metamodels and interfaces with the common metamodel and interface supplied by the repository. The life-cycle roles ascribed to the products are also simpler in this case.

Figure 6.15 illustrates the point-to-point life-cycle architecture resulting from enabling each of the tools pictured in Figure 6.8 with CWM adapters (for example, the large arrows that had represented product-wise meta data bridges in Figure 6.8 now represent lightweight, CWM adapter modules in Figure 6.15). Note that the actual meta data interchange *flow* between the products in Figure 6.15 is still exactly the same as the flow defined by the connecting bridges in Figure 6.8. However, from an *interface and metamodel mapping* perspective, all tools are integrated via a single, logical, CWM infrastructure layer. For example, the ODS is supplying meta data to the modeling tool using standard CWM meta data interfaces, and the modeling tool is supplying its meta data to its various consumers via the same standard interfaces. All of this meta data (actually, various portions of a single CWM model)

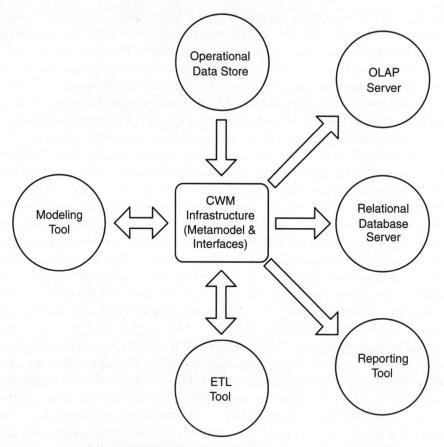

Figure 6.15 CWM-enabled point-to-point architecture.

are consistent with the single, CWM common metamodel. In principle, each tool participating in this architecture has only one metamodel that is publicly exposed—the CWM metamodel.

Standardization on the CWM metamodel and interfaces provides a point-to-point topology with a *logical central hub*. This hub is more conceptual than it is physical but provides essentially the same benefits as if we had introduced a physical central hub (that is, a meta data repository). For a collection of CWM-enabled tools, deploying a point-to-point architecture is no more expensive than building a centralized architecture. (The control and management advantages of the repository are missing, but for a relatively small number of interconnected tools, a strong requirement may not exist for central meta data management to justify the cost of a repository, anyway.)

What happens if we use a CWM-enabled repository to convert the point-to-point architecture into a centralized one? By saying that the repository is CWM-enabled, we mean that the repository's metamodel *is* the CWM metamodel and that the meta data stored in the repository consists of instances of the CWM metamodel. Note that how the metamodel and meta data storage schema is physically implemented under the covers (for example, as a relational database schema) doesn't really matter. Access to repository meta data must also be available via the standard CWM meta data interfaces (both via XML and programmatically).The repository must also provide a set of *system level* interfaces not defined by CWM, such as an interface for establishing a connection to the repository.

Figure 6.16 shows the centralized life-cycle architecture of Figure 6.10 with a CWM-enabled repository. Note that very little difference exists between this physically centralized architecture and the logically centralized architecture of Figure 6.16. In fact, from the perspective of standard meta data interfaces based on a common metamodel, essentially no difference exists between the two. Only the sources and targets of the meta data flows are different. There are going to be differences in terms of system level interfaces. For example, the

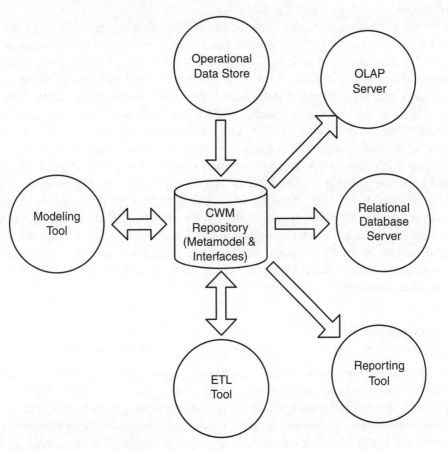

Figure 6.16   CWM-enabled centralized architecture.

interface used to connect to the repository probably will be different from the interface that would be used to connect to the OLAP server.

A need also exists to provide process-oriented interfaces for initiating the various types of interchange paradigms (for example, push-pull, request-response, subscribe-notify). These interfaces and their semantics are also outside the scope of the CWM specification. However, it is possible to hide the differences between the various system-level interfaces of various tools by providing a relatively simple *control framework* for the tools participating in a given environment. The basic control framework defines a number of fairly simple interfaces for implementing the basic meta data interchange sessions and interactions typically required in an integrated environment. A more complex control framework might implement the functionality required by completely automatic, dynamic, meta data environments (such as an active repository). Note that in a purely Web-centric environment using XML-based interchanges, supporting system-level interfaces is less problematic, as they are generally standardized in terms of the various Web services interfaces and protocols.

Figure 6.17 illustrates the concept of a CWM-enabled meta data environment. Two software tools, A and B, are enabled for CWM-based meta data interchange via CWM adapters. Adapter logic reads or writes tool-specific meta data (that is, meta data conforming to the internal metamodel of the tool) via each tool's proprietary meta data interfaces. Tool-specific meta data is translated to and from equivalent CWM meta data, according to a precisely defined mapping between CWM and tool-specific metamodels. (This mapping is defined as a part of the adapter module specification itself, and there are many possible ways, from a software engineering perspective, to design and implement this mapping logic.) CWM-compliant meta data is then somehow exposed to the interchange control framework. Note that the interchange control framework is not specified in any way by the CWM standard. Rather, it consists of the collection of system-level processes provided by the overall data warehouse or ISC implementation that manages and initiates meta data interchange and transfer. Such an overall control framework is necessary in any meta data-driven environment.

Summary

In this chapter, we discussed the need for a comprehensive meta data management strategy, acknowledging that no technology-based solution (including CWM) is ensured success without an overall strategy guiding its application. We surveyed the various patterns for meta data integration architectures and described both interconnection topologies and meta data interchange life cycles. We also examined why current approaches to deploying meta data inte-

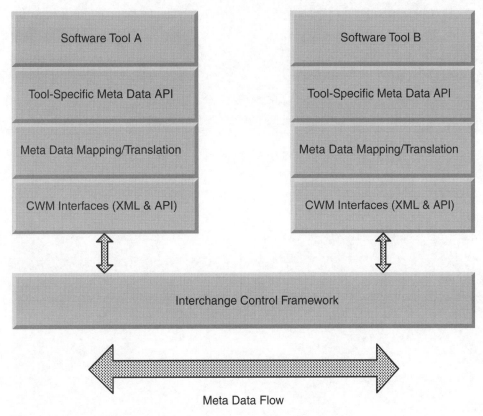

Figure 6.17   CWM-enabled meta data environment.

gration architectures (for example, via the building of meta data bridges) are complex and costly. We also demonstrated that CWM, as a model-based approach to meta data integration, simplifies the complexity and costs associated with building meta data integration architectures (regardless of interconnection topologies and life-cycle behaviors). CWM accomplishes this by moving much of the fundamental solution architecture out of the various tools and into the environment at large in the form of readily available, and universally understandable, models—*ubiquitous meta data* (META Group, Aug. 2000).

Implementing CWM

This chapter describes and contrasts general approaches for vendors implementing and using CWM. It covers the following:

- How the model was constructed
- How to extend the model using the internal mechanism provided for simple extensions and modeled extensions for more complex extensions
- How CWM can be used to provide interoperability
- How extensions affect interoperability
- Some sample implementation frameworks to provide interoperability

CWM provides a common foundation for data warehouse vendors and tools for the interoperability and interchange of meta data and possibly data. This common foundation was developed with no specific vendor tool in mind but rather represents a set of features and functions commonly found in many data warehousing tools. Tool vendors and application developers are provided a standard set of items by the OMG as part of the CWM specification.

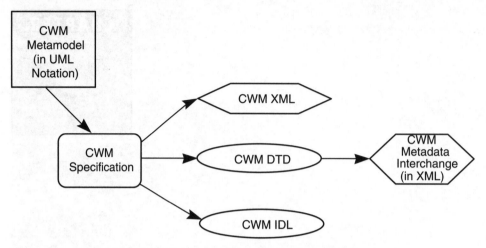

Figure 7.1 Materials supplied by the OMG for implementing CWM.

Figure 7.1 depicts the materials supplied by the OMG as part of the CWM specification. The specification itself has a complete set of objects and object definitions. In addition to the specification, the OMG supplies four other components with CWM. The complete CWM metamodel in UML notation is a set of UML diagrams that graphically demonstrates the CWM metamodel. An XML file that describes the CWM model is a MOF 1.3 compliant version of the CWM metamodel serialized into an XML document. The CWM DTD is a file that users of CWM can use to validate CWM interchange documents. Finally, the OMG also supplies a set of files that contain an IDL representation of the CWM metamodel.

CWM is not intended to solve all the problems faced by all the data warehousing tools and tool vendors in a single model. Rather, CWM is intended to provide a common representation of many of the commonly used features and functionality provided by many vendor and vendor tools. In many cases, CWM represents a lowest common denominator from the various tools analyzed to produce the CWM model. The model contains no vendor-specific representations or vendor-specific models. Given this approach, how then would a vendor (even a CWM working group member vendor) use CWM in the creation of a tool or to integrate into an existing tool? The first task for the vendor is to understand how the concepts in CWM were modeled and how those concepts relate to a tool-specific concept or, in some cases, concepts. The second task is understanding the vocabulary and nomenclature used by CWM, the model, and model definitions defined in the CWM specification. (These terms and object definitions may or may not match the way a specific vendor uses the same term or object.) Therefore, vendors implementing CWM must take great care when using objects and object definitions to ensure semantic usage equivalence.

The CWM working group consisted of a variety of companies representing different areas of the data warehouse landscape. Tools developed by the working group members have a great deal of overlap in features and functionality. This commonality led to the same type of information represented by different tools—some in common ways, and others in different ways. The challenge for the CWM team was to decide which features and functionality from the data warehouse space would be included in the public specification. When the features and functionality were settled, the next challenge was to develop a standard model and vocabulary, which could be used as a common representation among the various vendors and vendor tools with a defined semantic usage.

To achieve the goal of a common representation, the working group members identified various tools from which to analyze, gather, and model the requirements. In many cases, tool-specific representations for specific CWM concepts were evaluated and massaged into a model that was included into the overall CWM model. Throughout the CWM development process, the team reviewed many models from a variety of vendor tools and found that the tools had many of the common features and functions identified for the CWM standard.

Figure 7.2 depicts the functionality overlap of three sample warehouse tools: Tool X, Tool Y, and Tool Z. The tool-specific functionality is represented along the outside of the diagram as single lines, and the cross-hashed circle in the middle represents the overlap between the tools.

Given the overlap in tool functionality, a good starting point for the CWM working group was to evaluate the middle section of the diagram for inclusion into CWM. The number of tools the working group had to work with represented only a small subset of the actual number of tools in the marketplace. The final step in determining the supplied functionality was to further break down individual pieces and evaluate whether or not the concept was truly common or just common to the tools selected.

The resulting models (represented as the CWM Packages) in Figure 7.3 represent only what the working group determined were common across the board and generally useable by a large number of tools. The resulting representations try to provide the definitions in such a way that the largest number of vendors can leverage the definition in the greatest amount of common ways.

Extending CWM

CWM is a model that represents the common features and functionality available from various data warehouse tools. This approach to the model provides

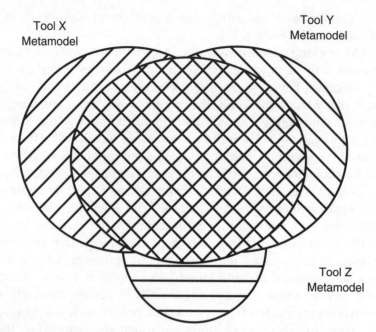

Figure 7.2 Functionality graphs of Tools X, Y, and Z.

vendors and tools with common definitions but probably lacks the complete set of information an existing tool or new tool would need to fully operate. The users of CWM will have to extend the given definitions to provide their tools with tool-specific definitions required for operation. Extending CWM can be categorized into two types of extensions:

- Simple extensions
- Modeled extensions

Simple Extensions to CWM

The built-in extension mechanism consists of using *stereotypes* and *tagged values*. This mechanism enables a user to assign any number of stereotypes or tagged values on any object. As a guide to understanding these concepts, let's look at the formal definitions from CWM.

A stereotype is defined as:

The stereotype concept provides a way of branding (classifying) model elements so that they behave as if they were instances of new virtual metamodel constructs. These model elements have the same structure (attributes, associations, operations) as similar non-stereotyped model elements of the same kind. The

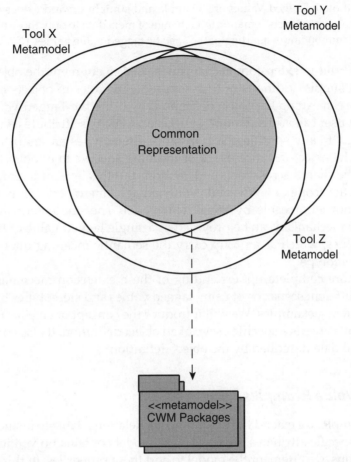

Tool X
Metamodel

Tool Y
Metamodel

Common
Representation

Tool Z
Metamodel

<<metamodel>>
CWM Packages

Figure 7.3 Common tool representations are used to create CWM packages.

stereotype may specify additional constraints and required tagged values that apply to model elements. In addition, a stereotype may be used to indicate a difference in meaning or usage between two model elements with identical structure. *(CWM, 2001)*

A tagged value is defined as:

A tagged value allows information to be attached to any model element in the form of a "tagged value" pair (i.e., name = value). The interpretation of tagged value semantics is intentionally beyond the scope of CWM. User or tool conventions must determine it. It is expected that tools will define tags to supply information needed for their operations beyond the basic semantics of CWM. Such information could include code generation options, model management information, or user-specified semantics.

Even though Tagged Values are a simple and straightforward extension technique, their use restricts semantic interchange of meta data to only those tools that share a common understanding of the specific tagged value names. *(CWM, 2001)*

CWM's built-in extension mechanism is used to augment the object definitions with simple additions or to assign semantic roles to objects in the system. Users can extend the object definitions by using the Tagged Value object. The CWM user can add any number of objects, such as attributes with associated values, to any specific object instance. Stereotypes are used to connote some special object instance usage or meaning specific to a tool. The stereotypes can be shared across tools and vendors, but this level of interoperability is beyond the scope of CWM and is only an agreement between two parties, which is not enforceable by the CWM model. The implementation of the stereotype mechanism can be provided as a single tagged value or by a set of tagged values, which as a group carry the semantic meaning intended for a specific stereotype.

For a more complete understanding of these extension mechanisms, let's examine different scenarios of using tagged values and stereotypes by looking at the following examples. We will introduce the concept of an object instance. An object instance is a specific usage of an object definition. It also contains the operational data described by the object definition.

Tagged Value Examples

In this example, we extend the definition of a Relational table to include several database specific attributes of a table. The model contains no vendor-specific models. Thus, we augment the model to add these properties. In this example, a tool needs to capture auxiliary information about the table not directly supplied by CWM. In this particular case, the information fits nicely as a set of tagged values associated with the Relational table object instance.

To create the extension, we start with the definition of a Relational table from CWM. (Note that Figure 7.4 contains a rendition of the Relational table definition. For example purposes only, this description has taken some liberty in the assignment of object attributes and associations for clarity of the example.) The Table object has a single attribute name, which is of type string, and the Table can contain any number of Column objects.

At runtime, a specific instance of the Table object can be created as the Product table with two columns: the ProductId and Description (see Figure 7.5).

Adding properties that are not otherwise supplied by the CWM model augments the runtime instance. In the example shown in Figure 7.6, we add three fictitious storage properties: disk_file, disk_block, and disk_percent.

This example shows that the CWM object definitions can be augmented with tool-specific information not native to the CWM model. Tools and ven-

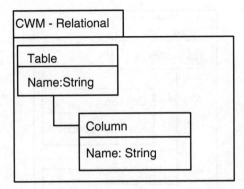

Figure 7.4 Sample CWM model, specifically a portion of the CWM relational model.

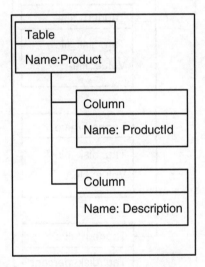

Figure 7.5 Sample instance of the CWM relational model.

dors can use this mechanism to store a wide variety of auxiliary information in CWM that is necessary for specific tools to operate. The next example of extending CWM will be to show how a tool can use either tagged values or stereotypes to connote a semantic meaning. Staying with tagged values, consider the case in which a tool would like to identify that a particular column in the preceding table should be used as the default display column of the table. A tool requires that one of the columns be identified as the display column at table creation time, because noncreation portions of the tool expect that a column is set up to play this role. The tool considers this meta data extension crucial to its operation, and a table definition is not complete without the assignment of the default display column. In this case, a tagged value can be

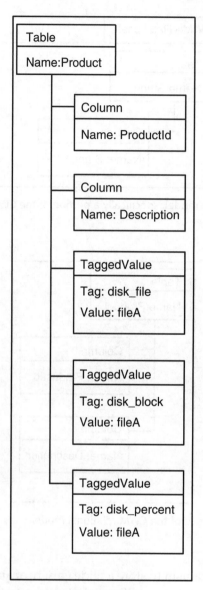

Figure 7.6   Tagged values added to a table instance.

used to associate a particular column to be used by a tool under the circum-stances defined by the tool. By adding the tagged value, the Column instance now carries the additional semantics required by the Tool (see Figure 7.7).

Stereotype Examples

Stereotypes can have much the same effect as tagged values on CWM objects; however, they have a broader definition in CWM: A stereotype can contain

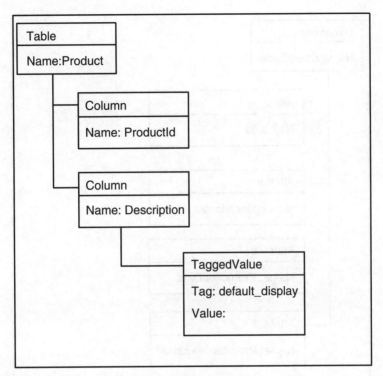

Figure 7.7 Tagged value representing semantic content.

any number of tagged values and can contain constraints. The latter mechanism gives a stereotype the appearance of creating a new virtual metamodel construct. Stereotypes are most useful in defining semantic roles to instances of CWM objects. These roles generally have a tagged value or a set of tagged values that further specify and/or qualify the desired role. To fully understand how to use a stereotype, let's examine the following example: A tool supports the definition of a periodic *dimension*. In order for a *dimension* to be periodic, it must supply the type of periodicity and the periodic unit and further identify two *dimension attributes* (by name) to be associated with a dimension's periodicity. One of the *dimension attributes* will represent the period of a dimension member, and another *dimension attribute* will represent the number of periodic units.

To illustrate the stereotype mechanism, consider a *dimension* instance first without the stereotype and then the same instance augmented with the periodic stereotype. (Note that Figure 7.8 contains a rendition of the dimension definition. For example purposes only, this description has taken some liberty in the assignment of object attributes and associations.)

In Figure 7.9, a stereotype definition, called the periodic stereotype is now attached to the Dimension instance. This stereotype contains four tagged values: one for type of periodicity, one for the unit of periodicity, one for the name

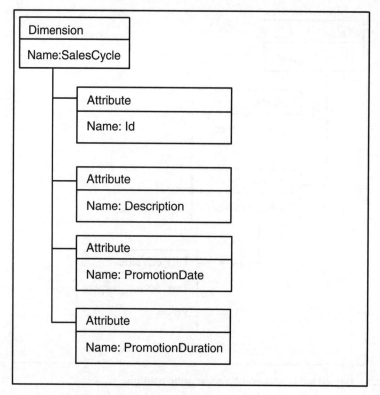

Figure 7.8 Sample dimension instance.

of the dimension attribute that contains the period, and one for the name of the dimension attribute that contains the number of periodic units in the period.

The CWM built-in extension mechanism is provided to overcome some of the tool-specific meta data requirements that were removed from the generic object model. The extension mechanism works well for a variety of uses (some have been mentioned previously); however, shortcomings of using both stereotypes and tagged values do exist, including the following:

- The tool must define and police the usage of both the stereotype and tagged value mechanism.

- Stereotypes and tagged values are not directly interchangeable. The semantic usage of these constructs is not conveyed in their definition. Therefore, tools may interpret the information differently.

- The stereotype definitions can change from release to release, making it necessary for a tool to either handle both definitions of the stereotype or to upgrade existing definitions.

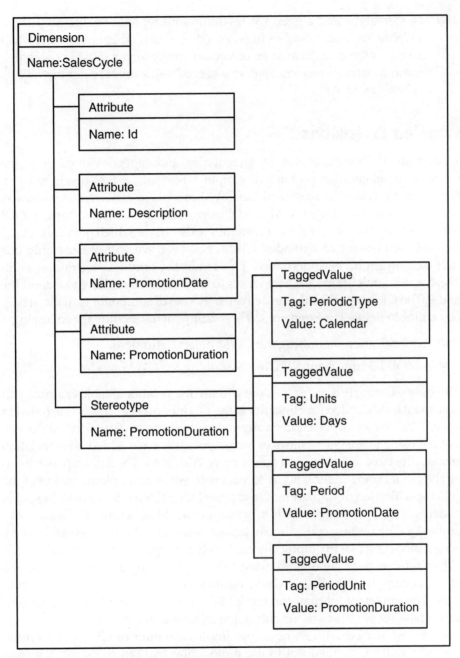

Figure 7.9   Dimension instance augmented with a stereotype.

■ Tagged values can have different semantic meanings for different tools. In this case, a tagged value may be used by more than one tool. If different tools are using the tagged value differently, one tool may inadvertently change a value expected by the other tool.

■ The stereotype and tagged values definitions will not be directly available through model-defined API definitions. This means that when looking at the definition of an object, an implementer must know that certain constructs are wrapped in a tagged value and are not directly available as an API call.

Modeled Extensions

To alleviate the shortcomings of stereotypes and tagged values or if the required model changes go beyond simple extensions, a tool needs to use a more robust mechanism to extend the CWM model. To achieve this endeavor, the vendor can extend the CWM model using standard Object-Oriented (OO) techniques. A number of OO techniques exist from which vendors could choose to implement an extended CWM; however, we will present only one such mechanism here—inheritance. This is not the only OO technique available, but it is straightforward and serves to help understand how to extend the model. The CWM specification is delivered as a set of components that can help the vendor to define the extensions. These components include the following:

■ A specification describing the CWM object definitions

■ A MOF 1.3 compliant XML file describing the CWM model

To fully examine this technique, we will use the Relational table example and implement the extended functionality using OO inheritance. This is illustrated in Figure 7.10. This example has been augmented to show an extension not directly possible using just tagged values or stereotypes. We have added an association between the table definition and one or more WidgetAs. The first step to extending the model using inheritance is to start with either an implementation of the CWM specification or by loading the supplied model file into some OO-capable modeling tool. The second step is to actually extend the definition. This activity can be done by writing code directly against some initial implementation or by using a modeling tool to graphically capture the extensions to the model.

If an implementer chooses to extend the model using a modeling tool, the MOF 1.3 compliant XML file could be imported into the tool as a starting point. The implementer then can model the extension using the tool and generate a new set of classes representing the extended model.

If we had started with some initial implementation of CWM, the implementer may have decided not to use a modeling tool but to extend the code directly using some software development tool. The following code fragment is not representative of an actual implementation of the CWM Relational table class definition but is for illustration purposes only. We have selected JAVA as the implementation language for the example.

```
Package CWM.Relational;
Class Table
{
      String      Name;
      Vector      Columns;
      void              setName(String input)
      {
            implementation specific code ....
      }
      String getName();
      {
            implementation specific code ....
      }
      void addColumn(Column input);
      {
            implementation specific code ....
      }
      void removeColumn(Column input);
      {
            implementation specific code ....
      }
      Vector getColumns()
      {
            implementation specific code ....
      }
}
```

We now add the extensions using OO inheritance. Notice that the new class name is also Table. This is possible because in JAVA class names are unique within the package. By adding a new package, the extended class definition can have the same name as the class in the CWM specification. This feature enables users of CWM to maintain the commonly used object name and still add the necessary extensions. This technique can be helpful in writing understandable code by not introducing class names that would be foreign to domain-specific applications.

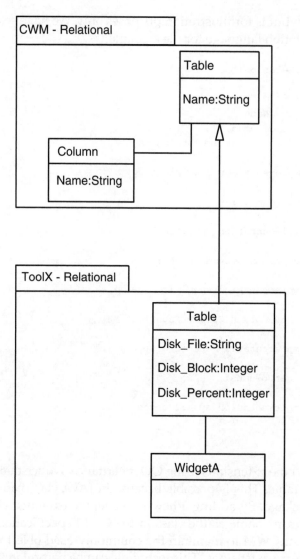

Figure 7.10 Model extension to CWM.

```
Package ToolX.Relational;
import CWM.Relational.Table;
class Table extends CWM.Table
{
     String disk_file;
     Integer disk_block;
     Integer disk_percent;
     WidgetA widgetA;
     void setDisk_file(String input)
     {
          implementation specific code ....
```

```
    }
    String getDisk_file();
    {
        implementation specific code ....
    }
    void setDisk_block(Integer input)
    {
        implementation specific code ....
    }
    Integer getDisk_block();
    {
        implementation specific code ....
    }
    void setDisk_percent(Integer input)
    {
        implementation specific code ....
    }
    Integer getDisk_percent();
    {
        implementation specific code ....
    }
    void setWidgetA(WidgetA input);
    {
        implementation specific code ....
    }
    WidgetA getWidgetA();
    {
        implementation specific code ....
    }
}
```

Modeling extensions to CWM is the preferred mechanism for additions that go beyond just simple extensions. In addition to providing extension capability beyond simple tagged values, it provides a cleaner programming model. Notice in the preceding example that the data types of several of the added class attributes are not string but reflect the implementers desired data type. Notice also that additional methods are generated for the class extensions. This type of extension mechanism makes the programming interface to the extended class more inline with a standard class interface definition.

Interoperability Using CWM

The CWM team consisted of a number of leading vendors in the data warehouse area. One of the main purposes of CWM is to provide interoperability between these vendors. Interoperability among vendors will enable the end-users to purchase tools and applications from vendors that will cooperate with each other. End-users then can buy best-of-breed tools from a variety of vendors without the cost of duplicated and/or separate administration.

Tools can interoperate by exchanging their meta data in a commonly understood format. In order to provide interoperability, some common understanding of the interchanged data and a common transport mechanism have to exist. CWM can be used to satisfy both interoperability requirements. First, the CWM model provides for the common understanding of the meta data semantics. Secondly, the CWM specification provides a Document Type Definition (DTD), which governs the serialization of instances of CWM objects into an XML file. To illustrate how CWM facilitates and promotes interoperability among different tools, consider the following initial scenario.

Figure 7.11 depicts a sample warehouse; a client has chosen a variety of different tools to perform various tasks within the warehouse. A modeling tool exists to plan the logical and physical implementation of the warehouse. A

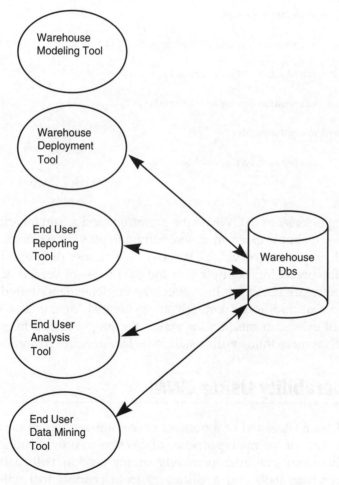

Figure 7.11 A set of data warehouse tools.

warehouse deployment tool can manage and control the creation, production, and maintenance of the warehouse. This tool may include the capability to schedule and implement the various transactions and transformations needed by an operational warehouse. A suite of end-user reporting and analysis tools is available. These tools range from simple reporting to complex data analysis and data mining.

As we move from tool to tool in Figure 7.11, we discover a great deal of meta data overlap among the various tools. The meta data about the warehouse is replicated and used by the different tools in different ways with different purposes. In Figure 7.11, the various tools shown must produce and maintain their own meta data information. As an example of common meta data information that could be shared, consider the meta data of the modeling tool. This tool might allow a user to graphically design both the logical and physical schema of the warehouse. These definitions could include very detailed information about the construction of the physical warehouse deployment. The deployment tool could certainly use this deployment information. In the preceding scenario; however, the tools are not connected. Thus, no process or methodology shares the deployment information. The preceding scenario contains many other possible opportunities for the tools to share meta data information and administration. Another opportunity for sharing meta data in Figure 7.11 comes from the end-user reporting and analysis tools. These tools could benefit from the knowledge about how the warehouse was designed and constructed. If these definitions could have be made available, the reporting and analysis tools wouldn't need to provide administration components to capture the physical deployment of the warehouse and could concentrate on providing administration for reporting and analysis only.

CWM can be used as the vehicle to provide interoperability for the various warehouse tools described here. If we alter the preceding scenario to include CWM, we can provide the common bond needed to allow the warehouse applications to cooperate and work together to share meta data information (see Figure 7.12).

By including CWM into the overall warehouse scenario, the tools can now interoperate with each other by importing and exporting their meta data information to and from the CWM common representation. Any tool that either imports or exports meta data can participate in this sharing methodology.

The main benefactors of interoperability are the clients. From an operational perspective, the end-user benefits from this because the administration of the warehouse has become simpler and more manageable. An end-user may not have to repeat the same administration tasks as they deploy tool after tool. Instead, the end-user will export the meta data definitions from one tool and import those definitions into a second tool. This process will give the second

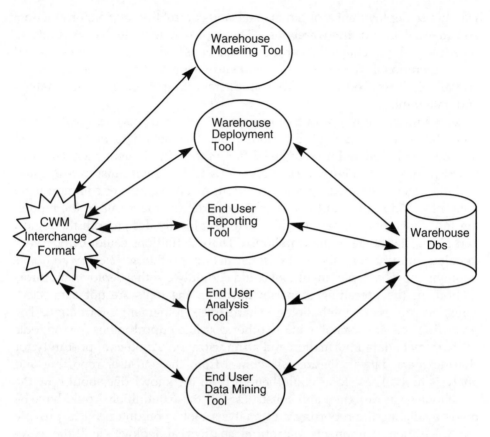

Figure 7.12 Using CWM to provide interoperability among data warehousing tools.

tool a jump-start on its configuration process. For example, the end-user could select the modeling tool to construct the logical and physical implementation of the warehouse. In addition, the end-user may enter specific deployment information via this modeling tool based on ease of use and presentation of information through this tool. When it comes time to deploy the warehouse, the end-user needs to use the warehouse deployment tool. Now the information from the design tool can be loaded directly into the deployment tool via CWM. This negates the need for the end-user to re-enter all the deployment information just added via the modeling tool.

To cement the importance of interoperability, consider a more complete example of warehouse administration and operations that can be improved using CWM:

■ A DBA uses a modeling tool to graphically design a warehouse.

■ The DBA uses the same tool to document and design a set of transformations to cleanse the raw data and produce a data mart for reporting and analysis.

- The DBA uses CWM to export the preceding designs and transformations to the common format.
- The DBA uses a deployment and scheduling tool to create and deploy the preceding designs. By importing the exported meta data definitions, a job is created based on the definitions from the design tool and scheduled for execution.
- The job is run, and the warehouse is created.
- The DBA can now use the same exported meta data to jump start the reporting and analysis tools. The DBA imports the definitions into the tool, and the tool is automatically ready to run.

In this scenario, we can see that CWM can provide interoperability across a wide range of tasks in the warehouse. CWM can be used to provide interoperability across the spectrum of tasks from concept to design to deployment to reporting and analysis.

Interoperability and Tool Extensions

In the preceding section, *Implementing with CWM*, we described several techniques to use and extend CWM. In this section, we describe how those extended implementations of CWM can still be used for interoperability. Note that this discussion relies on the fact the CWM was used as the basis of the tool model and uses the CWM DTD as defined in the specification. We start by categorizing the extensions into three generic types:

- **Proprietary attributes.** Tool-specific definitions not intended for interchange
- **Proprietary associations and classes.** Tool-specific areas not common and not intended for interchange
- **Sharable extensions.** Tool-specific extensions proposed for interchange via tagged value pairs

Proprietary Attributes

Proprietary attributes are added to the CWM model definitions for tool-specific purposes. The tool may want to keep these definitions and semantics private and, therefore, not want them to appear in the interchange with other tools (see Figure 7.13).

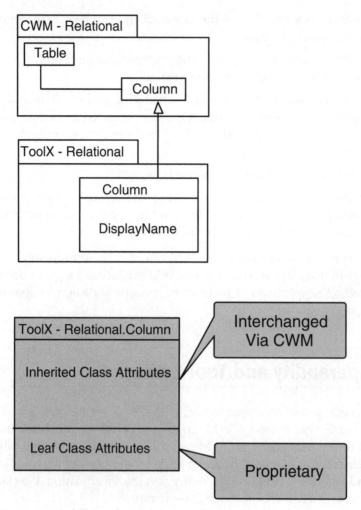

Figure 7.13   Interoperability and proprietary attributes.

Tool X has used the OO extension technique inheritance. The extended definition of Column has a new attribute, *DisplayName.* The semantics of Display-Name are for the sole and private use of Tool X. The intent is not to interchange the DisplayName value with other tools. However, this model can still be interchanged via the CWM DTD. No changes exist to the CWM model as provided. All the changes are below the CWM model, which means that none of the original model semantics or characteristics has been altered. Due to this OO feature, the implementer of Tool X could interchange the Tool X column definition as if it were a CWM column. Many techniques are available to the implementer, but one such technique would be to up-cast the Tool X Column object at runtime to be a CWM Column object. This up-cast would not natively change the runtime instance—only mask its real identity for the purpose of interchange. When the up-cast was done, the extra attribute would still be part of the actual class instance; except for the purpose of the export, only the core CWM model would be visible.

Proprietary Associations and Classes

The example shown in Figure 7.14 is an extension of the preceding one. In this case, the extended model is a reference to an object outside the scope of CWM, namely WidgetA. In this case as in the preceding one, we treat the extended

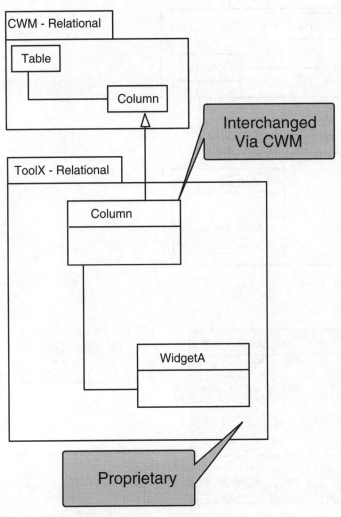

Figure 7.14   Interoperability and proprietary associations.

Column as a CWM column for the purpose of export. At the time the object instance is exported, the additional association will be invisible as was the *DisplayName* attribute in the preceding example.

Sharable Extensions

We now turn our attention to the extensions we want to interchange. In Figure 7.15, we intend the additional attribute to be part of the interchange. To accomplish this, we could still up-cast the Column object instance to be a

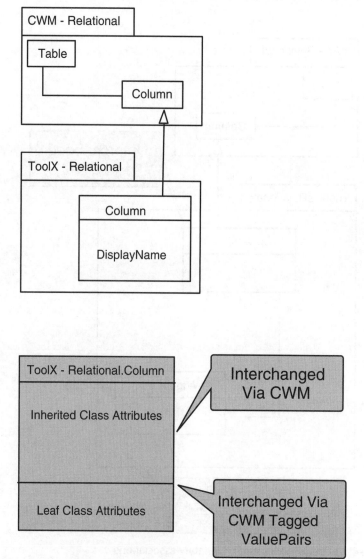

Figure 7.15 Interoperability and shared attributes.

CWM column instance; however, this time we must somehow include the additional attribute as a tagged value. The implementations will vary. For the sake of the example, we could create the tagged value pair in the process of exporting the instance data. The export would operate as before; however, the additional attribute would be included as a tagged value in the interchange file. In this example, we could have created the DisplayName attribute as a tagged value directly. This solution would have been equivalent, but the programming model would have been different; no exposed API would exist for the DisplayName attribute. To provide a friendlier interface to the extended object definition, object oriented inheritance was used. A projected interface to the extended attribute would most likely be setDisplayName and getDisplay-Name. The interface is a much more standard interface for the user of the class, and the CWM export details are hidden by the implementation.

In this last example, we will export an object that was not covered by the CWM model. This example is presented here to be complete and to highlight what is possible to interchange using the internal extension mechanism of CWM.

In Figure 7.16, the class WidgetA now inherits from ModelElement. This means that the entire contents of the WidgetA class can be interchanged as Tagged Values and stereotypes on a ModelElement. An additional Tagged Value or stereotype also must be added to indicate that this ModelElement is actually a class of type WidgetA. This type of interchange, although possible, assumes that the receiver of the augmented ModelElement will do the right thing. This technique is not recommended, but it is there as a viable transport mechanism for objects not covered by the CWM model.

Interoperability Frameworks and Implementing CWM

Interoperability using CWM is done via an XML document that contains instances of CWM objects. A number of techniques are available to tool vendors and tool implementers to provide interoperability using CWM. Those techniques can be categorized into two predominant mechanisms: transform direct and transform indirect interoperability implementations.

Transform Direct

In the direct transform method, a tool will transform the XML interchange instances directly into tool-specific objects. At no time will there be an implementation of a CWM object in memory. Using this method, a definition is read from the file; a tool-specific object is created; and the data is transferred to the tool object directly from the XML stream.

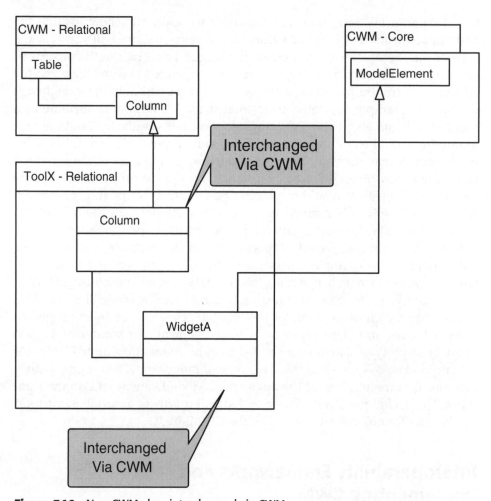

Figure 7.16   Non-CWM class interchanged via CWM.

Figure 7.17 depicts a typical interchange of meta data using the direct transform method. The key to this method is the use of some type of mapping methodology. This type of interchange works best when a one-to-one mapping is available from a CWM object to a tool-specific object. It is possible to use this method when the mapping is not one to one, but the following section provides a better mechanism when the CWM to tool object definitions are other than one to one.

Transform Indirect

Some sort of bridge, which moves data from the CWM model format to the tool's specific format, defines the indirect mechanism. This mechanism is

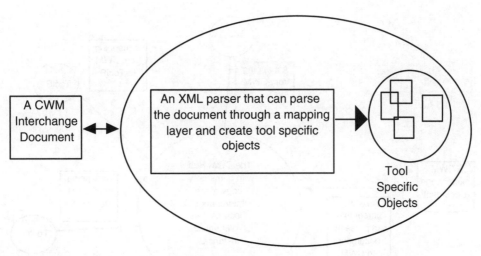

Figure 7.17 Transform-direct interoperability.

good for existing tools that want to interchange data and meta data with other tools that support CWM without rewriting the existing tool meta data model. In this approach, the tool generally reads the interchange document into some intermediate form, which is then transformed into the tool-specific representation by mapping the CWM model to the tool-specific model.

To illustrate how tools can use CWM in an indirect implementation, consider hub-and-spoke architecture first with CWM as the hub and some set of tools as the spokes. Indirect transformation would be an ideal choice for a vendor who needs to integrate a number of tools via CWM. A straightforward way to implement this would be to create an implementation of the CWM object model. This set of classes then would be populated by some CWM interchange document. The document instances would be read directly into the CWM class implementations. After the document was reconstructed in memory, the in-memory copy can be traversed moving the meta data from the CWM model definition to a tool-specific representation.

As shown in Figure 7.18, a vendor could use this approach to integrate a single tool or any number of tools. This approach reuses the code to move the document into memory. The vendor creates a new mapping to integrate a different tool.

In some instances, vendors will already have an integration strategy, which uses a hub-and-spoke architecture. In this case, the preceding architecture would change: The hub model would become a vendor-specific model created to provide interchange among existing tools, and CWM would become a new spoke. This is shown in Figure 7.19. When this was done, the pre-existing interchange mechanism would enable all tools supported by the hub with CWM.

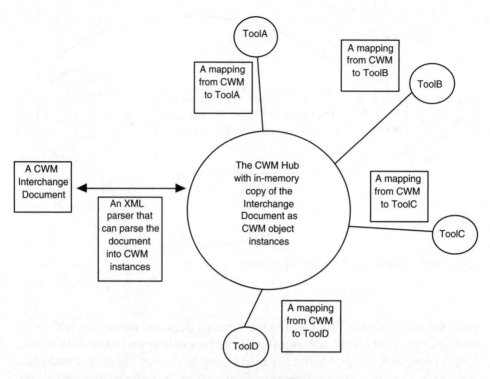

Figure 7.18 Hub-and-spoke architecture based on CWM.

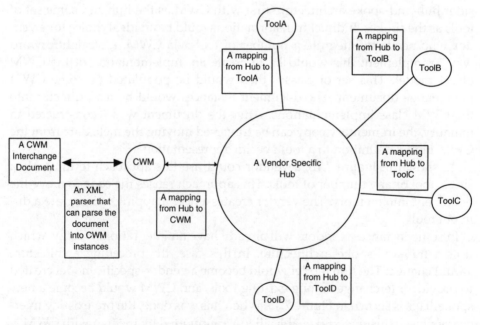

Figure 7.19 Hub-and-spoke architecture based on vendor-specific hub.

In a bridging architecture, the flow of data usually is done as a single isolated task. Figure 7.18 and Figure 7.19 give no indication as to the direction the data will flow, with one notable exception. The portion of the bridge, which reads and writes the CWM Interchange Document, must be bidirectional if a vendor wants compatibility both to and from any specific tool. In a number of instances, bidirectionality of the CWM spoke is not necessary:

- **Timing**. A tool may implement only one side of the bridge to gain speed to market.

- **End-user based reporting tools**. This class of tool may not need to write back to the CWM format because the definitions used by these tools use the predefined warehouse and build on top. It is not intended that the added definitions be shared.

- **Warehouse authoring tools**. This class of tool may be concerned only with creating the warehouse. It may not be able to nor consider it appropriate to enable users to change the warehouse definitions outside the context of this type of tool.

Summary

In this chapter, we saw that the CWM metamodel was constructed as a common set of features and functionality from a variety of existing data warehouse tools. Due to the fact that the model represents only a common set of features, an extension mechanism is built in. This internal mechanism is good for simple changes to the CWM metamodel. For larger, more complex changes, CWM users should model their changes using standard OO techniques.

The CWM metamodel provides interoperability among data warehousing tools by providing a standard XML definition for meta data interchange. Tools can interoperate by exchanging meta data definitions via files compliant with the CWM DTD. Tool extensions of the CWM metamodel can be either private or intended for interchange. If the extensions are intended for interchange, they must be interchanged using the built-in mechanism of tagged values and/or stereotypes.

Finally, we discussed a few sample implementation techniques. These methodologies are certainly not the only possible types of implementations. They have been used in some of the earlier adoptions of CWM in the context of the CWM interoperability demonstration. The CWM interoperability demonstration was performed by the CWM working group and several partners to show the viability of CWM. The interoperability demonstration provided interchange among various vendor tools and was first shown at the OMG technical meeting in March 2000. The interoperability demonstration has been shown many times since then at a number of different OMG meetings and meta data conferences.

The following are some of the implementation issues encountered when using either direct or indirect transform implementations of CWM. These experiences were taken from some of the teams that produced the interoperability demonstration.

- Transform Indirect, using CWM, as the hub in a hub-and-spoke architecture is a good and flexible overall design.

- Transform Direct works best when there is a pre-existing tool that has a one-to-one mapping between its object definitions and CWM.

- Transform Direct is a good choice when only a single point of interoperability is required and the mapping of tools to CWM is one-to-one or very close.

- If writing a new tool, use the CWM model directly if possible. The interoperability decision, Transform Direct or Transform Indirect, is then more based on whether single or multiple points of interoperability exist.

- Both Transform Direct and Transform Indirect interoperability is provided by an isolated XML file. In general, no information as to what came before the intended interchange exists, or there will be subsequent interchanges. Implementations should be aware that to provide complete round-trip interoperability, they must take into consideration how to merge into a pre-existing set of CWM objects.

CHAPTER

8

Conclusions

When IBM, Oracle, and Unisys proposed the CWM standardization effort to the OMG in May 1998, meta data interchange had been identified for some time as one of the most critical problems facing the data warehousing industry. No common solution, however, was available at the time or on the horizon. Meta Data Interchange Specification (MDIS) had been published by the Meta Data Coalition (MDC) and implemented by some vendors. However, it was getting little support in the industry because of its limited coverage of meta data types and the lack of open interchange format. As such, warehouse meta data interchange was limited to using a single vendor's proprietary format, such as IBM's Tag language, or using MDIS between a very limited number of vendors, such as between IBM and ETI.

It was against this backdrop that the OMG issued the Common Warehouse Meta Data Interchange (CWMI) RFP in September 1998. The objectives of the RFP were to do the following:

- Establish an industry standard specification for common warehouse meta data interchange.
- Provide a generic mechanism that can be used to transfer a wide variety of warehouse meta data.

■ Leverage existing vendor-neutral interchange mechanisms as much as possible.

Specifically, the RFP solicited proposals for a complete specification of the syntax and semantics needed to export and import warehouse meta data and the common warehouse metamodel, which may consist of a specification of the common warehouse metamodel, APIs (in IDL), and interchange formats.

The CWM standardization effort has been a resounding success after two and a half years of intense collaboration and hard work among eight cosubmitting companies: IBM, Unisys, NCR, Hyperion, Oracle, UBS, Genesis, and Dimension EDI. The OMG adopted CWM as an available technology, which means that it has gone through the finalization process and at least one submitting company has been able to demonstrate an implementation, in April 2001. Not only that, but CWM has become a showcase technology for the OMG as well as a core component of its new strategic direction on Model Driven Architecture (MDA), as shown in Figure 8.1. (See OMG's MDA resource page at www.omg.org/mda/index.htm.)

In this last chapter, we will discuss three important topics on CWM that illustrate its success, the reason for its success, and its relationship and significance to other industry standards on meta data. First, we will discuss CWM Enablement Showcase, which clearly demonstrates CWM's success for enabling meta data interchange among data warehousing and business intelligence tools and repositories. Second, we will discuss the model-driven approach used in CWM, which is a major reason for its success and which serves as an existence proof for the OMG's new strategic direction on MDA. Third, we will discuss the relationship and significance of CWM to other rele-

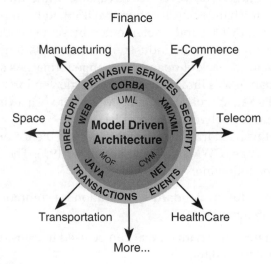

Figure 8.1 OMG MDA.

vant standards, both existing and emerging from OMG, W3C, and the Java community. Finally, we will conclude the book by peeking into the future evolution of CWM.

CWM Enablement Showcase

The CWM Enablement Showcase was first held at the OMG Orlando meeting in December 2000. It was a breakthrough event on meta data interchange for data warehousing and business intelligence. As shown in Figure 8.2, six vendors (Hyperion, IBM, Meta Integration, Oracle, SAS, and Unisys) demonstrated the ease of interchanging meta data, using CWM, between 10 different tools and repositories. In May 1998 when the CWM standardization effort was started, it was difficult to imagine that multiple vendors could interchange even relational meta data (catalog, schema, table, column, and so on), which were well known and relatively straightforward. Two and a half years later, as demonstrated by the CWM Enablement Showcase, it was almost trivial for multiple vendors to interchange not only relational, but also OLAP and warehouse process meta data. The warehouse process meta data being interchanged was pretty complex, representing the meta data involved in a customizable replication process from a source relational database to a target relational database. The types of meta data involved included relational, transformation, warehouse process, software deployment, and business information.

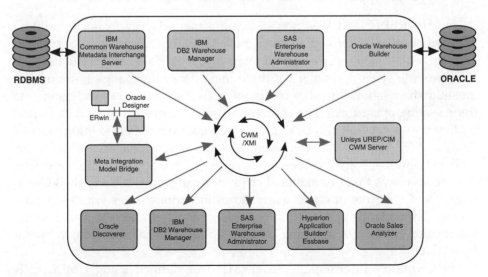

Figure 8.2 CWM Enablement Showcase.

The Showcase was structured along both horizontal and vertical dimensions. Horizontally, tools and repositories were arranged according to whether they played the role of meta data producer (top), meta data consumer (bottom), or both (middle):

- **Meta data producer.**   IBM CWM Interchange Server, IBM DB2 Warehouse Manager, SAS Enterprise Warehouse Administrator, Oracle Warehouse Builder

- **Meta data consumer.**   Oracle Discoverer, IBM DB2 Warehouse Manager, SAS Enterprise Warehouse Administrator, Hyperion Application Builder/Essbase, Oracle Sales Analyzer

- **Meta data consumer/producer.**   Meta Integration Model Bridge, Unisys UREP/CIM CWM Server

Vertically, tools were arranged depending on whether they interchanged relational meta data (left), warehouse process meta data (middle), or OLAP meta data (right):

- **Relational meta data interchange.**   From IBM CWM Interchange Server to Meta Integration Model Bridge to Oracle Discoverer or IBM DB2 Warehouse Manager

- **Warehouse process meta data interchange.**   From IBM DB2 Warehouse Manager to SAS Enterprise Warehouse Administrator or vice versa

- **OLAP meta data interchange.**   From Oracle Warehouse Builder to Hyperion Application Builder/Essbase or Oracle Sales Analyzer

Unisys UREP/CIM CWM Server, being a meta data repository, could be used with any of the preceding three meta data interchange flows, serving as an intermediate step for storing and managing meta data being interchanged.

To provide synergy among the three meta data interchange flows and to illustrate the relationships that commonly exist between relational meta data (representing operational data sources), warehouse process meta data (representing transformation and processing of operational data into informational data), and OLAP meta data (representing multidimensional analysis of informational data), a single business scenario was developed for the Showcase. The scenario was that of a national chain of retail stores, the so-called CwmStore, Inc. CwmStore operates many stores in various states with each store selling various kinds of products. The goal of the scenario was to define the information model, its mapping to a relational schema, and sample operational data.

The CwmStore information model (M1) was defined using UML and is shown in Figure 8.3. The information model consists of three classes repre-

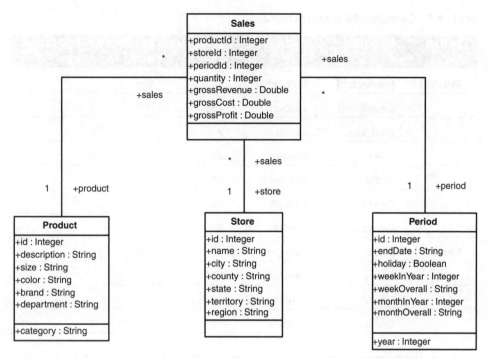

Figure 8.3 CwmStore information model.

senting major dimensions of CwmStore for business analysis—Product, Store, and Period—and a Sales Class representing key measures of CwmStore for business analysis—quantity, gross revenue, gross cost, and gross profit. The Sales class is connected to the other three classes through UML associations. Because its structure is shaped like a star with the Sales class in the middle, this kind of information model is commonly called a star schema. For convenience of analysis, each dimension class also contains level information. For example, the Store class contains territory and region attributes whose values can be used to form level-based hierarchies and analysis.

The CwmStore information model was mapped to a relational schema for representation and storage of operational data. The relational schema is shown in Table 8.1. It consists of three tables representing the three dimensions—Product, Store, and Period—and a Sales table representing the measures. The Sales table is related to the other tables through foreign key-primary key relationships. The mapping from the CwmStore information model to the CwmStore relational schema is straight forward, by nature of the star schema.

Relational meta data interchange involved exporting the CwmStore relational schema from DB2 UDB, using the IBM CWM Interchange Server, importing it into Meta Integration Model Bridge, and subsequently exporting

Table 8.1 CwmStore Relational Schema

TABLE	COLUMN	DATATYPE	LENGTH	PRIMARY KEY	FOREIGN KEY
Product	**product_id**	**integer**		**Yes**	
	Description	varchar	128		
	prod_size	varchar	7		
	Color	varchar	32		
	Brand	varchar	64		
	Department	varchar	64		
	Category	varchar	32		
Store	**store_id**	**integer**		**Yes**	
	Name	varchar	128		
	City	varchar	80		
	County	varchar	32		
	State	character	2		
	Territory	varchar	32		
	Region	varchar	16		
Period	**period_id**	**integer**		**Yes**	
	end_date	varchar	32		
	Holiday	character	1		
	week_in_year	integer			
	week_overall	varchar	7		
	month_in_year	integer			
	month_overall	varchar	8		
	Year	integer			
Sales	**product_id**	**integer**		**Yes**	**Yes**
	store_id	integer		Yes	Yes
	period_id	integer		Yes	Yes
	Quantity	integer			
	gross_revenue	double			
	gross_cost	double			
	gross_profit	double			

it from the Meta Integration Model Bridge and importing it into Oracle Discoverer or IBM DB2 Warehouse Manager. The CWM/XMI file used in the interchange is shown, in part, in Figure 8.4. This file, as can be expected, was generated using the CWM Relational package and its dependent packages, which include the CWM Object Model and Foundation packages. It can be seen that while the format and content of the file is formal and complete, therefore suitable for processing by any CWM-compliant tool, it is also quite readable by humans.

The CWM/XMI files generated for the interchange of warehouse process meta data and OLAP meta data, respectively, are similar in structure and content to that shown in Figure 8.5. However, they involve many more types of meta data and, therefore, are more complex. In the case of warehouse meta data interchange, the file was generated using the following CWM packages:

- Object model and foundation
- **Relational.** To represent the data source and data target of a customizable replication process
- **Transformation.** To represent replication transformations
- **Warehouse process.** To represent replication steps and activities and their scheduling

In the case of OLAP meta data interchange, the file was generated using the following CWM packages:

- Object model and foundation
- **OLAP.** To represent multidimensional analysis
- **Relational.** To represent the source of dimension members and that of cube data
- **Transformation.** To represent the mapping between OLAP constructs and that between the OLAP constructs and the constructs of relational sources

CWM and MDA

Many reasons exist for the success of CWM. Foremost is the willingness of major vendors to work together and develop a commonly agreed meta data interchange standard for data warehousing and business intelligence. Technically, the keys to the success of CWM are UML and XML. UML provides a single and powerful modeling language for modeling all types of warehouse meta data; XML provides a simple and universal data format for interchanging all these types of warehouse meta data. By nature, data warehousing deals with a very complex environment that involves many different types of data

```
INCLUDETEXT "G:\\cwmProj\\6.Book\\diagram\\9-5.xml" \c AnsiText  \*
MERGEFORMAT <XMI>
  ...
  <XMI.content>
    <CWMRDB:Catalog xmi.id="_1" name="CWMSTORE">
      <CWM:Namespace.ownedElement>
        <CWMRDB:Schema xmi.id="_1.1" name="GUEST" namespace="_1">
          <CWM:Namespace.ownedElement>
            <CWMRDB:Table xmi.id="_1.1.1" name="PERIOD"
              namespace="_1.1">
              <CWM:Classifier.feature>
                <CWMRDB:Column xmi.id="_1.1.1.1"
                  name="PERIOD_ID" length="10"
                  type="_11" owner="_1.1.1"/>
                <CWMRDB:Column xmi.id="_1.1.1.2"
                  name="END_DATE" length="32"
                  type="_19" owner="_1.1.1"/>
                <CWMRDB:Column xmi.id="_1.1.1.3"
                  name="HOLIDAY" length="1"
                  type="_8" owner="_1.1.1"/>
                <CWMRDB:Column xmi.id="_1.1.1.4"
                  name="WEEK_IN_YEAR" length="10"
                  type="_11" owner="_1.1.1"/>
                <CWMRDB:Column xmi.id="_1.1.1.5"
                  name="WEEK_OVERALL" length="7"
                  type="_19" owner="_1.1.1"/>
                <CWMRDB:Column xmi.id="_1.1.1.6"
                  name="MONTH_IN_YEAR" length="10"
                  type="_11" owner="_1.1.1"/>
                <CWMRDB:Column xmi.id="_1.1.1.7"
                  name="MONTH_OVERALL" length="8"
                  type="_19" owner="_1.1.1"/>
                <CWMRDB:Column xmi.id="_1.1.1.8"
                  name="YEAR" length="10"
                  type="_11" owner="_1.1.1"/>
              </CWM:Classifier.feature>
              <CWM:Namespace.ownedElement>
                <CWMRDB:PrimaryKey xmi.id="_1.1.1.11"
                  name="SQL001211141257580"
                  feature="_1.1.1.1" namespace="_1.1.1"
                  keyRelationship="_1.1.3.13"/>
              </CWM:Namespace.ownedElement>
            </CWMRDB:Table>
            <CWMRDB:Table xmi.id="_1.1.2"
              name="PRODUCT" namespace="_1.1">
              ...
            </CWMRDB:Table>
            <CWMRDB:Table xmi.id="_1.1.3"
```

Figure 8.4 CwmStore Relational meta data interchange file.

```
      name="SALES" namespace="_1.1">
   <CWM:Classifier.feature>
     <CWMRDB:Column xmi.id="_1.1.3.1"
       name="PERIOD_ID" length="10"
       type="_11" owner="_1.1.3"/>
     <CWMRDB:Column xmi.id="_1.1.3.2"
       name="STORE_ID" length="10"
       type="_11" owner="_1.1.3"/>
     <CWMRDB:Column xmi.id="_1.1.3.3"
       name="PRODUCT_ID" length="10"
       type="_11" owner="_1.1.3"/>
     <CWMRDB:Column xmi.id="_1.1.3.4"
       name="QUANTITY" length="10"
       type="_11" owner="_1.1.3"/>
     <CWMRDB:Column xmi.id="_1.1.3.5"
       name="GROSS_REVENUE" length="15"
       type="_15" owner="_1.1.3"/>
     <CWMRDB:Column xmi.id="_1.1.3.6"
       name="GROSS_COST" length="15"
       type="_15" owner="_1.1.3"/>
     <CWMRDB:Column xmi.id="_1.1.3.7"
       name="GROSS_PROFIT" length="15"
       type="_15" owner="_1.1.3"/>
   </CWM:Classifier.feature>
   <CWM:Namespace.ownedElement>
     <CWMRDB:PrimaryKey xmi.id="_1.1.3.12"
       name="SQL001211141258930"
       feature="_1.1.3.1 _1.1.3.2 _1.1.3.3"
       namespace="_1.1.3"/>
     <CWMRDB:ForeignKey xmi.id="_1.1.3.13"
       name="SQL001211141258940"
       feature="_1.1.3.1" namespace="_1.1.3"
       uniqueKey="_1.1.1.11"/>
     <CWMRDB:ForeignKey xmi.id="_1.1.3.14"
       name="SQL001211141258950"
       feature="_1.1.3.3" namespace="_1.1.3"
       uniqueKey="_1.1.2.10"/>
     <CWMRDB:ForeignKey xmi.id="_1.1.3.15"
       name="SQL001211141258941"
       feature="_1.1.3.2" namespace="_1.1.3"
       uniqueKey="_1.1.4.10"/>
   </CWM:Namespace.ownedElement>
 </CWMRDB:Table>
 <CWMRDB:Table xmi.id="_1.1.4" name="STORE"
   namespace="_1.1">
   <CWM:Classifier.feature>
   ...
 </CWMRDB:Table>
```

Figure 8.4 continued.

```
        </CWM:Namespace.ownedElement>
       </CWMRDB:Schema>
      </CWM:Namespace.ownedElement>
    </CWMRDB:Catalog>
    ...
    <CWMRDB:SQLSimpleType xmi.id="_11"
      name="INTeger" typeNumber="4"/>
    ...
    <CWMRDB:SQLSimpleType xmi.id="_19"
      name="VARCHAR" typeNumber="12"/>
    ...
  </XMI.content>
</XMI>
```

Figure 8.4 continued.

resources (relational, record-based, object-oriented, multidimensional, and XML), various types of transformation and analysis tools (ETL, OLAP, data mining, information visualization, and business nomenclature), as well as warehouse process and warehouse operation management. UML is capable of modeling the meta data for all of these entities, thus serving as the single modeling language. Also, by nature data warehousing involves many different tools from many different vendors, big and small. Therefore, for meta data interchange to be successful and prevalent, the interchange format used must be universal and must be cheap to implement and support. XML is ideal for this purpose, being simple, universal, and cheap to implement and support.

UML and XML by themselves, however, are not sufficient for the success of CWM. UML is a modeling language for meta data; XML is an interchange format for meta data. They are disjointed entities. To bring them together so that one can start with modeling meta data using UML and end up with interchanging meta data so modeled in XML, CWM uses a model-driven approach as shown in Figure 8.5. The development of the CWM specification starts with the CWM metamodel, which is represented in UML notation using a tool such as Rational Rose. When the CWM metamodel is developed, it is used to develop the CWM specification in text form by adding English text and OCL constraints where appropriate. The CWM metamodel is further used to automatically generate a CWM XML, a CWM DTD, and a CWM IDL, according to XMI and MOF, respectively. The CWM XML document is generated per the MOF DTD and represents a formal, tool-independent definition of the CWM metamodel. The CWM DTD can be used to validate XML documents used to interchange CWM meta data. The CWM IDL defines a language-independent API for accessing CWM meta data. In the future, as discussed in the next section, a CWM Java interface also will be generated per Java Meta Data Interface (JMI), which will define a Java API for accessing CWM meta data.

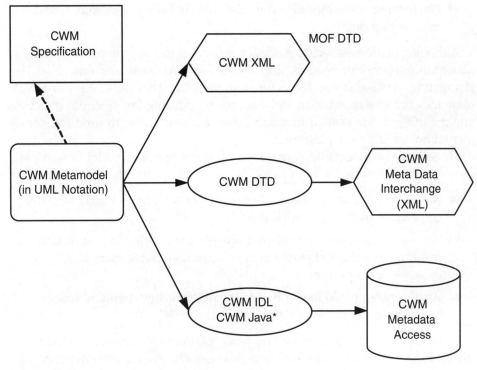

Figure 8.5 CWM model-driven approach.

The essence of the CWM model-driven approach is that everything starts with the CWM metamodel and, with the exception of the text-based CWM specification, everything is automatically generated. Anytime that something needs to be changed, the change is first made in the CWM metamodel and then propagated manually to the CWM specification and automatically to CWM XML, CWM DTD, and CWM IDL. This not only ensures consistency among all the CWM artifacts, but also enhances understanding because one only needs to focus on the CWM metamodel (and the CWM specification for OCL constraints).

Partly as a result of the success of the CWM model-driven approach, the OMG has recently embarked on a new strategic direction on MDA, as shown in Figure 8.1. MDA addresses integration and interoperability spanning the life cycle of a software system from modeling and design, to component construction, assembly, integration, deployment, management, and evolution. The following are definitions of models and their subtypes in MDA:

■ **Model.**   A formal specification of the function, structure, and behavior of a software system

■ **Platform-independent model.**   A model that abstracts away technological and engineering details

■ **Platform-specific model.** A model that contains technological and engineering details.

Although platform-specific models are needed to implement such models, platform-independent models are useful for two basic reasons. First, by abstracting the fundamental structure and meaning, they make it easier to validate the correctness of the model. Second, by holding the essential structure and meaning of the system invariant, they make it easier to produce implementations on different platforms.

Three basic ways exist to construct a platform-specific model from a platform-independent model:

■ A person could study the platform-independent model and manually construct a platform-specific model.

■ An algorithm could be applied to the platform-independent model resulting in a skeletal platform-specific model that is manually enhanced by a person.

■ An algorithm could be applied to the platform-independent model resulting in a complete platform-specific model.

Fully automated transformations from platform-independent models to platform-specific models are feasible only in certain constrained environments.

The CWM metamodel, specification, and generated artifacts fit in with MDA very well and can be looked at from two different perspectives. From the technology platform perspective (that is, if we think of XML, CORBA, and Java as different technology platforms), the relationships between the platform-independent model (the CWM metamodel and specification) and platform-specific models (CWM XML, CWM DTD, CWM IDL, and, in the future, CWM Java) are shown in Figure 8.6. All platform-specific models in this case are fully automatically generated from the platform-independent model. From the product platform perspective (that is, if we think of DMSII, IMS, Essbase, Express, and so on as different product platforms), the relationships between the platform-independent model (the CWM metamodel and specification) and platform-specific models (DMSII, IMS, Essbase, Express, and so on) are shown in Figure 8.7. All platform-specific models in this case are constructed by people from the platform-independent model.

CWM and Other Standards

For CWM to continue its initial success and prosper, it must evolve with other relevant standards, both existing and emerging. Even though data warehousing and business intelligence are major parts of an enterprise's information technology infrastructure, they are only parts of that infrastructure and not

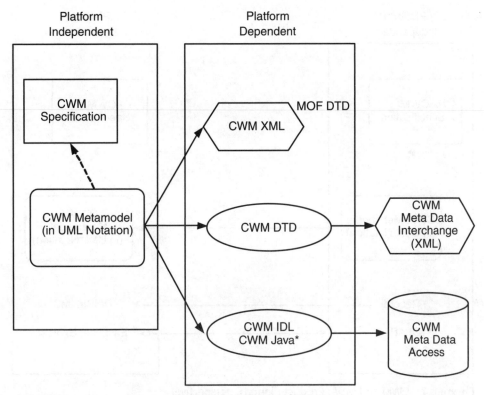

Figure 8.6 CWM and MDA: Technology-platform perspective.

the whole. Therefore, CWM, being the meta data interchange standard for data warehousing and business intelligence, must be consistent with and complement other relevant standards in the enterprise's information technology infrastructure.

OMG Standards

As discussed in Chapter 3, "Foundation Technologies," the following OMG standards are foundation technologies for CWM: UML, IDL, MOF, and XMI. These together form the core meta data standards adopted by the OMG. UML and MOF, together with CWM, also form the core components of the OMG MDA.

UML provides the UML notation and OCL as part of the metamodeling language for CWM. In addition, the UML metamodel, or a subset of it, was used as the design basis for the CWM Object Model package, which serves as both the base metamodel and the object metamodel for CWM. Specifically, the Object Model package was derived from the UML Foundation, Common_-Behavior, and Model_Management packages.

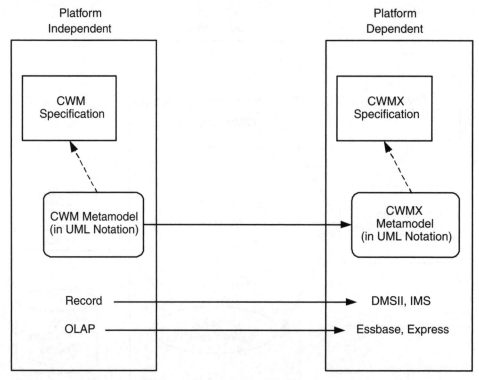

Figure 8.7   CWM and MDA: Product-platform perspective.

IDL provides an interface definition language for use in the CORBA environment. It is programming-language independent. Any programming language that has a defined IDL mapping and CORBA support can be used to implement IDL interfaces.

MOF provides the metamodeling architecture for CWM. Specifically, the MOF model provides the semantics of the metamodeling language for CWM; the MOF reflective interfaces provide generic APIs for accessing CWM meta data; and the MOF-to-IDL mapping provides the mechanism to generate CWM IDL interfaces for accessing CWM meta data.

XMI provides the meta data interchange mechanism for CWM. Specifically, XMI defines rules that can be used to automatically generate the CWM DTD, which can be used to validate any XML documents that contain CWM meta data. XMI also defines rules that can be used to generate XML documents that contain CWM meta data and that are valid per the CWM DTD. In the future, with the adoption by the OMG of XMI 2.0, XMI will in addition define rules that can be used to automatically generate the CWM XSD (for example, the XML schema definition for CWM), which can be used to validate any XML documents that contain CWM meta data.

Table 8.2 CWM and OMG Standards

CATEGORY	STANDARD	BASE TECHNOLOGY FOR CWM	DERIVED FROM CWM
OMG	UML	UML Notation OCL UML Metamodel	
	IDL	CORBA IDL definition	
	MOF	MOF Model MOF Reflective MOF-to-IDL mapping	
	XMI	XML DTD production XML document production XML schema production (future)	

The relationships between CWM and UML, IDL, MOF, as well as XMI are summarized in Table 8.2.

W3C Standards

In Chapter 3, we have discussed that XML, which is a W3C standard (see W3C), is a foundation technology for CWM. XML provides the universal format for interchanging CWM meta data. The XML specification defines the well-formedness rules for XML documents, the grammar rules for DTDs, and the validity rules for validating XML documents against its DTDs. In addition, the XML Namespace specification defines the mechanism for providing namespace support in XML documents and DTDs.

Recently the W3C has adopted XML Schema as a standard. XML Schema provides an alternative way to DTD for defining the structures of XML documents. There are many advantages of XML schema over DTD, including the following:

- DTD is based on a specialized syntax; XML Schema is based on XML.

- DTD treats all data (with few exceptions) as strings or enumerated strings; XML Schema supports a rich set of data types, comparable to those in SQL and Java.

- DTD uses a closed-content model that allows very little extensibility; XML Schema uses an open-content model, which allows one to extend vocabularies and establish substitution relationships between elements.

■ DTD allows only one association between a document and its DTD via the document type declaration; XML Schema supports namespace integration, which allows one to associate individual nodes of a document with type declarations in a schema.

Because of these advantages, XML Schema, rather than DTD, is expected to be used in the future to define the structures of XML documents, particularly those used to interchange data or meta data. As discussed previously, XMI 2.0 will define rules that can be used to automatically generate the CWM XSD (for example, the XML Schema definition for CWM).

XML Protocol, which originated from Simple Object Access Protocol (SOAP), is a standard being developed by the W3C which intends to define:

■ An envelope to encapsulate XML data for transfer in an interoperable manner that allows for distributed extensibility, evolvability, and intermediaries like proxies, caches, and gateways

■ An operating system-neutral convention for the content of the envelope when used for Remote Procedure Call (RPC) applications

■ A mechanism to serialize data based on XML Schema datatypes

■ A nonexclusive mechanism layered on an HTTP transport

Web Services Definition Language (WSDL) is a proposal made to the W3C for standardization. WSDL is an XML format for describing network services as a set of endpoints operating on messages containing either document-oriented or procedure-oriented information. The operations and messages are described abstractly and then bound to a concrete network protocol and message format to define an endpoint. Related concrete endpoints are combined into abstract endpoints (services). WSDL is extensible to allow description of endpoints and their messages regardless of what message formats or network protocols are used to communicate. Both XML Protocol and WSDL (or whatever is eventually standardized by the W3C in its place) are expected to become the foundation technologies for the CWM Web Services to be discussed in the next section.

Support for meta data search and query has been lacking for some time. The one exception is that for relational meta data, in which case one can use SQL for search and query, assuming that one has access to the schema tables. However, no such support exists for meta data represented in UML, not even standardized UML-based search or query languages. XPath and XQuery provide hope for such support, at least via the XML views of such meta data, with XPath used for simple search and XQuery used for search and query.

XPath is a W3C standard. The primary purpose of XPath is to address parts of an XML document. In support of this primary purpose, it also provides basic facilities for manipulation of strings, numbers, and booleans. XPath uses a compact, non-XML syntax to facilitate use of XPath within URIs and XML attribute values. XPath operates on the abstract, logical structure of an XML document, rather than its surface syntax. XPath gets its name from its use of a path notation as in URLs for navigating through the hierarchical structure of an XML document.

XQuery is an XML query language standard being developed by the W3C. It is designed to be a small, easily implementable language in which queries are concise and easily understood. It is also flexible enough to query a broad spectrum of XML information sources, including both databases and documents. XQuery provides for a human-readable query syntax, and XQueryX (the XML representation of XQuery) provides an XML-based query syntax. XQuery relies on path expressions defined in XPath for navigating hierarchical documents

The relationships between CWM and XML, XML Schema, XML Protocol, WSDL, XPath, and XQuery are summarized in Table 8.3.

Java Standards

In Chapter 3 we mentioned that Java has been the most widely used implementation platform for CWM and, therefore, is a foundation technology for CWM. A major reason for this is because Java can be written once and run anywhere. In particular, J2EE (see J2EE) has been the implementation platform of choice because of its support for enterprise computing, including Web technologies such as servlets and JSP that can work seamlessly with XML.

Table 8.3 CWM and W3C Standards

CATEGORY	STANDARD	BASE TECHNOLOGY FOR CWM	DERIVED FROM CWM
W3C	XML	XML document definition XML DTD definition	
	XML schema	XML schema structures and datatypes definitions (future)	
	XML Protocol	XML messaging protocol (future)	
	WSDL	Web Services interface definition language (future)	
	Xpath	XML Pattern language (future)	
	XQuery	XML query language (future)	

An important standard being developed through the Java Community Process (JCP) (see JCP) is Java Meta Data Interface (JMI), which will have direct relevance to CWM in the near future. JMI intents to specify a pure Java API that supports the creation, storage, retrieval, and interchange of meta data. The API is expected to implement the functionality of MOF in a way that will be compatible with the J2EE platform, although today one can use the MOF-to-IDL mapping and then the IDL-to-Java mapping to generate a Java API for CWM. That API is appropriate for use only in a CORBA environment. The API is nonintuitive to Java programmers, and it does not take advantage of the Java language or J2EE environment. After JMI is standardized, we should expect that in the future CWM Java will be automatically generated per JMI and published as part of the CWM specification, in a similar manner to CWM IDL.

All the standards we have discussed so far are existing or emerging foundation technologies for CWM. Two emerging standards, however, are technologies that derive, at least in part, from CWM. These are Java OLAP Interface (JSR-69) and Java Data Mining API (JSR-73).

JSR-69 intends to specify a pure Java API for the J2EE environment that supports the creation, storage, access, and maintenance of data and meta data in OLAP systems (for example, OLAP servers and multidimensional databases). The goal is to provide for OLAP systems what JDBC did for relational databases. JSR-69 intends to have a close alignment with JMI, the CWM OLAP and Multidimensional metamodels so that it can directly support the construction and deployment of data warehousing and business intelligence applications, tools, and platforms based on OMG open standards for meta data and system specification.

JSR-73 intends to specify a pure Java API for the J2EE environment that supports the building of data-mining models; the scoring of data-using models; and the creation, storage, access, and maintenance of data and meta data supporting data mining results and select data transformation. The goal is to provide for data mining systems what JDBC did for relational databases. JSR-73 intends to have a close alignment with JMI and the CWM data mining metamodel so that it can directly support the construction and deployment of data warehousing and business intelligence applications, tools, and platforms based on OMG open standards for meta data and system specification.

The relationships between CWM and Java, J2EE, JMI, JSR-69, and JSR-73 are summarized in Table 8.4.

The Future Evolution of CWM

CWM was adopted by the OMG as an Available Specification in April 2001. As a result, a CWM Revision Task Force (RTF) has been formed to solicit public

Table 8.4 CWM and Java Standards

CATEGORY	STANDARD	BASE TECHNOLOGY FOR CWM	DERIVED FROM CWM
Java	Java language	Java language definition	
	J2EE	Java implementation platform	
	JMI	MOF-to-Java mapping (future)	
	JSR-69		CWM OLAP metamodel
	JSR-73		CWM data mining metamodel

comments on the specification and to revise it based on resolutions of the comments and on feedback from CWM implementations. The following metamodels are expected to go through major revisions:

- **Data mining.** To incorporate feedback from the result of the JSR-73 standardization effort
- **XML.** To extend the metamodel to cover the new XML Schema specification adopted by the W3C

Separately, two RFPs were issued by the OMG in April 2001 to enhance CWM: CWM Meta Data Interchange Patterns RFP and CWM Web Services RFP. These two RFPs intend to enhance the ease of using CWM for meta data interchange and to enable such interchange using the new Web Services computing paradigm.

CWM Meta Data Interchange Patterns RFP

The construction and semantics of the CWM metamodel are such that the metamodel covers a broad spectrum of uses in the data warehouse. This design enables a user to interchange meta data for many diverse portions of the CWM metamodel. This flexibility, although expressively powerful, is at the same time problematic for tool implementors. The metamodel has no way to describe what a valid unit of interchange should be. As a result, it is possible to receive a portion of the CWM metamodel without sufficient context to reliably interchange the meta data. This was brought to light when the CWM team produced the CWM Enablement Showcase. To solve this issue, the participants agreed on what a valid unit of transfer was for the context of the Showcase. This methodology needs to be formalized for CWM.

Meta data interchange patterns are structural patterns for interchanged meta data content between typical DW and BI tools, which serve to constrain the total universe of possible meta data content that can be interchanged. They simplify tool construction and logic because an importing tool, for example, knows in advance what to look for. (It's search space is constrained to specific structural patterns, and it knows what the top-level anchor points for patterned-content are.) Similarly, exporting tools also have a guideline to follow in structuring their meta data for export.

The CWM Meta Data Interchange Patterns RFP, therefore, solicits proposals for a complete specification of the syntax and semantics of typical CWM meta data interchange patterns. Requirements on the proposals include the following:

- Proposals shall consist of (1) the specification of a generic mechanism for expressing CWM meta data interchange patterns and (2) the application of the generic mechanism to CWM. The generic mechanism must be specified in terms of MOF concepts, and the application of the generic mechanism to CWM must be based on and consistent with the CWM metamodel.

- Proposals shall address the interchange of all types of warehouse meta data specified in CWM, including foundation, resource, analysis, and management meta data.

CWM Web Services RFP

CWM describes the interchange of meta data. This is necessary, but not necessarily sufficient for interchanging DW/BI meta data over the Web. The major characteristic of the Web is that it consists of massive, loosely and infrequently connected, and asynchronous clients and servers. In such an environment, it is much more desirable and efficient to interchange information (including meta data) using a request-response model and in coarse-grain manners. CWM defines fine-grained metamodels for access and interchange of DW/BI meta data, using XML to interchange meta data and IDL to access meta data. CWM does not, however, define typical meta data interchange patterns nor define standard meta data interchange (request-response) protocols. Specifically, CWM does not define an enablement architecture that allows loosely coupled interchange of DW/BI meta data over the Web.

The CWM Web Services RFP, therefore, solicits proposals for the following:

- A complete specification of the syntax and semantics of standard CWM meta data interchange (request-response) protocols that is based on typical CWM meta data interchange patterns (as requested in the CWM Meta Data Interchange Patterns RFP).

■ A complete specification of the syntax and semantics of a CWM Web Services API that allow the loosely coupled interchange of CWM meta data over the Web and that is based on the standard CWM meta data interchange protocols.

This RFP is expected to solicit proposals that specify the protocols one can use to request specific patterns for interchange and to express the desired results of interchange, and the APIs one can use to do so over the Web. The Web Services API is expected to be dependent on the CWM interchange format (the CWM DTD) and be consistent with it.

CWM: The Solution to Meta Data Integration

With the decision by the Meta Data Coalition (MDC) in September 2000 to fold its meta data standardization effort into the OMG and the fact that Java Community Process (JCP) is extending OMG meta data standards into the Java platform (for example, JMI, JSR-69, and JSR-73), acceptance and support for CWM in the industry is rapidly growing. One should not be surprised to find CWM providing the common solution to warehouse meta data integration problems in the very near future. Looking a little further into the future, as W3C adopts newer standards on XML (for example, XQuery, XML Protocol, and WSDL) and as CWM evolves (that is, the CWM RTF, the CWM Meta Data Interchange Patterns RFP, and the CWM Web Services RFP) to incorporate these technologies, warehouse meta data integration using CWM should become even easier and more powerful.

Bibliography

Cited Works

Booch, Grady, James Rumbaugh, and Ivar Jacobson. (1999). *The Unified Modeling Language User Guide*. Reading, MA: Addison Wesley Longman, Inc.

Common Warehouse Metamodel Specification. (2001). Needham, MA: Object Management Group. Internet: www.omg.org/technology/cwm/index.htm or www.cwmforum.org/spec.htm.

Garter Group (Loureiro, K., Wallace, L., and Blechar, M.) (July 16, 1997). "Choosing the Right Repository: Functionality Criteria." Tutorials Research Note TU-450-1515. Stamford, CT: Gartner Group, Inc.

Garter Group (Blechar, M.) (February 1, 1999). "Meta Data Management Alternatives for DWs and Data Marts." Decision Framework Research Note DF-06-5074. Stamford, CT: Gartner Group, Inc.

Gartner Group (Blechar, M.) (January 28, 2000[a]), "Data Warehousing Business Meta Data Management Issues," Research Note TG-09-8992. Stamford, CT: Gartner Group, Inc.

Gartner Group (Blechar, M.) (January 28, 2000[b]). "Data Warehousing Technical Meta Data Management Issues." Tactical Guidelines Research Note TG-09-8995. Stamford, CT: Gartner Group, Inc.

Gartner Group (Blechar, M.) (July 28, 2000). "OMG's Common Warehouse Metamodel Specification." Events Research Note E-11-4175. Stamford, CT: Gartner Group, Inc.

Gartner Group (Blechar, M.) (August 25, 2000). "IT Meta Data Repository Magic Quadrant Update 2001." Markets Research Note M-11-8336. Stamford, CT: Gartner Group, Inc.

Java 2 Platform, Enterprise Edition, home page. Internet: http://java.sun.com/j2ee/.

Java Community Process, home page. Internet: http://jcp.org/.

Kimball, Ralph. (1996). *The Data Warehouse Toolkit.* New York: John Wiley & Sons, Inc.

Marco, David. 2000. *Building and Managing the Meta Data Repository: A Full Lifecycle Guide.* New York: John Wiley & Sons, Inc.

META Group. (November 10, 1997). "DW Metadata Management: Bottom Up, Top Down." Application Delivery Strategies, File No. 619. Stamford, CT: META Group, Inc.

META Group, (Doug Laney) (February 4, 2000). "Metadata Maelstrom Sinks Standards and Repositories." Application Delivery Strategies, File No. 825. Stamford, CT: META Group, Inc.

META Group, (Doug Laney) (August 7, 2000). "21st Century Metadata: Mapping the Enterprise Genome." Application Delivery Strategies, File No. 896, Stamford, CT: META Group, Inc.

OMG Model Driven Architecture resource page. (2001). Needham, MA: Object Management Group. Internet: www.omg.org/mda/index.htm.

Rumbaugh, James, Ivar Jacobson, and Grady Booch. (1999). *The Unified Modeling Language Reference Manual.* Reading, MA: Addison Wesley Longman, Inc.

Thomsen, Erik. 1997. *OLAP Solutions: Building Multidimensional Information Systems.* New York: John Wiley & Sons, Inc.

World Wide Web Consortium (W3C) home page. Internet: www.w3c.org.

Warmer, Jos, and Anneke Kleppe. (1999). *The Object Constraint Language: Precise Modeling with UML.* Reading, MA: Addison Wesley Longman, Inc.

Recommended and Related Readings

Arrington, C.T. (2000). *Enterprise Java with UML.* New York: John Wiley & Sons, Inc.

Gamma, Erich, Richard Helm, Ralph Johnson, and John Vlissedes. (1995). *Design Patterns: Elements of Reusable Object-Oriented Software.* Reading, MA: Addison Wesley Longman, Inc.

Inmon, William H. (1996). *Building the Data Warehouse, 2nd Edition*. New York: John Wiley & Sons, Inc.

Inmon, William H., Ken Rudin, Christopher K. Buss, and Ryan Sousa. (1999). *Data Warehouse Performance*. New York: John Wiley & Sons, Inc.

Kimball, Ralph, Laura Reeves, Marge Ross, and Warren Thornthwaite. (1998). *The Data Warehouse Lifecycle Toolkit: Expert Methods for Designing, Developing, and Deploying Data Warehouses*. New York: John Wiley & Sons, Inc.

Kimball, Ralph, and Richard Merz. (2000). *The Data Webhouse Toolkit: Building the Web-Enabled Data Warehouse*. New York: John Wiley & Sons, Inc.

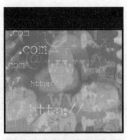

Index

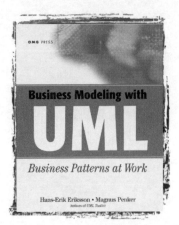